DARING TO EDUCATE

T0204549

DARING TO

EDUCATE

The Legacy of the Early Spelman
College Presidents

Yolanda L. Watson and Sheila T. Gregory

Foreword by Johnnetta B. Cole
Epilogue by Beverly Daniel Tatum

STERLING, VIRGINIA

COPYRIGHT © 2005 BY
STYLUS PUBLISHING, LLC

Published by Stylus Publishing, LLC
22883 Quicksilver Drive
Sterling, Virginia 20166–2102

Library of Congress Cataloging-in-
Publication Data
Watson, Yolanda L. (Yolanda Letitia), 1971–
    Daring to educate : the legacy of the early
    Spelman College presidents / Yolanda L.
    Watson and Sheila T. Gregory.—1st ed.
        p.   cm.
    Includes bibliographical references and
index.
    ISBN 1-57922-108-4 (hardcover : alk.
paper)—ISBN 1-57922-109-2 (pbk. : alk.
paper)   1. Spelman College—History.
2. Spelman College—Presidents.
3. Women's colleges—Georgia—Atlanta—
History.   4. African American women—
Education (Higher)—Georgia—Atlanta—
History.   I. Gregory, Sheila T.   II. Title.
LC2851.S685W38 2005
378.758′231—dc22   2004027299

ISBN: 1-57922-108-4 (cloth)
ISBN: 1-57922-109-2 (paper)

Printed in the United States of America

All first editions printed on acid free paper that
meets the American National Standards
Institute Z39-48 Standard.

First Edition, 2005

10   9   8   7   6   5   4   3   2   1

To my daughter, Gabrielle Moore, whose light I am certain will shine brightly when she continues our familial legacy and enters Spelman's hallowed and storied halls in the fall of 2011. I can't wait for your contributions to future Spelman history as student and leader. All I do is for you; you are my continual source of support, love, encouragement; and you are mommy's greatest work, to date. I love you!

To my angel, Carlton Moore, who oversaw my contributions to this project while on earth, and posthumously from heaven. You were my biggest fan and spoke life into the manifestation of this project even before it was conceived—I hope that you are proud!

To Spelman and Bennett Colleges for your enduring legacies as the only remaining historically black women's colleges in the United States. Like the African American women you serve, you have been weary, but not worn; bowed, but not bent; and tried, yet triumphant in your service to African American women the world over.

—Yolanda L. Watson

In memory of my Uncle Victor Gregory, who passed during the 2004 Christmas holidays and is now my guardian angel. To God be the glory, for without Him, none of this would have been possible.

—Sheila T. Gregory

ACKNOWLEDGMENTS

The authors and the publisher wish to thank Spelman College for their help and access to their archives and in particular to thank Spelman for permission to reproduce all the photographs in this book, courtesy of the Spelman College Archives, Atlanta, Georgia.

*   *   *

Thank you to John Von Knorring of Stylus Publishing for your belief in and commitment to this body of work and its potential contributions to the higher educational canon. Thanks to Judy Coughlin for your genuine personal interest in this research, and the accompanying care and meticulousness with which you reviewed and edited the book. Special thanks to Spelman Archivist Taronda Spencer (Spelman College C'80) for your incomparable assistance throughout every step of the process, and your facilitation of our access to the bountiful and wonderfully organized Spelman College archival material. Thanks to Brenda Banks (Spelman College C'71) for unknowingly fostering within me a love and commitment for historiography, and for piquing my interest in the treasure troves of dispersed, archive-worthy information on Spelman College long before the Spelman College Archives actually existed. Thanks to Spelman President Emerita and current Bennett College for Women President, Dr. Johnnetta B. Cole, for your contributions to this book, and for your passion and commitment to Black women's higher education which long ago inspired my love for Spelman, and the desire to tell of its early history. Thanks also to Spelman President Dr. Beverly Daniel Tatum, for your contribution to the book in the form of the epilogue, and for your charismatic leadership and commitment which will surely usher in future generations of "True Blue" Spelman Women poised to lead us into the next century. Special thanks to Spelman alumna Adrienne Lance Lucas (C'90) and Dr. Gwendolyn Bookman (Bennett College), for your help in facilitating the contemporary presidential contributions to the book.

To co-author and colleague Sheila Gregory, thank you so much for your belief in my previous Spelman research all those years ago during a chance encounter that led to our collaboration on this book and to our enduring friendship. I am in awe of your scholarship and it was my pleasure to work with you; I am so glad we did this—we must do it again! A special thank you to Spelman alumna Ms. Marguerite Simon (C'35) for your words of encouragement and inspiration related to the need for this book. Thanks to Dr. Robert Preston, Professor of History at Trinity University (Washington, D.C.) for the intellectual and anecdotal exchanges about women's collegiate education and the worthiness of the endeavor, which provided me with other perspectives from which to consider the Spelman curricular history. My sincerest appreciation to Drs. Wayne Urban, Philo Hutcheson, Jacqueline Rouse, and Janet Guyden for their encouragement, support, and review of early iterations of the research which formed the basis for this work. Thanks to Senior Pastor Dr. Kerwin B. Lee and the Berean Christian Church Family (Stone Mountain, Georgia) for your love and support. This church has been a stronghold for me during this past year, and for that I thank you.

A tremendous debt of gratitude to my mother, Dr. Joyce Morley-Ball, who knew that Spelman was the place for me, even when I didn't realize it. To my sisters Dr. Teknaya Watson (Spelman College C'96) and Ms. Natasha Ball (Spelman College C'00), with whom I have also been blessed to share the unique experience of Spelman sisterhood. For each of your unique displays of encouragement and support—I thank you—I couldn't have done any of this without you! Thank you very much to the New York State Chapters of the American Baptist Women's Society who sowed generous seeds into my initial matriculation at Spelman College. A tremendous thank you to those friends and family who encouraged me in limitless ways throughout various stages of the research, development, and completion of the book: Chioma Onyekwere, Ron Nance, Justina Giggers, Kevyn Giggers, Rachell Cobb-Valion, Bill Taylor, and Shaunté Parker. I love you all, and appreciate you in infinite ways. A special thanks to Lindberg Slade for your listening ear, as well as your thoughtful and incisive questions about this work. You are a treasure and a special friend! A tremendously special thank you to Mr. Wendell Spira for all of your support during the final stages of the book's completion.

—Yolanda L. Watson

*   *   *

To Sister Presidents, Johnnetta Cole and Beverly Daniel Tatum for their compelling contributions to this work.

I am grateful to several other persons. In acknowledging the generosity of others and the contributions they have made to this work, I begin with the women who participated in the socialization chapter of this book. Their thoughtfulness in describing their experiences at Spelman College and their willingness, patience, and candor in discussing their family background, personal experiences, and choices are the foundation of this book's intent.

To my first co-author on a book, Dr. Yolanda L. Watson, for her insights, incredible talent, and energy.

To my family at Clark Atlanta University, including the Dean of the School of Education, Dr. Pete Middleton: Chair of the Department of Educational Leadership, Dr. Melanie Carter: and my colleagues in the Department of Educational Leadership, Drs. Moses Norman, Trevor Turner, Ganga Persaud, and Leslie Fenwick. I want to give special thanks to Ms. Betty Cooke, our department secretary who sometimes anticipates my needs before I do and is always quick to assist me in whatever I may need. To Ms. Kendra Brooks, who completed the index for our book; Mr. Noran Moffett; and Dr. Coach David Propst, three of the most talented doctoral students I have ever had the honor to work with and mentor. Also, I would like to thank our CAU President, Dr. Walter Broadnax, and Provost, Dr. Dorcas Bowles, for setting such high standards and providing such encouraging support.

Most especially, I would like to thank my family and close friends whose love, patience and support helped me through these past two years; my husband and partner of twelve years, Anthony Jones, and our two beautiful children whom I consider to be my greatest blessing in life, Courtney and Anthony Jones. And with much love, respect and adoration, to my parents, Dr. Karl Gregory and Tenicia Gregory, who continue to set the example for myself and my siblings, Karin and Kurt Gregory. And to my sisters-in-law, Cynthia Sadler and Burma Jones, who continue to motivate me.

To my long-time friends, who have pushed and pulled me through, Bobby and LaJuan Jones, Karen Ferguson, Elena Robinson, Clifton Camp, Maureen Stapleton, Mary Carter, Augustus James, Barbara Reynolds and M. J. Warrender. To my newest kindred spirits, Linda Tillman, Senita Birbal, and Clairmont Barnes. And a special thanks to my mentors, not already mentioned, Drs. Otis Hill, George Keller, Vivian Gadsden, Dale Anderson, and Reginald Wilson.

To Pastor Marvin A. Moss, whose Sunday sermons at St. James United

Methodist Church give me insight and strength. And to my entire church family in Alpharetta, Georgia.

To John von Knorring of Stylus Publishers whose interest in and enthusiasm for our ideas made this project very rewarding and less stressful.

And for all Spelmanites and Black women and their families.

—Sheila T. Gregory

CONTENTS

FOREWORD   *xiii*
HEIR TO THE SPELMAN LEGACY
Dr. Johnnetta B. Cole

1. INTRODUCTION   *1*

2. THE HIGHER EDUCATION OF BLACK WOMEN   *39*

3. OUR WHOLE SCHOOL FOR CHRIST   *63*
The Packard and Giles Administrations (1881–1909)

4. NEW DIRECTIONS: TOWARD COLLEGIATE STATUS   *83*
The Lucy Hale Tapley Administration (1910–1927)

5. ONWARD AND UPWARD—THE CREATION OF A
LIBERAL ARTS INSTITUTION   *117*
The Florence Read Administration (1927–1953)

6. THE SOCIALIZATION OF SPELMAN STUDENTS   *133*

7. CONCLUSION   *155*

EPILOGUE   *163*
THE SPELMAN LEGACY LIVES ON
Dr. Beverly Daniel Tatum

BIBLIOGRAPHY   *173*

APPENDICES   *179*

INDEX   *201*

FOREWORD:
HEIR TO THE SPELMAN LEGACY

Dr. Johnnetta B. Cole

Before my tenure at Spelman College, I had not come from the tradition of college presidents, had not held the requisite number of administrative positions that mark our kind. Nor was I a typical faculty member; indeed, I was more given to the active exploration of theory and the impact of progressive engagement in those issues dear to me. I was a *teacher*, in that proud ritual that had wound back through centuries. The tutoring of young minds, the contest of fresh ideas, the digging through of mined texts in the search for new truth—that was my mission, my calling.

Nevertheless, in 1987, I accepted a mantle of responsibility crafted by the dedication of women and men who preceded me as President of Spelman College. I joined Spelman as the first African American woman to hold the position, and I began my tenure vibrantly aware of the expectations that now focused upon me. After a century of growth, Spelman required a new leader; I became a member of a unique group of women and men who had the audacity to imagine that a Black women's college could generate change agents for the entire world.

How hefty a task these other presidents had set for themselves and for me! Like them, I had been tapped to lead bright and dynamic African American women from adolescence into adulthood, from raw energy to refined action. Indeed, at Spelman, the presidency was exactly what I understood a *teacher* to be. Spelman College stood boldly for the proposition that education is integral and inseparable from social change. It was a school of teachers, dedicated to a prospect both lofty and courageous: to empower those who had long been among the most disenfranchised.

Presiding over Spelman College inducted me into a small cabal of leaders who numbered only six at the time I joined their ranks. Yet, those who had accepted the call in the years before me had not deserted the world they had created. As I walked the campus of my new home, their spirits surrounded me. More than names emblazoned on grand buildings raised in the late 1800s or the lush green Spelman Oval that held their indelible footprints, I was deeply aware of the wonder they had wrought over more than a century in the lively voices that hummed across the college grounds.

We had, we Spelman Presidents, come to our place from different starting points and with distinct comprehensions of what we could add to the institution. Still, we shared, in our ways, a common awareness of the needs of our charges. My immediate predecessors—Dr. Albert Manley and Dr. Donald Stewart—held my fundamental understanding of the whole needs of Black folk, particularly women and those who were our youngest members. From 1954 to my inaugural year of 1987, they had laid hands on the experiment that was Spelman as her students went through the turmoil of the Civil Rights struggle, the impassioned Women's Movement and the Black-Consciousness raising of the 1970s.

I asked each of the brother presidents—Dr. Manley and Dr. Stewart—to tell me of their time and their mission, as each walked with me across Spelman's campus. But it was the womenfolk, the righteous Sophia B. Packard and Harriet Giles, Lucy Hale Tapley and Florence M. Read, who also spoke to me. Four white women who understood what they had not lived, who saw what had not yet come to pass. In the eyes of freed slave women left behind in the rush to educate Black men at the close of the Civil War, Packard and Giles had seen the gleam of intellectual curiosity, and they stoked that fire. Tapley envisioned not simply a Spelman Seminary, a place of vocation and industry, but a Spelman College, a locus for academic rigor and exploration. Expanding on that vision, Read challenged Spelman's students and the wider world to truly embrace the liberal arts and to understand the place of African American women in that heritage.

I entered Spelman College, much as its students did, eager to learn of its glorious "herstory" and determined to add my mark. My bequest from these women leaders of Spelman was a passionate commitment to the education of Black women and all women who chose to enter her gates. The array of opportunities that I had the occasion to cultivate for those vibrant Spelman Sisters stood squarely on the foundation of those women.

This text, *The Legacy of Spelman College Presidents*, aptly details the remarkable accomplishment of Spelman's founders. Dr. Yolanda Watson and Dr. Sheila Gregory have excavated the chronicle of a college's founding and development through a detailed study of the lives and motives of the first four presidents of Spelman. Examined through the lens of curriculum, the cornerstone for academic learning, Drs. Watson and Gregory spin a tale of innovation and triumph while simultaneously adding to the scholarship of higher education. They explore the importance of the nature of study, and they set out the guiding principles that led these four women to their distinct, yet intertwined, administrations. Over the span of more than seventy years, Spelman evolved from a vocational training ground to a premier academic institution, and the lessons of her founders are essential to understanding her success.

Through an analysis of the curricular changes brought by each president, coupled with the important social and political contexts that surrounded those presidencies, this book presents a thoughtful discussion on the impact of a powerful woman's vision on the lives of other women. That these women achieved their goals for social uplift by charting a course for Black women is worthy of note and celebration. Moreover, that Packard, Giles, Tapley, and Read took on this fantastic mission, at a time when Black women were the most vulnerable of Americans, speaks to the promise of Spelman's future.

Like those who have come since my decade there, I owe a debt to the founding mothers of the nation's oldest continuously historically Black women's college. I have taught in the classrooms of their imaginings and helped to imagine new courses that could be because of the faith and courage of those who launched Spelman in the humble setting of a church basement. These remarkable women gave life to a dream that has sustained thousands of alumnae over the years. I was honored to contribute to that amazing "herstory," and I remain the proud inheritor of the legacy of the first Sister Presidents of Spelman College.

Dr. Johnnetta B. Cole
Seventh President of Spelman College

I

INTRODUCTION

From 1881 to 1953, dramatic curricular changes took place at Spelman College, the nation's oldest surviving historically Black college founded for the education of women. During the first seventy-two years of its history, Spelman was led by four presidents—all of them White women who were educated in northeastern seminaries and academies.[1] The identities of the college's first four presidents had a very profound impact upon the definition, creation, development, and revisions of the Spelman College curriculum.[2] The behaviors, leadership styles, and institutional culture instilled by these women presidents also helped to shape and define the roles and minds of thousands of young, Black, Spelman College students. This book examines the evolution of the Spelman College curriculum and explores the ways in which the Spelman culture socialized young Black women students during the administrations of its first four college presidents.[3]

Co-principals and Founders Harriet Giles and Sophia Packard served as heads of the institution from 1881 to 1888, when the Board of Trustees named Sophia Packard president, a position that she held until her death in 1891. From 1891 to 1909, Harriet Giles served as president of the institution. Lucy Houghton Upton served as the interim president from 1909 to 1910. From 1910 to 1927, Lucy Hale Tapley served as third president; and from 1927 to 1953, Florence M. Read served as the fourth president of Spelman.[4]

Spelman was the first educational institution for Black women to state formally that it offered college work. The academic leaders of the institution were well aware of the occupational areas its graduates would and could pursue and thus aimed to provide training to prepare its student body for careers as teachers in the public schools and skilled Christian workers for missionary and church work.[5] However, Spelman also sought to provide its students with

I

an education to be used for the uplift of the Black race.[6] Thus, high on the list of curricular priorities for Black women's colleges (such as Spelman)[7] were training in domestic activities, tacit training for leadership roles, and a version of liberal education that was beholden to the societal dictates established for the Black female in America.[8]

In 1860, there were approximately four million Black slaves, five hundred thousand free Blacks, and twenty-seven million Whites in the United States. Ninety-two percent of the Blacks in the United States during this time lived in the South, and eight million Whites did so as well. During the 1860s in the South, laws enacted by Whites prohibited the formal education of Blacks, particularly postsecondary education. In 1860, over 90 percent of the South's Black adult population was illiterate.[9] Black former slaves, however, demonstrated tenacity in their attempts to overcome this disadvantage. Prior to 1863, enslaved Black women who worked in the master's home received opportunities to associate with the White master's family, though not on an equal basis. This interaction provided chances for many "house" slaves to assimilate ideals and beliefs unknown to enslaved Blacks in the isolated fields. This "education by imitation" was the main source of learning, and for many Blacks perhaps served as their informal introduction to education. This relatively "privileged" status of Black women who served in the home of the slave master provided them with as much or more access to an informal, rudimentary education as the equally limited "imitation education" afforded Black slave men.[10]

On January 1, 1863, four million Black slaves (two million of whom were women) were emancipated after 250 years of enslavement.[11] With a tremendous disadvantage with respect to education and industrial skills, freed slaves were afforded little or no opportunity for social and economic success in the "land of the free." Acknowledgment of this disadvantage, and fear of perpetual educational and social inferiority inspired a determination within the freed slaves to achieve a formal education at any cost; this determination eventually became one of the most immediate sources of fear for White Americans.[12] In an effort to justify precluding formal education for newly freed Black slaves and free Blacks, Whites continued the proliferation of the following rationales: (1) the alleged intellectual inferiority of Blacks and (2) the belief that educated Blacks would "get out of their place" and inevitably compete with Whites in the economic, political, and sexual spheres.[13] These fears were so pervasive that they led to increased hostility, disparagement, and resentment of Black educational institutions by Whites, with subversive activities accompanying these sentiments. As a result of the combination of anti-Black-education beliefs and other negative activities, only twenty-eight Blacks earned bachelor's degrees from American colleges and universities prior to the Civil War.[14]

Despite the overt actions by Whites to thwart the formal educational attainment of freed Blacks (such as the creation of laws and policies that prohibited or minimized the education of Blacks), ex-slaves were quick to establish institutions to facilitate the achievement of what privileged Whites termed "the American dream" and what Blacks viewed as their only means of survival in the United States. After emancipation, free Blacks established a multitude of institutions such as African churches, African private schools, and African fraternal organizations in both northern and southern cities. The effects of establishing these institutions included the proliferation of venues for religious worship and the education of children and adults, as well as the establishment of entities through which to protect Black communities.[15] The founding, initial funding, and maintenance of these institutions within Black communities after 1865 came from freed and free Blacks as well as sympathetic (yet often paternalistic) Whites.[16] A scant few of these institutions were integrated, but were operated covertly to avoid the potential harassment and physical destruction of the facilities by angry Whites who were against integrated education for Whites and Blacks. By the end of the nineteenth century, most educational institutions were still segregated, and many Black educational institutions were forced to maintain clandestine operations or risk being shut down. Between 1865 and 1900, a number of Black colleges were established in the South, largely as a result of the desire of religious groups to increase the number of Black teachers and ministers.[17]

In 1865, approximately 4.5 million Blacks lived in the United States. Toward the end of the Civil War and throughout the period of Reconstruction, the responsibility for providing educational instruction for the mostly illiterate freed slaves rested with the federal government through its Bureau of Refugees, Freedmen, and Abandoned Lands (better known as the Freedmen's Bureau), which was established in 1865.[18] The Freedmen's Bureau provided elementary education to freed and free Blacks and poor Whites. Since the Freedmen's Bureau was not directly responsible for the day-to-day operation of schools, the cooperation and assistance of northern missionary societies were enlisted to expand the Bureau's efforts. Thus, the formidable task of educating newly freed Blacks was also undertaken by the church-related missionary societies in the North, as well as by Blacks themselves. The education of Black women became an important aspect of the missionary organizations' education of freed Blacks, particularly as Black women were needed to teach.[19] As the decision was made by White and Black men alike to educate Black women, four distinct issues emerged: whether or not Black women deserved or were capable of being educated; the extent to which this segment of the population should be educated; the type of education that Black women should receive; and the overall purposes of educating Black women.[20] Beyond the traditional reasons for educating Black women, in the early twentieth century the Black community began to recognize the need to train Black women for potential leadership roles in the community.[21] The resulting general sentiment that Black women should be trained to teach in order to uplift the masses soon became pervasive.[22]

The northern missionary societies initiated the development of a formal system of schools and colleges for Blacks. Some of the first missionary societies to do so included the American Missionary Association (AMA); the American Baptist Home Mission Society (ABHMS); the Northern Methodists; and the Southern Methodists. The establishment of formal educational institutions for Blacks by missionary organizations represents the tradition in which Spelman College was founded.[23]

The Founders of Spelman College,[24] Sophia B. Packard and Harriet Giles, were White missionary women, raised and educated in the female seminaries of the northeastern United States,[25] where both women had also gained a great deal of teaching and administrative experience.[26] In 1880, Packard traveled south as a representative of the Women's American Baptist Home Mission Society (WABHMS—of which she was a founding member[27]) to examine the aftermath of the recently ended enterprise of slavery and to gain a better understanding of the plight of the freedmen.[28] While traveling across the South, Packard was mortified by the difficulties newly freed Blacks were having acclimating to freedom, particularly as they had no sources of income and no homes to call their own.[29] She was particularly appalled at the plight of the Black female ex-slave in the South, and the seemingly prevalent perception that the status of these women was equivalent to that of the lowliest members in the American social hierarchy, a perception that she herself did not accept.[30] Her objection to this perception would later become evident in relation to her views about the purposes of Spelman: "We believe the day is coming when upon the solid basis now being laid, there shall arise many whose character shall be founded upon the rock, Christ Jesus, and all the glorious building shall be beautiful with love and purity and truth—instilled by the mothers whom we are training today."[31]

Packard immediately became determined to act in some way toward the amelioration of the social condition of Black females in the South, but unfortunately fell ill. She contacted her dear friend, Harriet Giles (who at the time was teaching in Boston), to come and care for her during her infirmity. While in the South, Giles also bore witness to the conditions of the post-emancipation South. She visited southern homes and schools, and even taught a Sunday school class at a Black church. After visiting and touring the South, she was equally mortified.[32] She immediately joined forces with Packard and the two returned to Boston in late April of 1880 intent upon founding an educational institution for Black women and girls in the South:

> . . . their eyes were opened [by the Southern trip] to the appalling need of help for the colored women and girls. The conviction was profoundly impressed upon them that their lives should be given to the education and Christianization of these downtrodden people. On their return North, this conviction deepened. . . . Even in the still night watches, a voice seemed to say: "Go South and help these women and girls who have never had a chance."[33]

Packard and Giles often declared that it was genuinely their duty and mission, sanctioned by God, to educate the masses of newly emancipated Negro women and prepare them for productive American citizenship, "We do not feel this is our work; it is God's work."[34] The Women's American Baptist Home Mission Society did not immediately concur with this proposed endeavor. However, Packard and Giles argued indefatigably for the opportunity to teach the former slave women. They used as a support the fact that while the Baptist denomination had established schools for Blacks (mainly males) in every Southern state, no provision had yet been made for the education of women and girls in the state of Georgia. This fact they found disturbing, particularly as Georgia, at that time, had the largest Black population, with a large proportion of that number being Baptist.[35]

With synchronized hearts, minds, spirits, and desires intact, and after finally having received the approval and support of the ABHMS, Packard and Giles vowed that the new school they endeavored to found would be committed to "train the intellect, to store the mind with useful knowledge, to induce habits of industry and a desire for general information, to inspire a love for the true and the beautiful, and to prepare the pupils for the practical duties of life."[36] The actions of these women were representative of the missionary zeal of many Northerners who had traveled South to "rescue" former slaves and their descendants in hopes of providing them with "higher education" which was, in those times, the single most effective path to what Albert Whiting terms an "expanded" life and upward mobility.[37] Reflecting upon their own seminary educations, Packard and Giles were convinced that similar educational experiences would equip students of the proposed new school for jobs (mainly in teaching and missionary work) as well as for the edification of their own Christian values and moral character.[38] The latter objective would become one of the most prevalent aspects of the institution, one that was particularly stressed in its curricular offerings.

On April 11, 1881, the Atlanta Baptist Female Seminary held its first class in the basement of Friendship Baptist Church in Atlanta, Georgia. The school's motto, "Our Whole School for Christ," clearly reflected the Founders' emphasis on religion and piety for its students.[39] The Atlanta Baptist Female Seminary's first class consisted of eleven students of varying ages.[40] These students were recruited through the efforts of local Black ministers who made personal calls and appeals to a number of church organizations, as well as through fliers and handbills distributed to announce the opening of the new school. Upon hearing of the opportunity to attend the Atlanta Baptist Female Seminary, Black families who were members of many local church congregations were some of the first to enroll their daughters, and many of the adult female church members enrolled as students themselves.[41] Most of the students in Spelman's first academic class were former slaves who were interested mainly in learning to read the Bible. They also wanted to write well enough to send letters to their children, who were often physically separated from them during slave trading.[42] These students, however, ended up receiving an education that encompassed a great deal more than the rudiments they were initially willing to accept.

The most compelling aspect of Spelman's early curricular history is that although the African American women studying at the institution were being educated to perform within their "proper spheres" (as were Southern White women)[43] of performing domestic work for others and serving as teachers for members of their own race, the Founders of Spelman believed strongly that the Spelman curriculum should consist of a diverse range of subjects for the edification of the total woman.[44] In this vein, the Founders sought to create a curriculum that would impart knowledge for racial uplift; knowledge and skills for personal domestic service (including the duties associated with the roles of wife and mother); knowledge and skills for professional vocational service; and contrary to popular White, southern culture, education in formal academic subjects.[45]

Using these diverse educational objectives as a foundation, this book recounts the evolution of the academic curriculum of Spelman College from its more practical, classical, and later traditional, southern orientation (while operating under the names Atlanta Baptist Female Seminary and later Spelman Seminary), to a more liberal arts focus (as Spelman College).

This book examines Spelman College's curricular evolution from 1881 to 1953 and relates it to the profound influence wielded by the first four presidents upon its students and the institution. The presidents' educational backgrounds, professional experiences, religious beliefs, and race significantly affected the content and areas of emphasis of the college's curriculum. Further, the institution's curriculum underwent significant changes over this period, as its first four presidents sought out a niche and purpose appropriate for the education of Black women. In 1953, Spelman College's curriculum turned in a significantly different direction as the first Black and first male president took over the helm of the institution. In conjunction with the changes to the general administration of the institution that accompanied the demographic changes of its leadership, the curriculum of post-1953 Spelman catered to a more activist student body—the Zeitgeist for the period, with the curriculum more reflective of the interests, concerns, and ideologies of a "new breed" of Spelman women.[46] Rather than attempting to address the complex and multi-faceted curricular issues associated with the post-1953 trajectory, this book focuses only on the pre-1953 Spelman.

A study of the curriculum of the post-1953 Spelman would necessitate a separate effort capable of adequately encompassing all of the social, educational, racial, and judicial complexities associated with the decades of the 1950s to the present. Thus, the post-1953 era is not incorporated into this study. Instead, this research focuses on the curricular foundation that paved the way for the curricular changes that would eventually pervade the post-1953 Spelman College.[47] The curricular foundation that spanned the years 1881 to 1953, although not often reflected in the public history of Spelman College, can be attributed to the power and legacy of four White women who purposefully and strategically determined the educational focus and opportunities for their Black female students.

This book utilizes the presidential administrations of the college as the organizational framework for the analysis of curricular development and socialization of students. This framework has been selected because dramatic changes in the foci and content of the curricula at the institution generally coincided with the goals of the president in charge of the institution.[48] During the period under study, college presidents held substantive roles in the leadership of their institutions. These presidents were truly academic leaders and often even taught courses within the institutions. The college presidents of this period were not solely the active fundraisers and external institutional liaisons often associated with the contemporary college president.[49] Four Spelman presidents officiated over the institution for Black women and girls from 1881 to 1953. These presidents had different notions about the form and substance of the Spelman curriculum, and thus used their respective presidencies as a means of shaping the curriculum. The use of the terms of the college presidents as the organizational framework for this study is not meant to discount the impact of the other actors and factors that influenced the curriculum or the socialization of students.

In addition to the impact of presidential influences upon the Spelman College curriculum, this book also attempts to identify other influences on the content and goals of the Spelman College curriculum at varying points in the seventy-two years under examination. However, the authors focus mainly on the internal institutional influences on the curriculum, while simultaneously acknowledging the existence of other relevant and no less important external forces.[50] The effect of external forces such as societal dictates, philanthropic interests,[51] accreditation agencies, and the like, upon the Spelman College curriculum is taken into account in many ways, for these internal actors were no doubt affected by external pressures.

This book generally discusses three types of curricula that have been operational at Spelman College over time: the formal academic curriculum, the "extracurriculum" and the "hidden curriculum."[52] The focus is, however, mainly on the operation of the formal academic curriculum, with examination of the operation of the other two as they impinged upon the former.[53] The book also describes the similarity of Spelman's curriculum to that of the northeastern White women's institutions that were the academic homes of

Spelman's New England-bred Founders as well as its administrative and faculty leadership.[54] Often referred to as either the Vassar, Wellesley, or Mount Holyoke of the South, the early curriculum of Spelman "has been likened to the curricula of Mount Holyoke and the Oread Collegiate Institute—schools from which the Founders graduated—as well as the curricula of institutions such as Oberlin College."[55]

This study also examines Spelman's persistent goal of creating Black female leadership for the uplift of Black communities. Essentially, the Founders of Spelman imbued in the faculty a philosophy that, beyond the training of students in domestic skills, incorporated the creation and development of "race women" who would use their formal educations for the religious and social uplift of their race:[56]

> Spelman's Founders never agonized over the need to offer their Black female students the classical education which male students were being offered elsewhere. Ever mindful of the peculiar history of Black women in this country and the realities of their everyday lives, the founders' primary aim was to provide training for teachers, missionaries and church workers. Equally important was the imparting of those practical skills that would make Black women good homemakers and mothers. Their philosophy of education (. . . . in many ways echoes [Booker T.] Washington), especially as it relates to Black women. . . . It is clear that the founders perceived their function to be enabling Black women to function in a world that had greatly restricted their opportunities rather than providing them with skills which they would be unable to use. . . . But [they] added that the literary work which [the students] were undertaking to build teachers and leaders of the race was also necessary.[57]

In what appears to be a contradiction to Spelman's racial uplift (through formal education) agenda, Spelman's curriculum (during certain periods) was, publicly, more closely aligned with Booker T. Washington's training philosophy related to the education of Black students than the "talented tenth" philosophy of W. E. B. DuBois.[58] Though DuBois' and Washington's views on the education of Blacks were widely touted as dichotomous, their views differed primarily with respect to the means to achieving the "education" as opposed to the end result of Blacks being educated. Washington's view, while more utilitarian in scope, could still be classified as racial uplift, since racial accountability and racial self-determination were part and parcel of his per-

spective on the ways that Blacks should be educated. DuBois describes the
two educational philosophies as follows:

> I believed in the higher education of a Talented Tenth who through their
> knowledge of modern culture could guide the American Negro into a higher
> civilization. I knew that without this the Negro would have to accept White
> leadership, and that such leadership could not always be trusted . . . Mr.
> Washington, on the other hand, believed that the Negro as an efficient
> worker could gain wealth and that eventually through his ownership of capi-
> tal he would be able to achieve a recognized place in American culture
>   . . . he proposed to put the emphasis at present upon training in the
> skilled trades and encouragement in industry and common labor.
>
> These two theories of Negro progress were not absolutely contradictory.
> Neither I nor Booker T. Washington understood the nature of capitalistic
> exploitation of labor, and the necessity of a direct attack on the principle of
> exploitation as the beginning of labor uplift.[59]

Spelman was not the only institution to stress industrial education during various periods throughout its history. From the 1880s to the 1930s, industrial
and vocational education became popular in curricula at many institutions
across the country (although not to the complete demise of liberal education).[60] This book seeks to demonstrate the varying ways in which each type
of education: classical (the trivium and quadrivium), liberal arts (education
for living which encompasses the arts, music, humanities, etc.), and industrial
education dominated, was subverted, or coexisted within the Spelman College
curriculum over the first seventy-two years of the college's history.[61]

This book examines Spelman College's curricular evolution over the period from 1881 to 1953. It is organizationally divided by the tenures of each of
the four college presidents who led the institution during this period. The
authors examine the ways in which the college's first four presidents influenced the formal academic curriculum and the extra and hidden curricula of
the institution. The authors look at how the formal academic curriculum per-
petuated classical, liberal, and industrial coursework, while the concurrently
operating extra and hidden curricula worked with the formal curriculum to
socialize Spelman students, thereby fostering the development of well-
rounded Black women capable of leadership and uplift of the Black race.

The First Four Spelman College Presidents—An Overview

In 1881, the Founders of Spelman Seminary sought to use their experience as missionaries and educators to assist in "saving the lost souls" of the former slave women of the South. This missionary zeal was a product of New England values and socialization, and a bit of ethnocentrism, coupled with a true desire to facilitate Black women's attainment of a better life for themselves and their families. One may be inclined to ask, "Why did the Founders choose to educate the *women* of the Black race?" The answer appears to lie in the Founders' backgrounds as women's activists, suffragists, and general purveyors of the belief that women were mentally and physically equipped to conduct the work that had traditionally been done by men. These sentiments probably contributed to their view that much hope for the uplift of the southern Blacks lay within the women of the race.

There is also cause to wonder if Sophia Packard and Harriet Giles intentionally set out not only to Christianize, but also to "westernize" these former slave women, based on the course of study that was pursued initially during the basement school days and later within former army barracks. Of course, equipped only with their own knowledge and educational experiences, as well as the sufficient belief that they had received superior educations in their northeastern seminaries and academies, these women sought to perpetuate "what worked" in their experience in the school they created for the "Negro women." This they did, and apparently ably so. The Founders struggled to create women who were like them, who met the standards of righteous and pious northeastern womanhood. These sentiments are not to be completely frowned upon as purely racist or ethnocentric, however, as they were generally the product not only of the way the Founders had been socialized to look at Black women (as savage and in need of taming or "saving"), but also of their own educational experiences which emphasized a variation of the trivium (grammar, rhetoric, logic) and quadrivium (geometry, arithmetic, music, and astronomy).

The Atlanta Baptist Female Seminary and subsequently, Spelman Seminary, under the Packard and Giles administrations (1881–1909), were created and cultivated in love and sincere Christian fellowship for the women and girls who attended the school. In none of the personal or professional correspondence of the Spelman principals or members of the faculty could we find a disparaging or unkind word spoken of the women and girls of Spelman

Seminary, their ability to learn, or their capacity for leadership. Great respect was also accorded the Founders, by students and faculty alike, even after their deaths. Succeeding presidents still sought to retain as much of the original aims of the Founders as they could in the Spelman curriculum.[62]

One very important lesson gained from this research is that the presidents of the college were clearly the most influential actors upon the curriculum of the institution. The first four presidents directly determined the course of study in which the women and girls would partake. As the position of dean developed in colleges throughout the country, the presidential control over areas such as curriculum lessened to some degree, but this was much less true at Spelman. Even as late as the Read administration, which lasted from the late 1920s to the early 1950s, the authority of the president over curriculum persisted.

The Packard and Giles administrations focused on imparting habits of industry and godliness to the women and girls of Spelman, along with intellectual education. Later, missionary work and normal training were of particular interest to the Founders, due to their adamant subscription to the belief that these women should extend their learning to the fields from whence they had come, to be shared with those less fortunate (educationally and spiritually) than they.

Miss Packard's and Miss Giles's strong philanthropic ties, beyond those with the Home Mission Society organizations, went a long way toward ensuring the viability of Spelman not just as an educational entity for women and girls, but one that eventually offered first-rate resources and curriculum. Their relationship with the early generations of the Rockefeller family ensured that resources of the highest quality would be made available to Spelman students. This commitment to the educational plight of African Americans was of utmost importance to John D. Rockefeller, whose mother had once opened her home as a stop on the Underground Railroad.[63] This spirit of philanthropy, the legacy of Mrs. Rockefeller, was embraced and enjoyed by many generations of Spelman students.

Miss Lucy Hale Tapley ushered in a new era to Spelman Seminary by initially focusing on the industrial needs associated with life in the South and society's limited expectations of Black women. She believed that education should be practical and applicable to daily living, a popular sentiment during that time, particularly as it related to Blacks. It must also be said that in this and other eras, the appropriateness of industrial and/or domestic education versus intellectual education was a pervasive issue of discussion with respect to White women's proper spheres. These differing approaches exemplify the very heavy influence that societal expectations and values can have and have had upon the academic enterprise and its curriculum. The curriculum of Spelman during the Tapley years clearly reflected a preponderance of vocational or industrial courses, but not completely to the detriment of academic or intellectual education. The constant improvements in the course offerings and the caliber of Spelman faculty members led to the upgrade of its status from Spelman Seminary to Spelman College.[64] This somewhat contradictory trajectory during the Tapley administration, in the industrial direction of the curriculum and the collegiate direction of the school, makes one wonder whether Miss Tapley wholly embraced the idea of practical education, or if her public endorsement of an industrial curriculum had more to do with responding to the interests of the philanthropic funding sources that supported Black higher education.

In essence, Lucy Hale Tapley built her Spelman presidential administration upon the religious, practical, and academic foundation established by the Founders, while simultaneously injecting a more vocational aspect into the institution that responded more to external forces—both societal and philanthropic. In so doing, Tapley was able to honor and respect the traditions and vision established by the Founders—of taking Spelman to an unsurpassed position of Black higher educational excellence tempered with education for racial uplift, while also retaining access to funding from external sources, which often required changing curricular priorities for Black postsecondary education.

Florence Read, the fourth president of Spelman College, brought a freshness of spirit and ideas to the institution and its curriculum. As president during what has been termed "the cultural explosion" in Black America, Miss Read availed herself of the opportunity to expose the Spelman students to new ideas and the fine arts. This exposure, combined with a curriculum comparable to that of other southern and some northern liberal arts colleges of the period, succeeded in propelling Spelman to the forefront of liberal arts education in the South, particularly among southern Black colleges.

The Read administration featured the most diverse (race and gender) faculty in the history of Spelman, as well as increased exposure and socialization opportunities for Spelman students, particularly due to the school's burgeoning fine arts program. Spelman drama and vocal students gained national and international recognition because of their accomplished fine arts faculty who, through the arts, were exposed to a world of opportunity, and who were in turn able to invite the world (almost literally) into Spelman's gates to witness their theatrical productions and other musical performances. In addition, guest lecturers, visiting and exchange professors, student academic exchange opportunities, and the like combined to make a Spelman education during the Read administration truly a more global experience.

A most poignant aspect of the curriculum of Spelman College in all the presidential administrations was the impact of non-academic portions of the curriculum on the students of Spelman. This book intentionally emphasizes the content of speeches given at building dedications, commencement ceremonies, and during guest lectures. In the estimation of the authors, these were some of the most compelling examples of the ways in which the hidden and extracurricula came together to create effective leadership from within the Spelman student body.

The women and girls of Spelman were incessantly inculcated with not only the expectation (via the allocation of human and capital resources) that they would and could excel academically and socially, but also (via the messages in speeches and lectures) with the belief that it was their responsibility to excel. The combination of religious, moral, and academic training found on Spelman's campus went a long way toward demonstrating these beliefs and expectations. Further, the principals, presidents, administrators, and faculty members went out of their way to serve as role models for the students. They demonstrated in word and in deed their commitment to the lifestyles and expectations that they so often "preached." Beyond their own actions, they went out of their way to bring the outside world to Spelman, even when the cruel and discriminating world was not quite ready to accept Spelman's students. Account upon account exists within the Spelman College Archives of instances where Spelman faculty members made special appeals and solicitations of museum curators, librarians, and the like to visit Spelman's campus to provide lectures to Spelman students, because "Negroes" weren't allowed to attend such public lectures in the segregated South.[65] Spelman students were also exposed to Black leaders from across the country in the fields of religion, medicine, education, the arts, and other areas. This exposure, by the presidents of the college, in the opinion of the authors of this book, tacitly demonstrated the presidents' acknowledgement of the potential that lay within each Spelman student to embody and emulate the great societal contributions of these religious, social, academic, and political leaders through their own future endeavors.

Dignitaries have abounded on the campus of Spelman, even from the time of its humblest beginnings, demonstrating to the students their worth, importance, and the esteem associated with being educated. Spelman students were constantly reminded of alumnae who were engaged in usual and unusual professions and activities. The important lesson for the students was that they could attain similar accomplishments, with their only limitation being their imaginations. These "pie-in-the-sky" types of ideals could have, on the surface, been harmful for Black, female students such as those at Spelman, who were limited by societal and legal constraints (e.g., discriminatory practices such as the separate-but-equal laws and policies referred to as "Jim Crow"). However, when examined within the context of the adversity that these former slaves and daughters of former slaves faced on a daily basis as Black women in the South, these dreams, as unrealistic as they may have seemed to some, probably helped to sustain these women and girls, and also to give them hope.

The Role of the College Curriculum

The study of academic curricula within educational institutions has always been a complex phenomenon, involving the examination of several factors that have impacted the way in which the curriculum has been developed, reformed, and otherwise altered. The study of the academic curricula of institutions of higher education is a particularly complex undertaking, considering the dynamic nature of higher education, as well as the constantly evolving nature of its component parts. "Curricular review is never easy. So many forces, external and internal, are at work on the curriculum, so many individuals have a concern with it, so many orientations compete as to the purposes that it might serve, so few effective mechanisms exist at the campus level for an examination of the curriculum in its totality, and so few leverages are available for constructive change . . ."[66]

The authors believe that the curriculum of institutions of higher education that have sought to provide a liberal education has been the most mercurial, while in other ways the most constant, of all of the curricular genres.

Influenced by a frank regard for public opinion, private resources and the peculiar circumstances of the various institutions in which college work has

been conducted, the [liberal arts] course of study remained uniform for such
extended periods of time that it naturally enough acquired a permanence
of opinion, private resources and the peculiar circumstances of the various
institutions in which college work has been conducted, the [liberal arts]
course of study remained uniform for such extended periods of time that it
naturally enough acquired a permanence of definition in the minds of its
friends that seriously hampered even incidental change.[67]

However, despite some of the confounding issues associated with the examination of academic curricula, the study of these curricula is necessary for
the evaluation of past educational practices of institutions of higher education
as well as for making projections of the academic futures of these institutions.
"Various writers claim that curriculum workers often have an inadequate appreciation of curriculum history and that future curriculum efforts are likely
to improve if they build on an understanding of the past."[68]

The academic curriculum has become more elaborate and convoluted
over time, as more and more diverse individuals have entered higher education. As women, members of ethnic minority groups, and other groups that
were not represented in the first graduating class of Harvard College (the long-
standing academic standard in higher education) have joined the ranks of
those in pursuit of postsecondary education, the academic curricula of many
institutions have changed to accommodate some members of these groups. In
other instances academic institutions have worked hard to circumvent the explicit recognition of these new groups in higher education by excluding issues
related to them from the academic curriculum.

The arrival of a new constituency on a college campus has rarely been an
occasion for unmitigated joy. Perhaps such students brought with them
much-needed tuition dollars. In that case, their presence was accepted and
tolerated. Yet higher-education [sic] officials, and often students from traditional constituencies, usually perceived the arrival of new groups not as a
time for rejoicing, but as a *problem* [emphasis in original]; a threat to an
institution's stated and unstated missions (official fear) or to its social life
(student fear) . . . In each case the entrance of a new group brought about
less-than-apocalyptic changes. In the case of relatively wealthy students in
nineteenth-century New England colleges, the arrival of poorer students led
to a decline in activities conducted by the student body as a whole and to a
rise of stratified eating and living arrangements. Ultimately the wealthier

students watched as the number of poorer brethren declined. Late in the nineteenth century the arrival of women on previously all-male campuses led to other forms of social segregation, which apprehensive administrators thought of abetting by segregating academic exercises by sex. Some years later, the arrival of a considerable number of Jewish students on east coast campuses caused concern lest gentile students seek out less "cosmopolitan" surroundings. Most recently, the arrival of significant numbers of black students on previously all-white (or almost so) institutions occasioned fears of "white flight" similar to what was perceived as happening in integrated elementary and secondary schools. In all of these cases, students adopted modest recourses [sic]—various informally segregated arrangements for living, eating, and socializing supplemented or took the place of officially sanctioned arrangements. Usually college authorities acquiesced in or even abetted these arrangements, believing them preferable to student exodus.[69]

The emerging issues related to the influx of more diverse groups into the higher educational milieu have led to renewed exploration of the purposes of the liberal arts curriculum by educational researchers and policy makers. The presence of these issues has also led to the initiation of in-depth investigations seeking to determine whether or not the college curriculum is the proper place to address the unique needs of each of the various ethnic, racial, and gender groups that have actively participated in higher education for over 150 years. According to Wegener,

> The burden thus placed upon a liberal curriculum is heavy, for one might seem obliged to incorporate within it what Lord Bacon called a "general and faithful perambulation of learning . . ."[sic] To put it bluntly, a liberal curriculum would seem to require us to teach everything intensively and reflectively, or, at least, to sample everything available in the intellectual world intensively and reflectively.[70]

Moreover, educators have often suggested that the college curriculum that is focused upon the liberal arts should also provide for the acculturation of America's youth:

> What are we to say about the culture of educational groups? First, educational groups are formed as a matter of policy with the defined objective of initiating pupils or students into culture. Because society does not provide, as a matter of common experience, the group affiliations which would trans-

mit all the cultural understandings we should wish, we form specialized groups to take over the task. Educators are responsible for controlling the experience of these groups.[71]

Such statements about the purposes of the college curriculum have led to what the Carnegie Foundation for the Advancement of Teaching has termed the "eternal points of tension" with respect to the aims of the college curriculum: scholarship versus training; attention to the past, the present, or to future; integration versus fragmentation; socialization into the culture versus alienation from the culture; student choice versus institutional requirements; breadth versus depth; skills versus understanding versus personal interests; theory versus practice; and ethical commitment versus ethical neutrality.[72] The authors' study of the curriculum development of Spelman College demonstrates the presence of these eternal points of tension over the course of the seventy-two years under examination.

In order to move effectively toward a clearer understanding of the enigmas associated with curriculum creation, development, and reform, common definitions of the substance of the college and university curriculum must be utilized as points of departure. The Carnegie Foundation for the Advancement of Teaching defines *curriculum* as "the body of courses that present the knowledge, principles, values, and skills that are the intended consequences of the formal education offered by a college."[73] However, the Foundation also offers two additional definitions of integral portions of the curriculum: the "extracurriculum" and the "hidden curriculum," which were not a part of the "intended consequences" of the formal college education, but existed on the college campus nevertheless. The definition of the *extracurriculum* provided by the Carnegie Foundation is: ". . . learning experiences provided informally through recreational, social, and cultural activities sponsored by colleges or by college-related organizations." The definition of the *hidden curriculum* is: ". . . learning that is informally and sometimes inadvertently acquired by students in interactions with fellow students and faculty members and inferred from the rules and traditions of the institution."[74] The definitions of the extracurriculum and the hidden curriculum within American colleges have been necessitated by the actions of their students:

When American colleges began to devote more official attention to academic programs and less to the behavior and personal development of students, it was the students themselves who filled the breach by organizing debating clubs, societies, sports activities, fraternities and sororities, and eventually scores of other activities that honored certain campus traditions, provided peer heroes, and supported the intellectual, emotional, and social development of students. The easy tendency to dismiss all of these activities as frilly and frivolous overlooks the fact that, while many extracurricular activities might deserve such characterizations, a substantial number of them were actually extensions of the educational enterprise. They made provisions for learning activities that could not (or at least were not) provided by the colleges themselves.[75]

Regardless of whether the curriculum, the extracurriculum, or the hidden curriculum is at work with respect to undergraduate education, one consistent notion that can be applied to the undergraduate institutions that develop their curriculum is that ". . . colleges do not always agree on the desired objectives of general education."[76] Jeanne Noble discusses three curricular philosophies that have been distinguished by Harold Taylor as prevalent in American colleges: rationalist, neo-humanist, and instrumentalist.[77] According to Noble, the rationalist approach places great emphasis on scholarship and is more interested in cultivating the intellect than developing the whole person. This approach does not usually place much value on extracurricular activities. The neo-humanist approach generally asserts that "it is important to transmit to the student, through instruction, that which man has learned and discovered throughout the ages. This philosophy has no other goals than those that lie within the cultural heritage itself."[78] The instrumentalist approach to the college curriculum, in contrast to both rationalism and neo-humanism, proposes education for self-fulfillment. According to Noble, within this approach, "general education should be devoted to helping each individual develop all his personal powers so that he may learn better to satisfy his own needs and share in caring for the needs of contemporary society."[79] The research for this book on Spelman College's curricular development seeks to determine whether or not any of these three curricular philosophies were in operation at Spelman as its curriculum evolved.

Beyond these approaches to examining the academic curriculum, which can assist in an understanding of the broad purposes of the college curriculum, Louis Franklin Snow argues:

> It is the ideal of the college that its graduates be prepared for citizenship by their course of study *within its wall*, in a way most fully to develop their best

powers of mind and establish their characters on the basis of integrity and truth. For each institution the problem has presented different phases. It is in this particular that the influence of the community upon the college has been felt. The ideals of the community have become the ideals of the college, and that college has done its most perfect work whose sympathy with the community has been most vital and close. Passing from the local to the wider environment, it will be seen that the college becomes most truly national which reflects and reproduces, in its curriculum, the national ideal.[80]

Despite Snow's assertion that the formation of the college curriculum does not exist in a vacuum,

> The undergraduate curriculum is often thought of as being insulated from influences outside the college . . . The curriculum is nevertheless responsive to the public interest and to changes in a college's relationship to professional and occupational groups, to the quality and level of preparation given to college students by high schools, to the levels of financial support available, to regulation and monitoring by governmental and accrediting agencies, and to the laws of survival and competition that govern the colleges' coexistence with other institutions of higher learning. The curriculum is particularly responsive to the growth of knowledge and to the rise and fall of subject fields in the public interest.[81]

However, there are still those educators who vehemently argue that

> . . . the determination of curriculum in higher education, at least at the undergraduate level, is largely a political matter usually settled by bargaining between entrenched departments and programs. As a result, the members of the academy, the professors, become their own body politic, or public, who influence the curriculum of higher education and offer many varied opinions about what liberal education was, is, and should be.[82]

The importance of these assertions is almost indisputable, as history itself has borne out the presence of internal and external forces having shaped the undergraduate liberal arts curriculum. Research on the academic history of Spelman College also demonstrates the continued presence of internal and external influences on the institution's curriculum.

Induction into Sisterhood: Spelman Culture and Expectations

The institutional values, norms and cultural values held by the first four women presidents also helped to shape and define the roles and minds of thousands of young Black students of Spelman College. This book examines the evolution of the Spelman College curriculum and explores the ways in which the Spelman culture, which evolved from the formal, hidden, and ex-tra- curricula, socialized young Black women students during the administrations of its first four presidents. According to R. K. Merton, *socialization* is defined as a process through which individuals acquire the values, norms, knowledge, and skills needed to exist in a given society.[83] A positive or negative socialization process can affect how successful the experience will be for the individual. How do institutional values or ideals shape the socialization of Spelman students and how are they transmitted through the internal environment by the administration to the student body?

The mission of women's colleges has always been to educate young girls in a supportive and nurturing environment where the development of self is most important. Many women's colleges were known by some as grooming schools, and most continue to promote "ladylike" behaviors as well as academic excellence, empowerment and community service.[84] Traditionally, historically Black women's colleges not only emphasized "ladylike" behaviors, but also the teaching of domestic skills, spiritual development, and rigid social controls. The main difference between historically Black women's colleges (HBWCs) and predominantly White women's colleges (PWWCs) is that PWWCs focus primarily on issues pertaining simply to gender, while HBWCs focus on how both gender and race affect the lives of Black women.

Traditionally, there has been little research published about Black women in higher education.[85] Today, the only two extant Historically Black Women's Colleges are Spelman College and Bennett College.[86] Despite the existence of HBWCs, PWWCs, and majority institutions with Black women students, much of the research on Black women in higher education has been overshadowed by research generalizations of women in higher education, which mostly reflect the experiences of White women.

Institutional Culture

Spelman College, like many other American educational institutions, boasts a cadre of tangible and intangible artifacts, which assist and have assisted in transmitting to current and future students the academic and social legacies of the institution. The iterative transmission of these legacies (often through legend or lore) to successive cohorts of Spelman students has successfully assisted in the creation and currently assists in the maintenance of the institutional culture of Spelman College.

Kuh and Hall articulate four key components of culture: *artifacts, perspectives, values,* and *assumptions*: "Artifacts are the tangible aspects of culture, the meaning and functions of which may be known by members."[87] The three main types of artifact are physical, verbal, and behavioral. Physical artifacts can be thought of as those that can be seen or touched by individuals and those that "provide them with immediate sensory stimuli as they carry out culturally expressive activities."[88] The most common physical cultural artifacts reviewed from Spelman College, to be discussed later, include Sisters Chapel, the Iron Gates, the Alumnae Arch, the Class Tree, the Spelman Messenger, the Grover-Werden Memorial Fountain, the Senior Bench, and Reynolds Cottage. Verbal cultural artifacts are, of course, transmitted orally by persons utilizing language, stories or myths and are manifested as either sagas or campus language. A saga is a "historical narrative describing the unique accomplishments of a group and its leaders, usually in heroic terms."[89] In comparison, Kuh and Whitt explain that campus language is "words, phrases, and tonal intonations" that identify a speaker as part of a particular group or organization.[90] The most evident verbal cultural artifacts of Spelman College include the College Motto and the Spelman College Hymn, the tenets of which are captured and embodied in every facet of the contemporary Spelman experience, including the Spelman College mission statement:

> Spelman is an outstanding historically Black college for women which promotes academic excellence in the liberal arts and develops the intellectual, ethical, and leadership potential of its students. Spelman seeks to empower the total person who appreciates the many cultures of the world and commits to positive social change.[91]

According to Manning:

> Myths and stories passed on from one student cohort to the next carry messages year after year about what the institution values and expects of students and others. At colleges with strong cultures, prospective students hear about

college traditions through stories told by paraprofessional admissions ambassadors and upper-class student leaders.[92]

Manning further asserts that behavioral cultural artifacts include rituals and rites of passage, cultural performances and traditions that serve to "express the traditions of the community, welcome and initiate new members, create a bridge between the here-and-now and the here-and-then, preview the passage from college living to outside college reality, express the community's beliefs and values, and celebrate members' accomplishments."[93] The traditions of Spelman College are filled with rituals that serve to give meaning to the past through their relevance to the present and future. The Parting Ceremony and the Rituals of Revitalization of Spelman are just two of the many rituals that communicate, through symbolization and celebration, Spelman's values, norms, ideals, and culture to its students as well as the faculty and administrators.

> To understand the type of educational institution created at Spelman, it is necessary to understand not only the philosophical underpinnings of the parent group but its view of Blacks who were the recipients of its largesse. Its members looked upon the experience of slavery as one which had morally, spiritually, and culturally bankrupted Blacks. Many of the missionaries believed Blacks to have emerged from the "dense darkness of ignorance dazed and terrorized by the new responsibilities of freedom."[94]

This book examines the physical, verbal, and behavioral cultural artifacts of Spelman College, which have either been created as an outgrowth of its academic, extra-, or hidden curricula, or have served as the progenitors of the same. The existence of these artifacts and their historical meanings and legacies are as integral to the history and fiber of the Spelman College experience as its Founders, its students, and the institutional leaders who helped to proliferate them.

The academic, social, and cultural knowledge, values, and beliefs gained by Spelman students from the late 1880s to the mid 1950s derived very heavily from the institutional culture of Spelman, which was fostered by its White, female academic and social leaders. This transmission of this very distinct and intentional set of social and educational values and beliefs contributed most notably to the unique socialization of the "Spelman Woman" as compared to other African American female collegians. In the early twentieth century, the process of socialization of Black college-educated women began and was greatly influenced by the religious beliefs and societal and moral values of Northern White women.[95] Corley explains, ". . . . Spelman graduates tended to continue organizing and forming women's groups for community better-ment or 'social uplift' and 'self-help' and contributed to the establishment of a Black middle class with White values."[96]

> Education can be viewed as a tool of liberation or a tool of socialization; perhaps both at the same time. The process of education for both groups of women was a radical act, one that was to exceed the visions of both sets of founders. Even the most controlled, carefully orchestrated education has unintended consequences. It raises aspirations and hopes: It allows the recip-ients to see themselves in a different way. As they are exposed to the world of new ideas, their consciousness of possible moves to a new level of aware-ness.[97]

This view of the purposes, functions, and potential outcomes of educating Black women is not only relevant in Historically Black Women's Colleges, but in Predominantly White Women's Colleges as well. For example, Tidball and her colleagues, in *Taking Women Seriously* (1999), examined Bryn Mawr and Bennett Colleges to ascertain the academic, social, and environmental fac-tors that contributed to the success of their African American women stu-dents. The resulting data were sorted into the following ten categories:

1. High academic expectations
2. Personal support and advising
3. Supportive peer culture
4. Strong institutional mission
5. Critical mass of African American women
6. Inclusion in the curriculum
7. Presence of role models
8. Emphasis on giving back to the community
9. Extracurricular involvement opportunities
10. Awareness of societal realities facing African American women

Tidball and her colleagues also noted seven major lessons about the institu-tional characteristics which contributed to the success of their African Ameri-can women students, based on the particular climates of these women's

colleges. These institutional characteristics included the possession of personnel, belief systems, and/or demographic qualities that

1. Clarify and communicate the mission
2. Believe students can achieve and hold them to it
3. Make students feel like they matter
4. Provide strong, positive role models
5. Have enough women to form a critical mass
6. Provide ample opportunities for student leadership
7. Include women in the curriculum

Historically, Spelman College has inherently and successfully integrated all of
the aforementioned success factors and lessons learned into its provision of
a well-rounded academic, social, and cultural environment for its students,
translating into significant graduation and graduate school entrance rates.[98]

In Tidball's 1974 article, she explores the reasons for the higher graduation rate of women from women's colleges than from coeducational institutions. Toward this end, she postulates:

> . . . the greater the women-faculty/women-student ratio, the greater the
> number of women graduates who subsequently achieve, While the average
> number of women achievers/women-faculty was the same in both groups of
> colleges (women's and coeducational), the women-faculty/women-student
> ratio in the women's colleges was twice as large as that in the coeducational
> school . . . Women teachers as role models for women students are thus a
> critical ingredient of a college environment that turns out talented women.
> In addition to serving as role models, women professors have also been
> found to be more concerned with emotional development of their students
> and with helping them attain a deeper level of self-understanding than are
> male professors.[99]

Fourteen years after Tidball's work was published, Rice and Hemmings re-
evaluated her findings and argued that if greater women role models in wom-
en's colleges were advantageous, then the "increasing visibility of senior
women faculty at coeducational institutions should also contribute to the success of coeducational college women alumnae."[100] Furthermore, Rice and
Hemmings concluded that the larger numbers of successful graduates from
women's colleges than from coeducational institutions can also be attributed

to other factors beyond the presence of more women faculty role models, such as a supportive educational environment or a highly selective admissions process.

In 1989, Smith examined 880 women graduates from women's colleges and coeducational institutions and concluded that:

> In general, each of the analyses supports the positive evaluation of women's colleges in terms of academic program and administration. The final analyses show that these colleges are rated higher on many institutional goals which are directed to academic, social, and civic development. Further, women's colleges are rated equally on their concern for career and professional objectives. The criticism that women's colleges ignore "real world" concerns is not supported by the perceptions of students who attend these schools.[101]

Spelman College is no exception to Smith's analysis. Historically, the concern of the academic and social leadership of Spelman College, for the professional and further academic growth and development of its students, has contributed to the benevolent experiences enjoyed by generations of Spelmanites. This book delves further into this phenomenon, as well as the impact that the unique institutional variables have had upon the education and acculturation of Spelman College students.

A Unique Socialization: The Case for Historically Black Colleges and Universities

In Wolf-Wendel's (previously known as Wolf) 1995 dissertation, she studied the socialization of undergraduate students from women's colleges and historically Black colleges and universities (HBCUs), disaggregating her data by race and gender. In her 1998 report, Wolf-Wendel contended that women's colleges and HBCUs have a more positive impact on their students.

> Compared to other institutional types, historically Black women's colleges produced the largest proportion of successful African American women in both analyses. The productivity ratios for historically Black women's colleges were up to 47 times greater than the ratios for predominately white coeducational institutions. Further, the productivity ratio means for historically Black women's colleges were up to 6 times greater than the means for historically Black coeducational institutions and up to ten times greater than

the means for predominately white women's colleges. In fact, in both analyses, the mean productivity ratio for the historically Black women's colleges was significantly higher than the means for all other institutional types.[102]

We contend that the socialization process of Black women at historically Black women's colleges (Spelman and Bennett Colleges) is very different from the socialization experienced by women attending coeducational HBCUs, PWWCs, and other institutions. Numerous socializing agents that have changed over time have contributed to the educational experiences of these generations of young Black women, particularly since the administrations of Spelman College's first four White women presidents; however, their effects have not necessarily decreased. Accordingly, these changes, as well as changing societal norms and perceptions, have influenced changes in the curriculum and the historical and contemporary expectations that society holds for the education of collegiate women in general.

According to the Spelman College charter, the institution emphasizes "learning for young colored women in which special attention is to be given to the formation of industrial habits and Christian characters."[103] These facets of the curriculum were certainly given specific attention, as a contribution to the training of the well-rounded Spelman woman, but not without equal attention to the more academic endeavors of Spelman students. In 1944, for example, Spelman hosted a conference entitled, "Current Problems and Programs in the Higher Education of Negro Women." This conference represented the first formal effort to examine the psychological and socioeconomic factors affecting the academic achievement of Black women within the higher educational milieu. The hosting of this conference on the campus of a college founded by White northeastern women specifically for African American women is therefore quite significant.

In Johnnetta Cole's 1984 book, *Conversations: Straight Talk with America's Sister President,* she offers several lessons learned from Spelman's successful track record of educating Black women that we consider in chapter 2 as we discuss the history of the undergraduate curriculum.

> In an atmosphere relatively free of racism and sexism, where teachers care and expect the very best, parents and kinfolk are involved, and the curriculum and those around the students reflect in positive ways who the students are—there are no limits to what individuals can learn and who they can

become . . . when we (black women) are empowered so, too, will be all African Americans. Women are the primary caretakers of children and, consequently their first teachers. So, as they sat, when you educate a man you educate an individual, but when you educate a woman, you educate a nation. That is why we must learn and we must teach.[104]

Notes

1. In the Northeast, during this period, religious academies and seminaries provided academic excellence as well as Christian conversion and piety. Academy and seminary educations took place at a lower academic level than in the "colleges." As a matter of fact, other institutions that combined secondary and collegiate forms of education loosely adopted the term "college" to describe their curricular offerings. For further discussion of seminaries and academies, see Barbara Miller Solomon, *In the Company of Educated Women* (New Haven, CT: Yale University Press, 1985), pp. 21–30.

2. The word *curriculum* is used in its broadest, most formal, academic sense, unless otherwise noted by the use of the terms *hidden curriculum* or the *extracurriculum*; each of the three terms is defined in greater detail later in this study.

3. For publications that speak to the social and curricular history of Spelman College, see: Florence Fleming Corley, *Higher Education for Southern Women; Four Church-Related Women's College in Georgia: Agnes Scott, Shorter, Spelman, and Wesleyan, 1900–1920* (Doctoral Book, College of Education, Georgia State University, 1985); Beverly Guy-Sheftall, *Spelman: A Centennial Celebration* (Atlanta, GA: Spelman College, 1981); Edward A. Jones, *A Candle in the Dark: A History of Morehouse College* (Valley Forge, PA: Judson Press, 1967); Albert E. Manley, *A Legacy Continues: The Manley Years at Spelman College, 1953–1976* (Lanham, MD: University Press of America, Inc., 1995); Florence Read, *The Story of Spelman College* (Princeton, NJ: Princeton University Press, 1961); and W.N. Hartshorn, ed., *An Era of Progress and Promise (1863–1910): The Religious, Moral, and Educational Development of the American Negro Since his Emancipation* (Boston, MA: Priscilla Publishing, 1910).

4. Guy-Sheftall, Spelman: A Centennial Celebration, p. 5.

5. See Spelman College Charter—State of Georgia, June 2, 1955 (as amended) in Spelman College Archives. See also Jeanne Noble, *The Negro Woman's College Education* (New York: Garland Publishing, 1987), p. 76; Guy-Sheftall, *Spelman: A Centennial Celebration*, p. 10; Stephanie Shaw, *What a Woman Ought to Be and To Do: Black Professional Women Workers During the Jim Crow Era* (University of Chicago Press, 1996), pp.1, 76; Patricia Roberts Harris, "Achieving Racial Equality for Women" in *Women in Higher Education*, p. 16; and Patricia Bell-Scott, "Black Women's Higher Education: Our Legacy," *SAGE: A Scholarly Journal on Black Women*, Vol. 1, No. 1, (Spring 1984): 841.

6. See Spelman College Archives, Presidents' Reports to the Women's American Baptist Home Mission Society, 1881–1911. See also Linda Perkins, "The Education of

Black Women in the Nineteenth Century," in *Women in Higher Education in American History*, eds. John Mack Faragher and Florence Howe (New York: W.W. Norton, 1988), p. 69. For discussion of role of Black colleges for purposes of developing leaders for racial uplift see Charles V. Willie and Ronald R. Edmonds, eds., *Black Colleges in America: Challenge, Development, Survival* (New York: Teachers College Press, 1978).

7. Although Spelman is the oldest surviving historically Black college for women, it was not the first and only such institution. Other educational institutions founded for the education of Black women during this era included: The Miner Normal School for Colored Girls (later Miner Teachers College)—Washington, D.C., founded by Myrtilla Miner in 1851; the Haines Normal and Industrial Institution—Augusta, GA, founded by Lucy Craft Laney in 1886 (later became co-ed); The National Training School for Women and Girls—Washington, D.C. founded by Nannie Helen Burroughs on October 19, 1909; The Palmer Memorial Institute—Sedalia, NC, founded by Charlotte Hawkins Brown in 1902 (later became co-ed); The Daytona Educational Industrial Training School (later merged with another college to become the co-ed Bethune-Cookman College)—Daytona, FL, founded by Mary McLeod Bethune on October 4, 1904; Scotia Seminary (later merged with another college to become the co-ed Barber-Scotia College)—Concord, NC; Tillotson College (later merged with another college to become the co-ed Huston-Tillotson College); and Hartshorn Academy—Richmond, VA, founded by Joseph C. Hartshorn in 1884 (merged with Virginia Union College in 1932). Also of note, although Bennett College, founded by Lyman Bennett, is now a Black women's college, when founded in 1873 it was co-educational and did not become a woman's college until 1926, so it was not, initially, among Spelman's contemporaries.

8. Beverly Guy-Sheftall, "Black Women and Higher Education: Spelman and Bennett Colleges Revisited," in *Journal of Negro Education* Vol. 51, No. 3 (1982): 278–285. For more thorough discussions of education for women's proper spheres, see the following books and articles whose entire texts deal with the issue (except where page numbers denote otherwise): Elizabeth Barber Young, *A Study of the Curriculum of Seven Selected Women's Colleges of the Southern States* (New York: Teacher's College, Columbia University, 1932); Mabel Newcomer, *A Century of Higher Education for American Women* (New York: Harper & Brothers, 1959); Emily Davies, *The Higher Education of Women* (New York: AMS Press, 1973); Helen Lefkowitz Horowitz, *Alma Mater: Design and Experience in the Women's Colleges from their Nineteenth Century Beginnings to the 1930s* (New York: Knopf, 1984); Florence Fleming Corley, *Higher Education for Southern Women: Four Church-Related Women's Colleges in Georgia: Agnes Scott, Shorter, Spelman, and Wesleyan, 1900–1920* (College of Education, Georgia State University, 1985); Noble, *The Negro Woman's College Education*; Linda M. Perkins, "The Impact of the 'Cult of True Womanhood' on the Education of Black Women," Lester F. Goodchild and Harold S. Weschler, gen. eds., *ASHE Reader on the History of Higher Education* (Needham Heights, MA: Ginn Press, 1989); Beverly Guy-Sheftall, "A Conversation with Willa P. Player," *SAGE: A Scholarly Journal on Black Women*, Vol. 1, No. 1 (Spring 1984): 16; and Linda Buchanan, *Not Harvard, Not Holyoke, Not Howard* (College of Education, Georgia State University, 1997).

9. J. B. Roebuck and K. S. Murty, *Historically Black Colleges and Universities: Their Place in American Higher Education* (Westport, CT: Praeger, 1993), p. 21.

10. During slavery, most of the male slaves worked on the plantation, while it was not uncommon to find Black women in the slave master's household tending to general household chores, caring for the children, or cooking for the master's family. Thus, slave women had more opportunity to carefully observe the lives of their White master and his family, while the slave men, who also learned a lot from imitation of the mannerisms and customs of the master, did not always have the ready access to the many facets of the life of the master and his family. This is not to say that female slaves who worked in the planter's home were excluded from fieldwork. Much to the contrary, if the crops required it, "house" slave women were also expected to join the other slaves in the field. For more information on this division of labor, see Kenneth Stampp, *The Peculiar Institution: Slavery in the Ante-Bellum South* (New York: Vintage, 1956), pp. 34–44.

11. Noble, *The Negro Woman's College Education*, p. 3.

12. The freed slaves' desire for knowledge and to achieve a formal education predated Reconstruction, and actually existed during slavery itself.

13. Roebuck and Murty, *Historically Black Colleges and Universities*, p. 23.

14. See Roebuck and Murty, *Historically Black Colleges and Universities* and Manley, *A Legacy Continues: The Manley Years at Spelman College, 1953–1976.*

15. Ibid, p. 2.

16. I make a distinction between "free Blacks" and "freed Blacks" wherein free Blacks were those who were considered free prior to Abraham Lincoln's Emancipation Proclamation, while freed Blacks were those whose freedom was granted as a result of the proclamation.

17. Bell-Scott, "Black Women's Higher Education: Our Legacy," p. 8. The most thorough and comprehensive discussion of the education of Blacks in this period can be found in James D. Anderson, *The Education of Blacks in the South, 1860–1935* (Chapel Hill, NC: University of North Carolina Press, 1988).

18. See Roebuck and Murty, *Historically Black Colleges and Universities* and Albert N. Whiting, *Guardians of the Flame: Historically Black Colleges; Yesterday, Today, and Tomorrow* (Washington, D.C.: American Association of State Colleges and Universities, 1991), p. 2.

19. Noble, *The Negro Woman's College Education*, p. 19 and Jeanne Noble cited in Paula Giddings, *When and Where I Enter: The Impact of Black Women on Race and Sex in America* (New York: William Morrow, 1984), p. 101.

20. Noble, *The Negro Woman's College Education*, p. 22.

21. Sheila T. Gregory, *Black Women in The Academy: The Secrets to Success and Achievement* (Lanham, MD: University Press of America, Inc., 1995).

22. Paula Giddings, *When and Where I Enter: The Impact of Black Women on Race and Sex in America* (New York: William Morrow and Company, Inc., 1984), pp. 20, 101.

23. For a more thorough discussion of missionary efforts to educate Blacks, see

complete text of article by Johnnetta Cross-Brazzell, "Bricks Without Straw: Mission-ary-Sponsored Black Higher Education in the Post-Emancipation Era," *Journal of Higher Education*, Vol. 63, No. 1, January/February 1992.

24. The name Spelman College or Spelman is used to represent the institution under study, despite the various names associated with the institution over the course of its development and maturity (e.g. Atlanta Baptist Female Seminary, Spelman Semi-nary, and later Spelman College).

25. Sophia Packard and Harriet Giles were both educated at New Salem Academy in Salem, Massachusetts. For more description of their educational attainments, see Read, *The Story of Spelman*, pp. 8–13.

26. While it was at New Salem that Packard and Giles became acquainted, their lifelong association as colleagues came about as they endeavored upon varying teaching and administrative posts in Petersham, MA, later Orange, MA. They then opened their own school in Fitchburg, MA in March 1859. This school was short-lived, and they both took positions at Suffield Academy (also referred to as the Connecticut Liter-ary Institution) in Suffield, CT. In 1864 they both resigned from Suffield Academy and took teaching and administrative posts at the Oread Collegiate Institute in Worcester, MA. For more information about their teaching and administrative experi-ences in New England, see Read, *The Story of Spelman*, pp. 11–25.

27. Read, *The Story of Spelman*, p. 30.

28. Guy-Sheftall, *Spelman: A Centennial Celebration*, p. 10 and Read, *The Story of Spelman*, p. 32.

29. Read, *The Story of Spelman*, p. 32.

30. Guy-Sheftall, *Spelman: A Centennial Celebration* p. 10. For a discussion of Black ex-slave women's receiving an education, see also Giddings, *When and Where I Enter*, p. 101.

31. Spelman Seminary Annual Report to Trustees of Spelman Seminary, *Spelman Messenger*, May 1909, p.12, in Spelman College Archives.

32. For a discussion of how Packard and Giles initially came south, and their initial impressions, see Guy-Sheftall, *Spelman: A Centennial Celebration*, p. 10 and Read, *The Story of Spelman*, pp. 32, 36.

33. Read, *The Story of Spelman*, p. 38.

34. Ibid, p. 55.

35. Read, *The Story of Spelman*, p. 36. Packard and Giles would later also indicate their selection of Atlanta as the site for the new school due to its "healthful climate, railroad connections, and spirit of enterprise," which "have made it largely the politi-cal, commercial and educational center of the state." See *Spelman Seminary School Cat-alogue, 1883–84*, p. 11, in Spelman College Archives.

36. Spelman Seminary Annual Report to Trustees of Spelman Seminary, *Spelman Messenger*, April 1917, p. 1, in Spelman College Archives.

37. Whiting, *Guardians of the Flame*, p. 2.

38. On the similarity of Spelman's early academic curriculum and student policies to that of Suffield Academy and the Oread Collegiate Institution, see Read, *The Story of Spelman*, pp. 13, 19, 21, 23, 44.

39. Guy-Sheftall, *Spelman: A Centennial Celebration*, p.31.

40. See Read, *The Story of Spelman*, p. 50. Packard entered into her diary the fact that she received a visit from Rev. William Jefferson White of Augusta (who was an educational, religious, and political leader of Blacks in Georgia; publisher and editor of *The Georgia Baptist* newspaper; as well as founder of the Atlanta Baptist Seminary in Augusta— later Morehouse College) who expressed objections to the school teaching students who were less than fifteen years old. After pressure also mounted on this issue from a committee of Black ministers convened by Rev. White, Miss Packard and Miss Giles sent all of the under-fifteen children away. See *Diary of Miss Packard*, April 13, 1881, no page number, Box: Sophia B. Packard, in Spelman College Archives.

41. For a discussion of the types of students who attended Spelman and other Black Southern colleges during this and latter periods, see E. Franklin Frazier, *Black Bourgeoisie* (New York, The Free Press, 1957) and Willard B. Gatewood, *Aristocrats of Color in the South* (Bloomington, IN: Indiana University Press, 1990). See also Read, *The Story of Spelman*, p. 44. At this point in Spelman's history students simply "came" to Spelman, there were no formal admissions procedures as such.

42. Guy-Sheftall, *Spelman: A Centennial Celebration*, p. 19. These former slaves gained information about the whereabouts of their children through the Freedmen's Bureau. Miss Packard and Miss Giles also mentioned that many of the oldest pupils in the school did not want an education to teach in schoolrooms, but instead to read the Bible and for religious and moral instruction within their churches. See *Annual Report to WABHMS from Packard and Giles*, 1883, p.13.

43. The "proper spheres" were defined differently for Black and White women. White women's proper spheres included the home, and in limited fashion, the professional world, but always was regarded as being subordinate to the position of White men. The Black women's proper spheres included subordination not only to White men, but also to White women and Black men.

44. For discussion, see Manley, *A Legacy Continues*, p. 27; Letter from Miss Giles to Rev. Morgan, January 24, 1901, in Box: "Harriet E. Giles," Folder: Correspondence, Spelman College Archives; and *Annual Report to WABHMS from Packard and Giles*, 1883, pp. 11,12.

45. Guy-Sheftall, *Spelman: A Centennial Celebration*, p.29; See also Read, *The Story of Spelman*, and Spelman Archives—Spelman Messenger newsletters (1885–1953).

46. See Manley, *A Legacy Continues*, pp. 15–90 for discussion of political awareness, solidarity, and activism among Spelman students during the post-1953 era. See pp. 27–35 for a discussion of initial academic curricular changes during the Manley administration. This is not to say that Spelman's curriculum was completely devoid of these components prior to the Manley administration (1953–1976); evidence indicates that as early as 1900, Spelman/Morehouse annex courses in history and sociology dealing with the African-American experience (developed by W.E.B. Du Bois, then an Atlanta University professor) were being taught. For a discussion of these courses, see Corley, *Higher Education for Southern Women.*, p. 238. It must also be said that the induction of the "contemporary Black college" model (whereby Black students intentionally at-

tend Black colleges in search of political and social solidarity, self- and cultural awareness, etc.) at Spelman College really began to come into existence during the Read and
Manley administrations, and has persisted throughout successive administrations.

47. The post-1953 Spelman College witnessed its first Black president (male), its
first Black female president, and most recently its first alumna president. President
Emeritus Albert E. Manley served as Spelman's fifth president 1953–1976; Spelman's
sixth president, Donald Stewart, served 1976–1987; Spelman's seventh, and first Black
female president, Johnnetta Cole, served 1987–1997; Spelman's eighth, and first
alumna president (and wife of Albert E. Manley—deceased), Audrey Manley, became
the president of Spelman College in 1998.

48. This is not to say that the Spelman Board of Trustees was powerless. On the
contrary, the Spelman Board of Trustees held much sway over many of the matters
related to the institution, but the power and authority to raise funds and craft the
curriculum of Spelman College rested heavily with the president of the institution,
with certain matters of course going before the Board for approval.

49. Regarding the more involved role of the college president as educator, and not
solely as fundraiser or liaison with external entities, see Laurence Veysey, *The Emergence of the American University* (Chicago, IL: University of Chicago Press, 1965). Note:
Though Veysey's work generally focuses on the period from 1910–1920, the notion of
the presidents as academic leaders held true at Spelman College beyond this decade,
and well into the Read administration.

50. For a general discussion of the various types of internal influences upon the
college curriculum, see Bruce A. Kimball, "Curriculum History: The Problems in
Writing About Higher Education," in Craig Kridel, ed. *Curriculum History: Conference
Presentations from the Society for the Study of Curriculum History* (Lanham, MD: University Press of America, 1989), p. 60. In addition to the college's presidents as internal
influences, Spelman's faculty also had a profound impact on the institution's curriculum. For an example of this impact, see *Annual Report of Spelman Seminary*, 1924–24,
p. 2 in Spelman College Archives, which details the colleges and technical schools from
which Spelman's faculty members hailed, e.g. Columbia University, Boston University, University of North Dakota, Mount Holyoke, Wellesley, Smith, Colby, Cornell,
Penn State College, Framingham State Normal College, Ypsilanti Teachers College,
Barnard, Skidmore, Gordon Bible College, and Northwestern College. This book addresses the question of whether the alma maters of the faculty impacted the curriculum.

51. See Perkins, "The Education of Black Women in the Nineteenth Century," p.
163, in Faragher and Howe, *Women and Higher Education in American History,* for
discussion of ways in which White philanthropic organizations and members of society
viewed education of Blacks for "education's sake" as impractical, and thus not worthy
of funding. Philanthropic organizations began to agitate for the provision of a more
"practical" education for Blacks in higher education, particularly Black women. This
pressure upon the college curriculum for Black women led to the emergence of large
vocational and professional departments on college campuses seeking to train Black

female teachers, nurses, and domestic workers. This book also demonstrates how philanthropic interests, such as those of the General Education Board, manifested support for Spelman's stated curricular objectives which combined practical with intellectual education.

52. The Carnegie Foundation for the Advancement of Teaching, *Missions of the College Curriculum* (San Francisco: Jossey-Bass ., 1977), pp. xii, xiii, defines curriculum as "the body of courses that present the knowledge, principles, values, and skills that are the intended consequences of the formal education offered by a college." The Foundation asserts that the hidden curriculum and the extracurriculum are not part of the intended consequences of the formal college education, but exist on the college campus nevertheless. The Foundation therefore defines the extracurriculum as "learning experiences provided informally through recreational, social, and cultural activities sponsored by the colleges or by college-related organizations." The Foundation further defines the hidden curriculum as "learning that is informally and sometimes inadvertently acquired by students in interactions with fellow students and faculty members and inferred from the rules and traditions of the institution."

53. For general guidance on the development of college curricula in institutions of varying types (though attention to Black colleges was minimal in both texts), consult Frederick Rudolph, *Curriculum: A History of the American Undergraduate Course of Study Since 1636* (San Francisco: Jossey-Bass Publishers, 1977) and Laurence R. Veysey, *The Emergence of the American University* (University of Chicago Press, 1965). For curriculum theory, see: Louis Franklin Snow, *The College Curriculum in the United States* (New York: Teachers College, Columbia University, 1907); Barry J. Fraser, "An Historical Look at Curriculum Evaluation," in *Curriculum History: Conference Presentations from the Society for the Study of Curriculum History*, Craig Kridel, ed. (Lanham, MD: University Press of America, 1989). For discussion of liberal curriculum and transmission of culture via curricula, see Charles Wegener, *Liberal Education and the Modern University* (Chicago: University of Chicago Press, 1978); David O. Levine, *The American College and the Culture of Aspiration, 1915–1940* (Ithaca, NY: Cornell University Press, 1986); and Lawrence Stenhouse, *Culture and Education* (New York: Weybright and Talley, 1967). For discussion of Black women's relationship to curriculum see Barbara Sicherman, "The Invisible Woman: The Case for Women's Studies in *Women in Higher Education*, W. Todd Furniss and Patricia Albjerg Graham, eds. (Washington, D.C.: American Council on Education, 1974).

54. For discussions of curriculum development in the women's colleges, see the complete texts of the following books which specifically address the issue: Corley, *Higher Education for Southern Women. . . .*; Newcomer, *A Century of Higher Education*; Elizabeth Barber Young, *A Study of Curriculum of Seven Selected Women's Colleges of the Southern States* (New York: Teachers College, Columbia University, 1932); Barbara Miller Solomon, *In the Company of Educated Women* (New Haven, CT: Yale University Press, 1985); Christie Ann Farnham, *The Education of the Southern Belle: Higher Education and Student Socialization in the Antebellum South* (New York: New York University Press, 1994) and Lynn D. Gordon, *Gender and Higher Education in the Progressive Era* (New Haven, CT: Yale University Press, 1990).

55. Bell-Scott, "Black Women's Higher Education," p. 9. For further discussion of influences of Northeastern women's seminaries and academies on Spelman College's curriculum see Corley, *Higher Education for Southern Women* and Shaw, *What a Woman Ought to Be and To Do.*

56. Although the term "race woman" is generally used to discuss a woman's foray into social reform and race/social injustice protest work, the Founders and subsequent presidents of Spelman College believed that by serving as leaders amongst the race as teachers, missionaries, and church workers, with the possible accompanying role of social activist, then these women were indeed uplifting their race and were therefore "race women."

57. Guy-Sheftall, *Spelman: A Centennial Celebration*, p. 27–29.

58. Spelman, like many educational institutions for Blacks, was often at the financial mercy of White philanthropic organizations. It was often asserted by W.E.B. DuBois that the financial support of Black higher educational institutions was contingent upon recommendations by Booker T. Washington (what DuBois referred to as the "Tuskegee Machine"). That is, those institutions that openly supported Washington's philosophy related to industrial education were favored for funding considerations. DuBois, on many occasions, recounted his version of the story about Atlanta University's inability to receive funding from organized philanthropy due to his affiliation with the institution and the concurrent controversy between himself and Booker T. Washington, which lasted from 1903 until about 1908. According to DuBois, during that period of time the controversy became increasingly personal and bitter and unfortunately dragged the university in the middle of it. Thus, it is no surprise that Spelman, though it did indeed subscribe to a "dual function" of education—academic and practical, may have publicly emphasized the domestic and industrial arts components of its curriculum early on in its history. For more discussion about the "debate" between DuBois and Washington and its effects on Black postsecondary institutions, see the following: Cedric Robinson, *Black Marxism: The Making of the Black Radical Tradition* (Atlantic Heights, NJ: Zed Books Ltd., 1983), pp. 266–278; W.E.B. DuBois, *Dusk of Dawn: An Essay Toward an Autobiography of a Race Concept* (New Brunswick, NJ: Transaction Publishers, 1984), pp. 67–87; W.E.B. DuBois, *The Souls of Black Folk* (New York: Bantam Books, 1903, 1989) pp. 30–43, pp. 53–62; Frederick Rudolph, *Curriculum: A History of the American Undergraduate Course of Study since 1636.* (San Francisco: Jossey-Bass, 1977), pp.148–149, pp.167–169; and Guy-Sheftall, *Spelman: A Centennial Celebration*, pp. 27–31. For a discussion of Atlanta University during this period, see Clarence A. Bacote, *The Story of Atlanta University: A Century of Service, 1865–1965* (Atlanta, GA: Atlanta University Press, 1969).

59. W.E.B. DuBois, *The Autobiography of W.E.B. DuBois* (International Publishers, New York, 1968).

60. Bell-Scott, "Black Women's Higher Education," p. 9.

61. The classical curriculum consisted generally of the trivium (grammar, rhetoric, and logic) and the quadrivium (arithmetic, music, geometry, and astronomy). The liberal arts curriculum generally focused on providing education for "acculturation,"

while industrial education prepared students for vocations and equipped them with useful skills. For more in-depth discussion of the three curricular types see Chapter 2 of this book, "The Higher Education of Black Women."

62. See Presidents' Reports (1910–1953) in Spelman College Archives.

63. Read, *The Story of Spelman*, pp. 80–83.

64. Improvements in the course offerings included upgrades of the course content from lower-level courses (on par with secondary education) to those commensurate with collegiate-level courses offered at reputable institutions of higher education.

65. For discussion, see also Read, *The Story of Spelman*, p. 325, 326.

66. Carnegie Foundation for the Advancement of Teaching, *Missions of the College Curriculum* (San Francisco: Jossey-Bass, 1977), p. xii, xiii.

67. Snow, *The College Curriculum*, p. 78.

68. Barry J. Fraser, "An Historical Look at Curriculum Evaluation," in *Curriculum History: Conference Presentations from the Society for the Study of Curriculum History*, Craig Kridel, ed. (Lanham, MD: University Press of America, 1989), p. 114.

69. Harold S. Weschler, "An Academic Gresham's Law: Group Repulsion as a Theme in American Higher Education," Lester F. Goodchild and Harold S. Weschler, gen. eds., *ASHE Reader on the History of Higher Education*, (Needham Heights, MA: Ginn Press, 1989), p. 389. See also, pp. 390–398 of this text for more thorough discussion of the group repulsion concept as it relates to each of Weschler's "repulsed" groups.

70. Charles Wegener, *Liberal Education and the Modern University* (University of Chicago Press, 1978), p. 98.

71. Lawrence Stenhouse, *Culture and Education* (New York: Weybright and Talley, 1967), p. 56.

72. Carnegie Foundation for the Advancement of Teaching, p. 1, 2.

73. Carnegie Foundation for the Advancement of Teaching, *Missions*, p. xiv.

74. Ibid.

75. Ibid, p. 94.

76. Jeanne Noble, *The Negro Woman's College Education* (New York: Garland, 1987), p. 76.

77. Spelman College's history demonstrates the existence of each of Harold Taylor's curricular philosophies, over the period 1881–1991.

78. Noble, *The Negro Woman's. . . .*, p. 77.

79. Ibid, p. 78.

80. Snow, *The College Curriculum*, pp. 13, 14 [emphasis added].

81. Carnegie Foundation for the Advancement of Teaching, *Missions,* pp. 62, 63.

82. Bruce A. Kimball, "Curriculum History: The Problems in Writing About Higher Education," in Craig Kridel, ed. *Curriculum History: Conference Presentations from the Society for the Study of Curriculum History,* (Lanham, MD: University Press of America, 1989), p. 60.

83. R.K. Merton, *Social Theory and Social Structure.* (Glencoe, IL: Free Press, 1957).

84. Tidball et al., *Taking Women Seriously.* Phoenix, AZ: Oryx Press, 1999.

85. Guy-Sheftall and Bell-Scott, "Finding A Way: Black Women Students and the Academy." In C. S. Pearson, D. L. Shavlik and J. G. Touchton (Eds.), *Educating the majority: Women challenge tradition in higher education*. New York: Macmillan Publishers, 1989.

86. See endnote 7 for more information about colleges founded for Black women.

87. G. D Kuh and J. E. Hall, "Cultural Perspectives in Student Affairs." In G. D. Kuh (Ed), *Cultural Perspectives in Student Affairs Work*, (pp. 1–20). Baltimore, MD: American College Personnel Association, 1993, p. 4.

88. G. D. Kuh and E. Whitt, "The Invisible Tapestry: Culture in American Colleges and Universities." *ASHE-ERIC Higher Education Report*, No. 1. Washington, D.C.: ERIC Clearinghouse on Higher Education, 1988, p. 19.

89. Ibid, p. 18.

90. Ibid.

91. Spelman College. *Spelman College Annual Report, 1998–1999: Measuring Up to the Mission*. Atlanta, GA: Spelman College, 1998.

92. K. Manning, "Properties of Institutional Culture." In G. D. Kuh (Ed), *Cultural Perspectives in Student Affairs Work*, (p. 21–36). Baltimore, MD: American College Personnel Association, 1993, p. 23.

93. Manning, *Ritual, Ceremonies, and Cultural Meaning in Higher Education*. Westport, CT: Bergin and Garvey, 2000, p. 8.

94. Cross-Brazzell (1992), p. 31.

95. See Corley for more explanation.

96. Ibid, p. 276.

97. Cross-Brazzell, Johnnetta. *Education As a Tool of Socialization: Agnes-Scott Institute and Spelman Seminary, 1881–1910*. Doctoral Dissertation, University of Michigan, 1991, p. 239.

98. Spelman College, 1998.

99. Tidball, p. 52.

100. J. K. Rice and A. Hemmings. "Women's Colleges and Women Achievers: An Update." *Signs: Journal of Women in Culture and Society*, 13(3), 1988, pp. 556–557.

101. D. Smith, "Women's Colleges and Coed Colleges: Is There a Difference for Women?" *Journal of Higher Education*, 61(2), 1989, p. 193.

102. Wolf-Wendel, L. E. "Models of Excellence: The Baccalaureate Origins of Successful European American Women, African American Women, and Latinas." *Journal of Higher Education*, 69(2), 1998, pp. 165, 166.

103. Bell-Scott, p. 10.

104. Cole, Johnnetta B. *Conversations: Straight Talk with America's Sister President*. Anchor Books: New York, 1994, pp. 181, 182.

2

THE HIGHER EDUCATION
OF BLACK WOMEN

The study of academic curricula within educational institutions has always been a complex phenomenon involving the examination of several factors that impact the way in which the curriculum is developed, reformed, and otherwise altered. The study of the academic curricula of institutions of higher education is a particularly complex undertaking considering the dynamic nature of higher education, as well as the constantly evolving nature of its component parts. "Curricular review is never easy. So many forces, external and internal, are at work on the curriculum, so many individuals have a concern with it, so many orientations compete as to the purposes that it might serve, so few effective mechanisms exist at the campus level for an examination of the curriculum in its totality, and so few leverages are available for constructive change. . . ."[1]

Our belief is that the curricula of institutions of higher education, such as Spelman, that have sought to provide a liberal education for their students, are the most mercurial, while in other ways the most constant, of all of the curricular genres.

> Influenced by a frank regard for public opinion, private resources and the peculiar circumstances of the various institutions in which college work has been conducted, the [liberal arts] course of study remained uniform for such extended periods of time that it naturally enough acquired a permanence of opinion, private resources and the peculiar circumstances of the various institutions in which college work has been conducted, the [liberal arts] course of study remained uniform for such extended periods of time that it

naturally enough acquired a permanence of definition in the minds of its friends that seriously hampered even incidental change.[2]

However, despite some of the confounding issues associated with the examination of academic curricula, the study of these curricula is necessary for the evaluation of past educational practices of institutions of higher education as well as for making projections about the academic futures of these institutions. "Various writers claim that curriculum workers often have an inadequate appreciation of curriculum history and that future curriculum efforts are likely to improve if they build on an understanding of the past."[3]

The academic curriculum has become more elaborate and convoluted over time, as more and more diverse individuals have entered higher education. As women, members of ethnic minority groups, and other groups that were not represented in the first graduating class of Harvard College (the long-standing academic standard in higher education) have joined the ranks of those in pursuit of postsecondary education, the academic curriculum of many institutions has changed to accommodate some members of these groups. In other instances, academic institutions have worked hard to circumvent the explicit recognition of these new groups in higher education by excluding issues related to them from the academic curriculum.

The arrival of a new constituency on a college campus has rarely been an occasion for unmitigated joy. Perhaps such students brought with them much-needed tuition dollars. In that case, their presence was accepted and tolerated. Yet higher-education [sic] officials, and often students from traditional constituencies, usually perceived the arrival of new groups not as a time for rejoicing, but as a *problem* [emphasis in original]; a threat to an institution's stated and unstated missions (official fear) or to its social life (student fear) . . .

In each case the entrance of a new group brought about less-than-apocalyptic changes. In the case of relatively wealthy students in nineteenth-century New England colleges, the arrival of poorer students led to a decline in activities conducted by the student body as a whole and to a rise of stratified eating and living arrangements. Ultimately the wealthier students watched as the number of poorer brethren declined. Late in the nineteenth century the arrival of women on previously all-male campuses led to other forms of social segregation, which apprehensive administrators thought of abetting by segregating academic exercises by sex. Some years later, the arrival of a considerable number of Jewish students on east coast campuses caused concern lest gentile students seek out less "cosmopolitan" surroundings. Most recently, the arrival of significant numbers of black students on previously all-white (or almost so) institutions occasioned fears of "white flight" similar to what was perceived as happening in integrated elementary and secondary schools. In all of these cases, students adopted modest recourses [sic]—various informally segregated arrangements for living, eating, and socializing supplemented or took the place of officially sanctioned arrangements. Usually college authorities acquiesced in or even abetted these arrangements, believing them preferable to student exodus.[4]

The emerging issues related to the influx of more diverse groups into the higher educational milieu have led to renewed exploration of the purposes of the liberal arts curriculum by educational researchers and policymakers. The presence of these issues has also led to the initiation of in-depth investigations which have sought to determine whether or not the college curriculum is the proper place to address the unique needs of each of the various ethnic, racial, and gender groups that have actively participated in higher education for over 150 years. According to Wegener:

> The burden thus placed upon a liberal curriculum is heavy, for one might seem obliged to incorporate within it what Lord Bacon called a "general and faithful perambulation of learning . . ."[sic] To put it bluntly, a liberal curriculum would seem to require us to teach everything intensively and reflectively, or, at least, to sample everything available in the intellectual world intensively and reflectively.[5]

Moreover, educators have often suggested that the college curriculum focused upon the liberal arts should also provide for the acculturation of America's youth:

> What are we to say about the culture of educational groups? First, educational groups are formed as a matter of policy with the defined objective of initiating pupils or students into culture. Because society does not provide, as a matter of common experience, the group affiliations which would transmit all the cultural understandings we should wish, we form specialized groups to take over the task. Educators are responsible for controlling the experience of these groups.[6]

The aforementioned statements about the purposes of the college curriculum have led to what the Carnegie Foundation for the Advancement of Teaching has termed the "eternal points of tension" with respect to the aims of the college curriculum: scholarship versus training; attention to the past, the present, or the future; integration versus fragmentation; socialization into the culture versus alienation from the culture; student choice versus institutional requirements; breadth versus depth; skills versus understanding versus personal interests; theory versus practice; and ethical commitment versus ethical neutrality.[7] This study of the curriculum development of Spelman College will demonstrate the presence of these eternal points of tension over the course of the seventy-two years under examination.

In order to move effectively toward a clearer understanding of the enigmas associated with curriculum creation, development, and reform, common definitions of the substance of the college and university curriculum must be utilized as points of departure. The Carnegie Foundation for the Advancement of Teaching defines curriculum as "the body of courses that present the knowledge, principles, values, and skills that are the intended consequences of the formal education offered by a college."[8] However, the Foundation also offers two additional definitions of integral portions of the curriculum: the "extracurriculum" and the "hidden curriculum" which are not a part of the "intended consequences" of the formal college education, but exist on the college campus nevertheless. The definition of the extracurriculum provided by the Carnegie Foundation is: ". . . learning experiences provided informally through recreational, social, and cultural activities sponsored by colleges or by college-related organizations." The definition of the hidden curriculum is: ". . . learning that is informally and sometimes inadvertently acquired by students in interactions with fellow students and faculty members and inferred from the rules and traditions of the institution."[9] The definitions of the extracurriculum and the hidden curriculum within American colleges have been necessitated by the actions of their students:

> When American colleges began to devote more official attention to academic programs and less to the behavior and personal development of students, it was the students themselves who filled the breach by organizing debating clubs, societies, sports activities, fraternities and sororities, and eventually scores of other activities that honored certain campus traditions, provided peer heroes, and supported the intellectual, emotional, and social development of students.

The easy tendency to dismiss all of these activities as frilly and frivolous overlooks the fact that, while many extracurricular activities might deserve such characterizations, a substantial number of them were actually extensions of the educational enterprise. They made provisions for learning activities that could not (or at least were not) provided by the colleges themselves.[10]

Regardless of whether the curriculum, the extracurriculum, or the hidden curriculum is at work with respect to undergraduate education, one consistent notion which can be applied to the undergraduate institutions that develop their curriculum is that ". . . colleges do not always agree on the desired objectives of general education."[11] Jeanne Noble discusses three curricular philosophies that have been distinguished by Harold Taylor as prevalent in American colleges: rationalist, neo-humanist, and instrumentalist.[12] According to Noble, the *rationalist* approach places great emphasis on scholarship and is more interested in cultivating the intellect than developing the whole person. This approach does not usually place much value on extracurricular activities. The *neo-humanist* approach generally asserts that "it is important to transmit to the student, through instruction, that which man has learned and discovered throughout the ages. This philosophy has no other goals than those that lie within the cultural heritage itself."[13] The *instrumentalist* approach to the college curriculum, in contrast to both rationalism and neo-humanism, proposes education for self-fulfillment. According to Noble, within this approach, "general education should be devoted to helping each individual develop all his personal powers so that he may learn better to satisfy his own needs and share in caring for the needs of contemporary society."[14] Spelman College exhibited each of these philosophies during the evolution of its first seventy-two years of curricular history.

Beyond these approaches to examining the academic curriculum, which can assist in an understanding of the broad purposes of the college curriculum, Louis Franklin Snow argues:

It is the ideal of the college that its graduates are prepared for citizenship by their course of study *within its wall*, in a way most fully to develop their best powers of mind and establish their characters on the basis of integrity and truth. For each institution the problem has presented different phases. It is in this particular that the influence of the community upon the college has been felt. The ideals of the community have become the ideals of the college, and that college has done its most perfect work whose sympathy with the community has been most vital and close. Passing from the local to the wider environment, it will be seen that the college becomes most truly national which reflects and reproduces, in its curriculum, the national ideal.[15]

Despite Snow's assertion that the formation of the college curriculum does not exist in a vacuum,

> The undergraduate curriculum is often thought of as being insulated from influences outside the college. . . . The curriculum is nevertheless responsive to the public interest and to changes in a college's relationship to professional and occupational groups, to the quality and level of preparation given to college students by high schools, to the levels of financial support available, to regulation and monitoring by governmental and accrediting agencies, and to the laws of survival and competition that govern the colleges' coexistence with other institutions of higher learning. The curriculum is particularly responsive to the growth of knowledge and to the rise and fall of subject fields in the public interest.[16]

However, there are still those educators who vehemently argue,

> . . . . the determination of curriculum in higher education, at least at the undergraduate level, is largely a political matter usually settled by bargaining between entrenched departments and programs. As a result, the members of the academy, the professors, become their own body politic, or public, who influence the curriculum of higher education and offer many varied opinions about what liberal education was, is, and should be.[17]

The importance of these assertions is almost indisputable, as history itself has borne out the presence of internal and external forces having shaped the undergraduate liberal arts curriculum. Research on the academic history of Spelman College also demonstrates the continued presence of internal and external influences on the institution's curriculum.

History of the Undergraduate College Curriculum

The Carnegie Foundation divides the history of the college curriculum into three eras that were heavily influenced by extrinsic factors—two of which coincide with the roughly seven-and-a-half decades under study in this research.

The first of these three eras, 1636–1870, the authors call the era of the "Ivory Tower." According to the authors, general education was prevalent during this period, which was marked by a more or less standard curriculum that was considered "liberal." During this era, higher education reflected the "high culture" of the period whereby a student's passage through the curriculum identified him as a member of a distinct class of persons. The curriculum of this period was controlled by a guild of college teachers, many of whom were also ministers.[18] The ministerial focus of early Spelman makes this era relevant to this research, though Spelman was not yet established during this time.[19]

The second era, from 1870 through the 1960s, is called the era of the public service institution. During this era more attention was paid to the production of new knowledge and the cultivation of what would later be referred to as "human capital." Also, manpower needs in the market greatly influenced college enrollments and the college curriculum.[20] The characterization of this era, which coincides with the period studied in this book, is relevant to research findings related to the Spelman College curriculum.

The third era outlined by the Carnegie Foundation authors dates from 1977, and thus is not relevant to this research. This era however, is summarized as that of the "academic shopping center." During this period the concept of electives grew in importance, and students became a little better organized and on many campuses wielded more direct control over curricular policy.[21]

As evidenced by the Carnegie Foundation's periodic division, the focus of the academic curriculum of institutions of higher education has changed drastically over time, though the curricula have remained relatively unchanged. However, many commonalities have also existed among American colleges since 1636 despite these changes. For instance, "All members of the elite and educated classes in America through the middle of the nineteenth century studied a curriculum of languages and texts. . . ."[22] Similarly,

> This general limitation of the curriculum to a series of prescribed subjects variously taken from the classics, mathematics, science, history, and philosophy marks a great step toward uniformity in the course of study in the college of the United States. In 1842, Francis Wayland asserts that the studies "in all the Northern Colleges are so nearly similar that students, in good standing in one institution, find little difficulty in being admitted to any other." The catalogues reveal that by 1825 this general system is well established.[23]

The early colleges sought only to provide the tools of learning—logic, mathematical skills, and language—that cultivated a student body knowledgeable in the art of communication, disciplined thought, and reason. The curriculum that was believed to accomplish the above consisted of the classical trivium—grammar, rhetoric, and logic, and the quadrivium—arithmetic, music, geometry, and astronomy. Physical sciences were first introduced into American colleges in the nineteenth century. Early in the 1800s the classical curriculum came under attack by educators. During the 1860s and 1870s, scientific studies of evolution, beginning with Charles Darwin's *The Origin of Species* (1859), gained popularity. By 1900, a potpourri of subjects ranging from manual labor and calisthenics to engineering and home economics began to compete with the classics, philosophy, and sociology, within the academic marketplace, all vying for recognition as legitimate subjects within liberal education. Modern languages were also introduced in the nineteenth century. Between 1870 and 1915, incremental yet monumental changes took place in the college curriculum. The social and behavioral sciences (which emerged from moral philosophy and metaphysics courses) came of age during the twentieth century, along with the arts and professions such as architecture, forestry, business, and agriculture.[24] Harvard University, which had long served as the prototype for curriculum development for undergraduate students, gradually allowed its students to choose all courses under the elective system, with only English composition being a required course based on the recommendations of the Redbook Committee's 1945 report.[25] Subsequently, Stanford, Columbia, and Indiana Universities made similar changes.[26]

As was often typical of curricular changes that took place during this and subsequent periods, "The Harvard Report's significance . . . rested more with its philosophical presentation of general education than with this course of study." This report demonstrated the effects that the undergraduate college curriculum can also have on the external community rather than merely vice versa. Toward this end,

> Daniel Bell states that the purpose was not primarily to reform the program at Harvard, but instead to "formulate a complete educational philosophy for American society." . . . The undergraduate curriculum was merely a vehicle for the Committee to address the more fundamental topics of Western Heritage, democracy, vocational education, and liberal education.[27]

This education for democracy, good citizenship, and for vocational considerations would soon have a very profound impact upon the way in which Black and White women were educated in American colleges and universities.

Historical Reasons for Educating White and Black Women

When women became active participants in higher education during the early nineteenth century, they did so within four fairly distinct types of institutions. These types of institutions

> have shared in the practical realization of college standards for American women; the coeducational college; the "annex-plan," a scheme to enable women to receive instruction from a university not coeducational; the woman's college which is coordinated with a university, but maintains a degree of autonomy as far as the content of its curriculum and the appointment of its instructors are concerned; and the separate college for women.[28]

Each of these institutional types attempted to craft curricula which would suit the needs (however those needs were so defined) of the (mainly White) women who attended.

Elizabeth Barber Young argues that during the first half of the nineteenth century, educators and citizens advocated an equality of intellectual opportunity for girls and boys (that is, White girls and boys): "In the expression of opinion bearing on this subject there was frequently implied a willingness that intellectual opportunities be given woman for the purpose of enabling her to develop the capacity both to meet the obligations of life as an individual and to meet them in the way which her own conscience dictated."[29] However, even this encouragement of "equality of intellectual opportunity" for girls and boys was related strictly to those tasks deemed appropriate to women's proper spheres.[30] The prevailing sentiment of the period was that ". . . no education would be good which did not tend to make good wives and mothers; and that which produces the best wives and mothers is likely to be the best possible education."[31]

And in instances in which education for motherhood and domesticity was not enough, education for acculturation of these women was important.

> Clearly, girls cannot be kept at school indefinitely till they marry. When they leave school, say at eighteen, what are they to do next. The answer must

chiefly depend on circumstances. Where the resources of the parents are such that there is reasonable certainty of an abundant provision for the future, an education corresponding with that given by the universities to young men—in other words, "the education of a lady," considered irrespectively of any specific uses to which may afterwards be turned—would appear to be the desideratum. And clearly the education of a lady ought to mean the highest and the finest culture of the time.[32]

So, it appears from the literature on women's participation in higher education that postsecondary education for women was tolerated, but not wholly encouraged as it was for men: "No one indeed would go so far as to say that it is not worthwhile to educate girls at all. Some education is to be held indispensable, but how much is an open question."[33] Thus,

> In the early days of women's education, less emphasis was placed on achieving in the disciplines. More emphasis was placed on general education for the varying roles that it was assumed women would always hold in our society. For example, you studied academic subjects, but you studied them against the backdrop of functional aspects of living, such as what will this do to improve community life? How will this enable one to become a better mother and partner to her husband? What will women be able to do to improve the quality of life?[34]

Education of women for their "proper sphere" was a dominant theme for many years; however, "as the better educated women began to play more active roles in society outside the home, this development brought demands for further curriculum changes" which precipitated the development of "college grade" curricula for women.[35] Elizabeth Barber Young cites three critical developmental periods in the emergence of curriculum of "college grade." Young characterizes the first period, 1836–1861, as encompassing a critical spirit by institutions of higher education with respect to the type of training provided to women via the seminary and the women's academy. Further, Young posits that liberal views were abundant during this period, which emphasized the offering of subjects commensurate with those offered within the men's colleges. During this period, a very small, select, well defined, and economically elite group of women were served by the early women's colleges. There was "a large amount of freedom . . . allowed students in the choice of subjects, which tended to give advantage in the [White] Southern college, as in the seminary and boarding school, to studies that contributed to a social and leisurely mode of living."[36]

The second period that Young outlines in her discussion of the emergence of the women's college curriculum of "college grade" is 1861 to 1886, an era which encompassed the Civil War and Reconstruction. Young defines these years as a time in which the ornamental branches of the women's college (music, art, elocution, and other courses thought to refine a woman) were being sustained. ". . . Together with the fact that the central academic curriculum failed to incorporate the courses offered by the 'ornamental' and vocational departments, set the practice within these institutions at variance with a homogenous program."[37] The last period that Young describes is 1886 to 1927. Young characterizes these years as marked by increasing definiteness within institutions with respect to the requirements for entrance and graduation with the degree of Bachelor of Arts and by the establishment of policies that tended to direct students away from their pursuit of preparatory, irregular, and special courses into more academic channels.[38] Thus, among White women's colleges, "the curriculum offerings were similar to those of men's colleges, but the graduation requirements were not. The course of instruction emphasized English, French, and science (geography, geography of the heavens, chemistry, astronomy, and especially botany) because of the qualifications of its faculty in those areas."[39]

For African American women during this period, the route to academic, more "liberal education" was less well defined. Often the education to which African Americans had access was more denigrating than uplifting:

> A major goal of a liberal education, particularly in the humanities, has been to learn to place oneself in the perspective of an honored cultural tradition. Presumably this objective inspired the original survey courses on Western Civilization, with their emphasis on the Judeo-Christian and Greek intellectual traditions. That women occupied a degraded position in Greek society or blacks in the Western hemisphere was, of course, considered beside the point. Educators assumed that all groups attending college partook equally of this tradition; if they did not, it was nevertheless the only one worth aspiring to. . . . Thus, by assuming that a highly selected set of facts constituted the Western tradition, the curriculum fostered notions of racial inferiority and hindered blacks from acquiring a positive self-image.[40]

Despite the presence of an academic curriculum that was not representative of the experiences and lives of African Americans, higher education was still the best alternative for African American women whose options were otherwise limited.

> These women were educated to the best abilities of their families and communities, not in spite of their being black women but because they were black and female and would otherwise have few economic alternatives to a lifetime of "work-oxen and hoes," "brooms and cook-pots." In the minds of many parents, their daughters would be far too vulnerable to economic and sexual exploitation as female domestics or agricultural laborers. Formal education, and the people who made it possible, were "highways" around those limitations.[41]

Although African American parents of African American girls sought to protect their daughters from perpetual domestic or agrarian service by assisting them with the attainment of higher education and public careers, "traditional norms of domesticity were also important aspects of respectability. In fact knowing how to perform mundane domestic tasks was not enough; these women learned that they should do them well."[42] Thus, high on the list of priorities of colleges for Black women were training in domestic activities, training for leadership roles, and a version of liberal education that was beholden to the societal dictates established for the Black female in America.[43]

According to Paula Giddings,

> No matter what their thirst for knowledge, it was particularly important for [Black] women to get an education because the majority of them had to work. Since their occupations were limited to "teaching in colored schools or domestic service,". . . . an education not only had a dramatic impact on their status and quality of life, but often shielded women from the sexual harassment that many of them confronted in white homes.[44]

Thus, it is clear that the reasons for educating Black and White women were very different—the former often for short-term escape from sexual subjugation and long-term social subjugation, and the latter to establish social parity with men. Despite their often divergent paths toward higher education, however, Black and White women's presence within the higher educational enterprise precipitated significant changes not only in their ability to obtain a postsecondary education, but also in the ways in which they were educated, as well as the objectives of their being educated.

Curricular Differences between Black and White Women's Colleges

As the impetus for the pursuit of higher education differed for Black and White women, the curriculum created to educate these two groups of women differed as well. The education of women however, subdivided not just along racial lines, but also along geographic lines. The education of southern women (Black or White) often lagged behind the education received by northern women (Black or White).[45]

In the first twenty-five years of the nineteenth century, the institutional education of girls in the South was undertaken largely through boarding schools and academies which were without "collegiate assumptions."[46] More than half of all women who were set upon continuing their formal education beyond the secondary level tended to enroll in normal schools and teacher's colleges. The curricula of these schools differed widely from those offered at the women's liberal arts colleges. The normal schools and teacher's colleges had a very specific purpose—to prepare teachers—mainly of arithmetic and English grammar, never of calculus and Greek grammar as was being taught in the liberal arts colleges dominated by men. Moreover, the normal schools had much less stringent requirements for admission than the liberal arts colleges, and the majority of the former did not offer a four-year course of study leading to a degree.[47] The assumed lack of rigor and competitiveness of the normal school education (as compared to the higher education offered for men), as well as the obvious disparity between what was being learned by males enrolled in college and what was being learned by females enrolled in college, caused the gradual move away from normal training and toward liberal education in the women's colleges.

Florence Fleming Corley outlined three discernible periods with respect to southern (White and Black) women's engagement within the undergraduate college curriculum: 1836–1861; 1861–1886; and 1900–1920. During the first period, 1836–1861, the American public showed dissatisfaction with the "finishing school" idea of the female seminaries, academies, and collegiate institutes. The curriculum emphasized the classical languages, higher math, natural science, and philosophy during this period. There was also a major Latin language influence on the women's college, which was considered to be essential to a rudimentary education in 1836. In most male colleges Greek was the companion language to Latin, but Greek was rarely taught prior to the

Civil War in women's colleges.[48] The "finishing school" curricula of women's colleges offered fewer advanced courses in reading, writing, arithmetic, and French, and emphasized the arts to prepare women for their prospective roles as wives and mothers. In the church-related schools, Bible was taught and required, and piety was emphasized. Education for Black slaves during the period was forbidden, although many freed Blacks did indeed receive formal education.[49]

Corley also sees the period from 1861 to 1886 as being pivotal in the curricular development of women's colleges. During this period, the Civil War and Reconstruction caused higher education for White women in the South to fall behind that of their northeastern counterparts. This educational lag occurred for several reasons. First, during these critical years in the mid to late 1800s, educator and feminist Emma Willard's ideas, such as the importance of religion in women's education, seclusion for women, work-study programs, and teacher training, were being implemented at Troy Seminary in New York. Second, the proliferation of large educational endowments on the campuses of the northern White women's colleges brought faster progress to these institutions, while their southern counterparts were left merely attempting to emulate the accomplishments of the northeastern institutions.[50]

Between 1861 and 1886, although religious education was a component of the collegiate curriculum for women, it "was not of the same caliber as that given to the future clergymen [who attended the men's colleges]."[51] It was also during this period that the women's colleges maintained for a long time the requirement of studying mathematics for graduation. This was occurring during an era of standardization when higher mathematics no longer held a position as a study of general interest. As a result of this, selected colleges for women began to develop curricula for the Bachelor of Arts degree without the calculus requirement. However, spherical trigonometry was required for either entrance or graduation, as was geometry, depending upon the institution.[52] This waxing and waning in the importance of mathematics in the curricular history of women's colleges demonstrates the lengths that these institutions would go to emulate the education being received by their male counterparts. As exemplified by the description above of the curriculum that was pervasive among the northern and southern women's colleges of this period, ". . . a careful study of the curriculums [sic] of the major women's colleges in 1918 concludes that they were not marked by any particular originality; they were rather, a 'safe imitation' of those of the men's colleges."[53]

A major difference between the college curriculum for women and men was the existence for women of coursework described by educational historians as consisting of the "ornamental subjects" of music, art, and elocution. These subjects were mainstays in many southern colleges during this period and "became specialized and vocational areas of study in both Black and White women's schools during the latter part of the nineteenth century."[54] The older women's colleges had always promoted the study of Greek, Latin, and mathematics, but also emphasized the importance of the sciences. Women in the leading northeastern women's colleges were encouraged to engage in the sciences, and excelled in them accordingly.[55] "Although this achievement in the sciences still held in the early twentieth century, elite women's colleges (like comparable schools for men) were increasingly emphasizing cultural studies. An important curricular development occurred in the burgeoning humanistic disciplines."[56] Meanwhile, during this same period, colleges for men de-emphasized cultural studies, and saw no place or value for "ornamental subjects" in the curriculum for college men.

The period of the 1880s was very significant in the history of the Black women's college curriculum in that courses in domestic science, nursing, and missionary training became available to some Black women in the South, particularly in Georgia.[57] Also during this period, Spelman College was founded (in 1881); "[Spelman] was the first educational institution for Negro women to state that it offered college work. Aware of the occupational areas the graduates would pursue, Spelman aimed to provide training for teachers for the public schools and skilled Christian workers for missionary and church work."[58] Linda M. Perkins argues that beyond the academic preparation for teaching and missionary work, "unlike White women, Black women were encouraged to become educated to aid in the improvement of their race." She adds that the Black female college curriculum reflected this encouragement.[59]

The third significant period in women's curricular development, according to Corley, was 1900 to 1920. This period signified changes in course offerings. Many northern and southern women's colleges began the twentieth century still clinging to the traditional classical curriculum, with a strong emphasis on ancient languages and literature, mathematics, natural science, and philosophy. This curriculum was prevalent in the Black schools for women (and men) as well. White philanthropic organizations and White members of society viewed Blacks being educated "for education's sake" as impractical, and began to agitate for the provision of a more "practical" education for

Blacks in higher education, particularly for Black women. Because of this pressure upon the college curriculum for Black women, large vocational and professional departments began to emerge on Black women's college campuses seeking to train Black female teachers, nurses, and domestic workers.[60] Meanwhile, Black and White southern women's colleges continued to look toward the northeastern women's colleges at the turn of the century as models for curriculum development, and continued to follow the lead of the northeastern women's colleges with respect to becoming standard, accredited colleges.[61] During this period there also emerged a trend in the women's colleges (and some of the coeducational institutions) wherein the curricula designed for women students became more correlated with life activities.[62]

> Training in the domestic arts was a very important part of the formal schooling the [Black] women undertook even at the liberal arts colleges and universities. Women at Atlanta University first pursued these courses in the classrooms, then practiced in several dormitory rooms designed to simulate a traditional home. . . . Both normal and college students at Spelman took domestic courses. And here too, by the early 1900s all seniors, five at a time, lived in the Practice Cottage and assumed full responsibility for all the housecleaning, meal planning, and food purchase and preparation.[63]

The issue of the practical utility of education for women crossed the racial divide. White and Black female collegians (unlike their male counterparts) "were caught between the attraction of using their education in professional ways and keeping in mind that a woman's usefulness was not equated with professionalism."[64] In the early 1900s,

> Most institutions, both coeducational and women's colleges included domestic studies as a part of the female collegiate course. Only the oldest eastern women's colleges self-consciously avoided the issue. To them, such studies were a waste of the precious undergraduate years. Domestic science courses such as those being offered at Cornell and the University of Illinois in the 1880s constituted a step backward into the kitchen.[65]

However, although countenanced in some women's colleges, "early attempts to introduce home economics into the curriculum of leading White women's colleges met with failure." These courses were not considered as intellectually rigorous or as competitive as the courses being taken by males in the leading liberal arts colleges whom the northeastern, White women's colleges were perpetually attempting to emulate.[66]

Despite attempts by northern women's colleges to deviate from a curriculum related to domesticity, the combination of science with traditional home economics types of courses gave greater validation and acceptance to home economics as a viable course of study for women in women's and coeducational colleges. A ready example of the infusion of science into a traditionally domestic curriculum was in the areas of health and hygiene. The latter fields were two easy targets for conversion into the home economics course of study because "the field of study in which the women's colleges clearly pioneered was health. Courses in hygiene and physiology were standard offerings in nearly every women's college from the beginning. They were usually required at a time when they were rarely found in the men's colleges."[67] According to Frederick Rudolph, "Domesticity made less headway as a curricular value in the new woman's colleges where the creation of courses and programs of study that opened up new careers for women—in social work, public health, and education—widened woman's social role without raising her consciousness unduly or threatening men."[68]

In the early 1900s curriculum additions within the White women's colleges also included progressive "social efficiency"[69] courses such as normal school training, business, and physical education. Although similar courses were offered for Black women, most Black women's colleges did not offer business or physical education courses at the college level until much later.[70]

The major differences between the early college curricula at Black and White women's liberal arts schools was in the number of courses available to their students. It was not until the 1920s and 1930s that significant numbers of elective courses were offered at Black colleges, while colleges such as Wellesley had been doing so since the 1880s.[71] After 1920, English and the modern languages began to appear in the curriculum of Black and White women's colleges. According to Elizabeth Barber Young, these courses have "become the keystone of the arch of liberal culture as represented by the Bachelor of Arts curriculum."[72] Social sciences have not had much of an impact on the women's college curriculum except through the history requirement that has served as the groundwork for students possessing special interests in such subjects as languages, religion, sociology, and economics. Philosophy had been much of a constant even within the women's college curriculum during the first half of the nineteenth century, but over time it has shifted from being logic based (theoretical) to more ethics based (or practical). Religion was always an important subject in the women's college curriculum; however, its importance decreased among the White women's colleges by the end of the nineteenth century, while just the opposite occurred within the Black women's colleges. This was due to the believed need to "Christianize" or "save" the descendants of promiscuous Black women who had engaged in sexual activity, albeit nonconsensual, with White planters during slavery.[73]

> While the black community encouraged black women to seek an education "for the good of the race," black male educational leaders tempered their acceptance of educated women by advocating that their education be "different." Major curriculum recommendations centered around moral and Christian education. While moral education was a common concern in the higher education of all women, black men appeared especially sensitive about the sexual abuse of black women by white men during slavery and Reconstruction.[74]

This notion was extended by White male and female educators of Black women whose preconceived notions about Black women were holdovers from the pre-emancipation era and advertently and inadvertently affected the college curriculum for Black women:

> The interesting observation here is that the one role of her past that did come up in discussions concerning the Negro woman's education related to her foremother's role as concubine. The Negro woman's new role carried not only the stigma of being a Negro but also a new sense of inferiority in being a woman. All of this surely must have influenced her self-concept negatively. Authorities prescribed a rigid moralistic curriculum. This is not to say that white women were not also exposed to severe rules concerning the governing of their conduct. Indeed, curriculum builders of Negro colleges were doubtless influenced by the nature of education for white women. But it appears that many of the Negro woman's rules and regulations may have possibly been predicated on reason relating to her foremother's sex role as slave. Overnight she was to so live that by her ideal behavior the sins of her foremother's might be blotted out. Her education in many instances appears to have been based on a philosophy which implied that she was weak and immoral and that at best she should be made fit to rear her children and keep house for her husband. Nevertheless, though to some of the educators the ideal education may have been that of education for home-

making, there was a practical need for teachers. And while on the one hand educators stressed moral education and education for homemaking, they also recognized that they must recruit teachers from among the ranks of Negro women.[75]

Black women were educated in the liberal arts tradition, but to a lesser extent than their northeastern, White, female, collegiate counterparts. Similarly however, White southern women also received a comparatively less "liberal" undergraduate education than their northern counterparts and, at varying points through early higher education history, were expected to receive higher education only as appropriate to their externally defined "spheres." Hence, the curricula designed for White and Black southern women were "extrinsically prescribed," and lagged behind the curricula developed for White women attending the elite women's colleges of the Northeast. Although the external determination of coursework suitable for the women's college curriculum applied to the northeastern women's colleges as well, this phenomenon was much more pronounced in the South.

The entire history of curriculum development for women seems to have simulated a "cat and mouse" game wherein each educational milieu has attempted to emulate the curricular content of the other; for instance, Black women's colleges sought to emulate the curricular content of White women's colleges in the Northeast (as many of their founders and teachers hailed from these institutions); southern White women's colleges also sought to emulate the curriculum of these northeastern, White women's schools; and the northeastern White women's schools sought to imitate the undergraduate curriculum which White men studied while in college.

Spelman College, an institution of higher education founded for Black women, did not depart from the trend of Black women's colleges seeking to emulate the curricular content of White, northeastern, women's colleges. The founders of Spelman College, both of whom were products of northeastern female seminaries, had taught and served in administrative capacities in several noted New England academies prior to their founding of the college.[76] Undoubtedly, their experiences in the northeastern seminaries and academies influenced their creation of curricula for Spelman students. However, social reality also influenced the way in which the Spelman curriculum was crafted:

Unlike their White counterparts in the North (the birthplace of higher education for American women), Spelman's founders never agonized over the need to offer their black female students the classical education which male students were being offered elsewhere. Ever mindful of the peculiar history of black women in this country and the realities of their everyday lives, the founders' *primary* aim was to provide training for teachers, missionaries and church workers. Equally important was the imparting of those practical skills that would make black women good homemakers and mothers. Their philosophy of education (. . . . in many ways echoes [Booker T.] Washington), especially as it relates to black women. . . . It is clear that the founders perceived their function to be enabling black women to function in a world that had greatly restricted their opportunities rather than providing them with skills which they would be unable to use. . . . But [they] added that the literary work which [the students] were undertaking to build teachers and leaders of the race was also necessary.[77]

This ethos would serve as the crux of the Spelman curriculum for at least its first forty-six years in existence.

Notes

1. Carnegie Foundation for the Advancement of Teaching, *Missions of the College Curriculum* (San Francisco: Jossey-Bass Publishers, Inc., 1977), pp. xii, xiii.

2. Snow, *The College Curriculum*, p. 78.

3. Barry J. Fraser, "An Historical Look at Curriculum Evaluation," in *Curriculum History: Conference Presentations from the Society for the Study of Curriculum History*, Craig Kridel, ed. (Lanham, MD: University Press of America, 1989), p. 114.

4. Harold S. Weschler , "An Academic Gresham's Law: Group Repulsion as a Theme in American Higher Education," Lester F. Goodchild and Harold S. Weschler, gen. eds., *ASHE Reader on the History of Higher Education*, (Needham Heights, MA: Ginn Press, 1989), p. 389. See also, pp. 390–398 of this text for more thorough discussion of the group repulsion concept as it relates to each of Weschler's "repulsed" groups.

5. Charles Wegener, *Liberal Education and the Modern University* (Chicago, Illinois: University of Chicago Press, 1978), p. 98.

6. Lawrence Stenhouse, *Culture and Education* (New York: Weybright and Talley, Inc., 1967), p. 56.

7. Carnegie Foundation for the Advancement of Teaching, p. 1,2.

8. Carnegie Foundation for the Advancement of Teaching, *Missions*, p. xiv.

9. Ibid.

10. Ibid., p. 94.

11. Jeanne Noble, *The Negro Woman's College Education* (New York: Garland Publishing, Inc., 1987), p. 76.

12. Spelman College's history demonstrates the existence of each of Harold Taylor's curricular philosophies, over the period 1881–1991.

13. Noble, *The Negro Woman's . . .*, p. 77.

14. Ibid., p. 78.

15. Snow, *The College Curriculum*, pp. 13, 14 [emphasis added].

16. Carnegie Foundation for the Advancement of Teaching, *Missions,* pp. 62, 63.

17. Bruce A. Kimball, "Curriculum History: The Problems in Writing About Higher Education," in Craig Kridel, ed. *Curriculum History: Conference Presentations from the Society for the Study of Curriculum History*, (Lanham, MD: University Press of America, 1989), p. 60.

18. Carnegie Foundation for the Advancement of Teaching, *Missions*, p. 3.

19. Spelman women were not educated for induction into a distinguished class of persons, however.

20. Ibid., pp. 3, 4.

21. Ibid., p. 4.

22. Bruce Kimball in Kridel, "Curriculum History," p. 56.

23. Snow, *The College Curriculum*, p. 141.

24. For discussions of this historical curricular development see Barbara Miller Solomon, *In the Company of Educated Women* (New Haven, CT: Yale University Press, 1985), pp. 79, 80 and Carnegie Foundation for the Advancement of Teaching, p. 25.

25. Harvard Committee, *General Education in a Free Society* (Cambridge, Mass.: Harvard University Press, 1945), pp. 195–201.

26. Kridel, *Curriculum History: Conference Presentations*, p. 161.

27. Kridel, *Curriculum History: Conference Presentations*, p. 162.

28. Elizabeth Barber Young, *A Study of the Curriculum of Seven Selected Women's Colleges of the Southern States* (New York: Teachers College, Columbia University, 1932), p. 3.

29. Ibid., p. 197.

30. For more thorough discussions of women's spheres see Young, *A Study of the Curriculum of Seven Selected Women's Colleges*; Newcomer, *A Century of Higher Education*; Emily Davies, *The Higher Education of Women* (New York: AMS Press, Inc., 1973); Helen Lefkowitz Horowitz, *Alma Mater: Design and Experience in the Women's Colleges from their Nineteenth Century Beginnings to the 1930s* (New York: Alfred A. Knopf, Inc., 1984); Florence Fleming Corley, "Higher Education for Southern Women: Four Church-Related Women's Colleges in Georgia, Agnes Scott, Shorter, Spelman, and Wesleyan, 1900–1920" (Dissertation, College of Education, Georgia State University, 1985); Noble (1987); Linda M. Perkins, "The Impact of the 'Cult of True Womanhood' on the Education of Black Women," Lester F. Goodchild and Harold S. Wechsler, eds., *ASHE Reader on the History of Higher Education*, (Needham Heights, MA: Ginn Press, 1989).

31. Davies, *The Higher Education of Women*, p. 11.

32. Ibid., p. 72.

33. Ibid., p. 38.

34. Beverly Guy-Sheftall, "A Conversation with Willa P. Player," *SAGE: A Scholarly Journal on Black Women* Vol. 1, No. 1 (Spring 1984): 16.

35. Corley, "Higher Education for Southern Women," p. 157.

36. Young, *A Study of the Curriculum of Seven Selected Women's Colleges*, p. 195.

37. Ibid., p. 196.

38. Ibid., p. 196.

39. Corley, "Higher Education for Southern Women," p. 24.

40. Barbara Sicherman, "The Invisible Woman: The Case for Women's Studies" in *Women in Higher Education* , W. Todd Furniss and Patricia Albjerg Graham, eds. (Washington, D.C.: American Council on Education, 1974), p. 160.

41. Stephanie Shaw, *What a Woman Ought to Be and To Do; Black Professional Women Workers During the Jim Crow Era* (Chicago, Illinois: University of Chicago Press, 1996), p. 1. Also see Patricia Roberts Harris, "Achieving Equality for Women" in *Women in Higher Education*, p. 16.

42. Shaw, *What A Woman Ought to Be and To Do. . . .* p. 26.

43. Beverly Guy-Sheftall, "Black Women and Higher Education: Spelman and Bennett Colleges Revisited," in *Journal of Negro Education* Vol. 51, No. 3 (1982):278–285.

44. Paula Giddings, *When and Where I Enter: The Impact of Black Women on Race and Sex in America* (New York: William Morrow and Company, Inc., 1984), p. 101.

45. For discussion see Young, *A Study of the Curriculum of Seven Selected Women's Colleges*; Newcomer, *A Century of Higher Education*; Corley, "Higher Education for Southern Women;" and Lynn D. Gordon, *Higher Education in the Progressive Era* (New Haven, CT: Yale University, 1990).

46. Young, *A Study of Seven Selected Women's Colleges*, p. 3.

47. Newcomer, *A Century of Higher Education,* p. 88.

48. Young, *A Study of Seven Selected Women's Colleges*, p. 200.

49. Corley, "Higher Education for Southern Women," p. 158.

50. Corley, "Higher Education for Southern Women," p. 160.

51. Newcomer, *A Century of Higher Education.* p. 73.

52. Young, *A Study of Seven Selected Women's Colleges*, p. 201.

53. Newcomer, *A Century of Higher Education*, p. 87.

54. Corley, "Higher Education for Southern Women," p. 160.

55. According to Young, *A Study of the Curriculum of Seven Selected Women's Colleges*, natural philosophy, chemistry, botany, and other scientific studies were not considered science although they were being taught in the Southern women's colleges.

56. Solomon, *In the Company of Educated Women*, p. 83.

57. Corley, "Higher Education for Southern Women," p. 161.

58. Noble, *The Negro Woman's College Education*, p. 19.

59. Perkins in Faragher and Howe, "The Education of Black Women," p. 69.

60. Corley, "Higher Education for Southern Women," p. 163.

61. Corley, "Higher Education for Southern Women," p. 170.

62. Young, *A Study of the the Curriculum of Seven Selected Women's Colleges*, p. 207.

63. Shaw, *What a Woman Ought to Be and to Do. . .* , pp. 77,78.

64. Young, *A Study of the Curricula. . . .,* p. 85.

65. Solomon, *In the Company,* p. 85. See also Newcomer, *A Century of Higher Education,* p. 89.

66. Newcomer, *A Century of Higher Education,* pp. 89,90.

67. Ibid., p. 101.

68. Rudolph, *Curriculum: A History of the American Undergraduate Course of Study,* pp. 124, 125.

69. Although not formally defined by Corley, based on the context provided in the text, "social efficiency" courses were those which would presumably aid the female in being more efficient in both the public and private spheres, thereby adding to her "finishing." The text suggests that in essence these courses would facilitate the female's ability to conduct herself most appropriately and efficiently in relation to matters of business or the home. See Corley, "Higher Education for Southern Women," p. 168.

70. Corley, "Higher Education for Southern Women," p. 168.

71. Shaw, *What a Woman Ought to Be and to Do,* p. 285.

72. Young, *A Study of the Curriculum of Seven Selected Women's Colleges,* p. 203.

73. Young, *A Study of the Curriculum of Seven Selected Women's Colleges,* p. 205; Solomon, *In the Company,* p. 92.

74. Perkins in Faragher and Howe, "The Education of Black Women," p. 91.

75. Noble, *The Negro Woman's College Education,* p. 24.

76. Beverly Guy-Sheftall, *Spelman: A Centennial Celebration* (Atlanta, Georgia: Spelman College, 1981), p. 10.

77. Ibid., pp. 27–29 [emphasis added].

3

OUR WHOLE SCHOOL FOR CHRIST

The Packard and Giles Administrations (1881–1909)

During the Harriet Packard and Sophia Giles presidential administrations, Spelman's curriculum underwent significant growth, as did its physical plant, which facilitated this growth. At the beginning of the Packard/Giles administration at Spelman, the institution operated more in the way of a Sunday School, a training school for manners and social graces, and a one-room schoolhouse ill-equipped to teach little more than the rudiments of reading, writing, and arithmetic. By the end of the Giles administration in 1909, the school had burgeoned into an educational institution with quality medical facilities and a varied, well-structured curriculum (including a collegiate-level course of study), on par with the normal and academic schools of the North. Much of this development could be attributed to the founders' ties with philanthropic individuals and organizations.

The curriculum of Spelman College from 1881 to 1909 (the combined presidencies of its founders) very heavily reflected the tenets and educational philosophies of its founders, who sought to purify and educate newly freed Black women for missionary work, household industry, and racial uplift. Early academic life at Spelman College under its founders did not feature the practical and classical curriculum that pervaded many women's educational institutions of the period. The school began as the Atlanta Baptist Female Seminary, in the basement of Friendship Baptist Church, in a coordinate arrangement with the Atlanta Baptist Seminary (now Morehouse College). The founders, who were among the institution's only four teachers in the "basement school," as it has been called, were faced with great challenges in their endeavor to educate the former slave women and their daughters. First, the New England missionaries desired to "save the souls" of these "heathen" women through the conversion of "lost souls." Second, they felt it imperative to imbue the women with practical skills for use in their households and in their communities. Third, they believed that their efforts to educate these women and girls would be in vain unless the knowledge was shared with those who were unable to attend the school, so they sought to create "teachers" and "missionaries" who could go forth into their communities and share with others all that they had learned from the White, New England, educators. Sophia B. Packard and Harriet E. Giles reflectively shared their view of the task before them with the members of the American Baptist Home Mission Society (ABHMS):

> It is very essential that these colored people shall be Christianized as well as educated. Hence the importance of schools where the Bible is taught daily, and constant attention is paid to morality, truthfulness, and honesty. There are hundreds of places in Georgia where they have no schools, and the people are growing up in ignorance and vice, led by preachers as ignorant as themselves. We had no idea of the heathenism existing in our own country till we came to Atlanta. Our school has one object, namely to educate Christian women and girls to go out into the dark places and tell them of Jesus. Many go out this summer vacation, and we trust they go full of love and do great good.[1]

These sentiments, condescending as they were, were always evenly tempered with the sentiment that Atlanta Baptist Female Seminary students should be developed and socialized for leadership positions in their communities:

> For many years to come [Negro] girls will need to be trained religiously and intellectually, that at home, in social life, and in church they may be leaders in morality and religion. The conviction grows stronger year by year that, if the race is to be transformed and brought out of darkness, these girls must be kept and trained under religious influences a series of years instead of one or two.[2]

All aspects of the formal and informal curriculum of the Atlanta Baptist Female Seminary reflected these goals and ideas. Packard and Giles taught ten or eleven classes daily, for five-and-a-half days each week. Additionally, each one conducted four prayer meetings and four Bible readings; taught two Bible classes a week; made thirty-five to forty-five religious visits; and still found the time to distribute about two hundred Bibles and religious pamphlets in one month.[3] The early courses taught in the basement school were rudimentary. The students learned the basics of reading, writing, and arithmetic. They also learned about personal and domestic hygiene and [northeastern] norms of conduct,[4] and of course they learned about the Bible and were strongly encouraged to accept Jesus Christ as their personal savior.

The education the early Atlanta Baptist Female Seminary students received also came to include a very basic form of normal training.[5] In 1883, Ms. Caroline Grover, one of the original teachers in the basement school, started the "model school" to train student teachers. Within a month, twenty-four children under the age of fifteen were enrolled as students, with Atlanta Baptist Female Seminary girls studying to become teachers in the model school classrooms.[6]

As word of the basement school spread, attendance grew significantly.[7] The basement of Friendship Baptist Church was very damp and musty, and largely lacking in the conditions necessary for educating students, as well as the equipment needed to facilitate their learning. The principals of Atlanta Baptist Seminary, Packard and Giles, appealed to Dr. Henry L. Morehouse, Field Secretary of the American Baptist Home Mission Society (ABHMS)[8] for bigger and more comfortable accommodations for the newly established school. After many such appeals, and careful consideration of the request, on December 30, 1882, the ABHMS agreed to make the down payment on a nine-acre tract of land adjacent to the Atlanta Baptist Seminary. The property had formerly served as army barracks for Union officers during the Civil War.[9] The unspoken intention of this financial agreement was to make the property available for the joint use of the all-male Atlanta Baptist Seminary and the all-female Atlanta Baptist Female Seminary, both affiliated with the ABHMS, thereby effectively unifying the disparate institutions.[10] Packard and Giles very firmly expressed their disapproval of this proposal which, contrary to their desires, would effectively create a coeducational institution. They argued that "it was their experience that in coeducational schools the courses were primarily for men, and training for women received only secondary consideration; they also believed that the special education which women required could best be accomplished apart from the constant companionship with men."[11]

Packard and Giles formalized their sentiments in their annual report to the trustees of the WABHMS, retrospective of their initial visit to the South:

> The visit of several days at Atlanta strengthened our convictions of the wisdom of continuing this as a *separate girls school*. It will involve extra expense, but it will secure results in giving so many eager women and girls the best moral and religious teaching under the most favorable circumstances.[12]

Ever faithful to their determination to maintain this school for girls, Packard and Giles continued in their educational endeavors and sought to raise funds to pay off the mortgage on the property. This freed the school from the mandatory coeducation associated with the ABHMS payment in full for the property. In the meantime, the basement school was closed the weekend of January 31, 1883, and the school was relocated to the barracks property while funds to pay off the mortgage continued to be sought.

By 1883, the Atlanta Baptist Female Seminary boasted an enrollment of close to three hundred students.[13] The move to the barracks property facilitated the opening of the school's boarding component, thereby allowing accommodation of the large numbers of students who were enrolled. The school, while it retained its basic educational components and its religious training, with the increase in physical space began to expand its reach to include applied normal training.

An Industrial Department was opened by April 11, 1883 in which the students were taught the various types of work associated with maintaining a household, such as cooking, ironing, washing clothes, sewing, and cleaning. Similarly, all the work of the boarding department of the school was conducted by the students, so as to provide them with hands-on experience in domestic skills they were acquiring via their coursework. It is worth noting that the founders did not view this domestic training as regressive or belittling. Instead, they viewed this nonacademic training as necessary for these women whom they considered to be lacking in the basic, necessary skills for survival at home and abroad:

> That industrial training is being introduced into the colored schools gradually, year by year, is cause for rejoicing. Every girl thoroughly trained in this department will be a missionary of wise management and practical knowledge in the domestic arts, a leavening power, not only in towns and villages,

but in the country where they have no knowledge of even the most common utensils in the household.[14]

. . . Instead of losing in the intellectual, there is a decided gain in thoroughness because of the industrial work; and even the graduating class, who have been with us six years, bear testimony to the advantage it will be to them, and are still eager to engage in it. The training of eye and hand not only increases their power of observation, and gives precision to their work, but prepares them for homes of their own. And what an untold blessing it will be to the Congo Mission Circle when they enter upon their chosen work in Africa.[15]

Further, the industrial course was viewed as a very respectable course of study within the curriculum, due to the structured requirements mandated for receipt of an industrial studies certificate. In the industrial course students were required to "attend school at least two years, be of good moral character, and serve creditably in the various branches taught in the Industrial Department, including cooking, washing, ironing, chamber work, and plain sewing."[16] The hands-on industrial training combined the use of religion and missionary zeal, and served to socialize Spelman students for "service" at home, within their social life, and in church. In addition, the program emphasized the vocational aspects of education.

Beyond the practical educational components of the curriculum, the Atlanta Baptist Female Seminary expanded its academic courses to include English, mathematics, grammar, literature, and geography. This expansion facilitated the creation of a college preparatory department that was in essence a high school.[17]

While the work of the school carried on, Spelman's co-principals continued to solicit funds to secure the mortgage on the barracks property. Comparatively meager funds totaling twenty-five dollars had been raised through the diligence of an Educational Society consisting of "basement school" students, and rather sizable donations had been sent to the founders by northern White philanthropists, Black ministers, and churches in the South. However, a deficit still loomed.[18]

John D. Rockefeller, a wealthy gentleman from Ohio, later to become a well-known philanthropist, had been introduced to the founders in June of 1882 by one of their former pupils from Suffield Academy in Massachusetts. At the time of their initial introduction to Rockefeller, Packard and Giles successfully solicited funds for a building for the education of "Negro girls."[19] They decided to call again upon the wealthy Northerner for assistance in meeting their impending deadline of satisfying the remainder of the mortgage debt on the barracks property. On the occasion of the seminary's third anniversary (April 11, 1884), Rockefeller made a surprise visit to the school and presented the founders with a gift for the remaining amount of the outstanding mortgage on the nine-acre property. It was upon receiving this financial gift that Packard suggested that the name of the institution be changed in honor of the Rockefeller family. Rockefeller assented and agreed to name the institution Spelman Seminary, in honor of his parents-in-law, Mr. and Mrs. Harvey Buel Spelman.[20] This gift is very significant to the curricular development of the institution in that without it, the Atlanta Baptist Female Seminary would have been subsumed into the structure of the Atlanta Baptist Seminary. This could have, according to the sentiments expressed by Packard and Giles, very adversely affected the type of education its female students received.[21] Thus Rockefeller is credited with effectively saving the dream of the founders by providing the financial gift that established the school for women:

> We believed, as we often said, that we could not overestimate the good influence of such a school for the colored people; and we prayed and worked to secure the money. Gifts varying from $1 to $1000 were received from our New England men and women; but Mr. J. D. Rockefeller of Cleveland, Ohio, responded most generously to our appeal, and gave a little more than half of the $11,500. The relief and gratitude felt by the [American Baptist Home Mission] Society for this noble gift can never be known save by Him, who in answer to our prayer, prompted Mr. Rockefeller to give it. At his request and by the unanimous vote of the Woman's Board, the name was changed to Spellman [sic] Seminary, in honor of the father of Mrs. Rockefeller, a devoted friend of the colored people.[22]

With this immense financial gift as a start, the work of Spelman Seminary was continuously enhanced by similar gifts toward the education of the Black women of the South. The John F. Slater Fund provided financial compensation for teachers in the Industrial Department at Spelman Seminary. The Fund held profound and vested interests in rural, industrial, elementary, secondary, and teacher-training education.[23] Thus, it was in keeping with these interests that the Slater Fund donated a printing press to the Seminary during the 1884–85 academic year. Students were trained within the Industrial Department on the operation of the press, typesetting, and accuracy and as soon as possible began to publish printed material for the school such as the school catalogue, invitations, and other public materials. This press would soon also be used to print *The Spelman Messenger*, the Seminary's student publication and communication mechanism with the "outside world."[24]

A nurse-training school came to fruition within the Spelman Seminary curriculum, due to the founders' recognition of the paucity of trained nurses for the care of Black people, as well as the difficulty associated with obtaining nurses, trained or otherwise. Therefore, the principals of Spelman viewed education in the field of nursing as a necessity, as they believed it would open another vocational avenue to their students.[25] In 1884, Dr. Sophia Jones, a Black woman from Canada, who had received her educational training at the University of Michigan Medical College, became affiliated with the Seminary as a medical caretaker for ill students, as well as a teacher in the professional nurse-training course.

As students were being educated in the practical skills necessary for life, the academic coursework of Spelman in the late nineteenth century was also considered indispensable to the school's curriculum. These courses included mathematics, English, grammar, literature, geography, and natural philosophy; many extracurricular activities were also provided for the students. Vocal music was offered for an extra charge of two dollars per month.[26] The Congo Mission Circle was established as an organizational link to the Congo for those students interested in doing missionary work in Africa. From the Seminary's inception until about 1889, weekly lectures continued to be given to all students in the areas of physiology and hygiene. These were considered of utmost importance due to what the founders' termed "the great ignorance of the colored people in the care of the sick and of their own health."[27] Further, each morning was devoted to Bible Study, in conjunction with separate courses in Bible instruction.[28]

The conversion to Christianity was a diligent and pervasive component of the Spelman Seminary curriculum and socialization. Solicitation for converts to Christianity manifested itself in many ways on the Spelman campus during the Packard and Giles administrations. Beyond the formal solicitations via Bible study and general Christian education, one of the most influential conversion methods was through student organizations such as the Young Women's Christian Association (YWCA), the Society of Social Purity (an organization that emphasized piety and a religious lifestyle), the White Shield

Societies (organizations to which girls pledged lives of chastity), the Christian
Endeavor Societies (organizations that sought to convert students to Christianity), as well as the Bands of Hope (temperance groups) and the Christian
Temperance Workers who studied temperance as a science.[29] These organizations encouraged conversion to Christianity, and embraced what the founders
deemed to be the most important areas of Christian work: temperance and
the proper manner of conducting prayer meetings and Bible readings.[30] Re-
cords were arduously maintained of the names and number of boarding and
day students who had been converted to Christianity, and non-converting students were looked upon disparagingly.[31] The following account of a Spelman
"model school" student's temperance efforts, in which the founders no doubt
took great delight, was provided in an annual report of the principals of Spelman Seminary in 1888:

> . . . But the improvements in the [Model School] children has been marked
> and especially have the efforts to give them instruction in temperance and
> religion been blessed. They have carried this instruction to their homes, and
> the influence for good on their parents has been manifest. During the tem-
> perance campaign in Atlanta one little girl would plead with her father every
> night to vote the dry ticket. At last she prevailed upon him to attend a tem-
> perance meeting, and the result was he voted for prohibition. A number of
> these little girls have become Christians and have been baptized. Some of
> them who have unconverted parents never fail when writing to urge them
> to become Christians.

The principals of Spelman took great pride in such efforts by Spelman students, as these efforts were viewed as evidence that the religious education
their students were receiving at the institution was not only reaching them,
but in the spirit of mission work, also reaching the "dark places."[32] There was
no question that religious socialization, Christianity in particular, was paramount in the minds not only of the principals of the Seminary, but also of
the teachers of the students, who subscribed very heavily to similar tenets and
had also been trained in religious academic environments.[33]

A pious, simple, Christian lifestyle was also reflected in the rules and regulations of the school. For example, prayer meetings were not listed under
activities or the formal curriculum in the early years of Spelman Seminary,
but instead under the "Regulations" section. Along with mandatory prayer
meetings, students were expected to be "courteous and polite to their school-

mates and respectful and obedient to their teachers." According to the school catalogue, "No students are wanted or retained, who have not sufficient character to appreciate their advantages, and to listen to reasonable advice and admonition." The catalogue expounds, "Neatness, cleanliness, industry, and economy, are with us indispensable virtues."[34] The rules of the institution became progressively more cumbersome as the institution aged. Provisos were added that prohibited students from hosting visitors on campus on Sundays and prohibited parents from sending "provisions" to the students. Similarly, all students were required to return to their home communities at the close of the school year.[35] These regulations were thought best for the "proper" Christianization of these women:

> Our boarders are always under our oversight; they are separated from debasing home surroundings and friends; they breathe an atmosphere of refinement and purity; they have daily instruction in our industrial departments; they are required to give their evenings to silent study; they spend their Sabbaths in worshipping God together in our chapel, and in studying the Bible,—their thoughts are turned continually to earnest Christian living. We can even *see* the changes in them from month to month. . . .

> We always look forward to the long summer vacation with anxiety. Our girls will then be thrown into severe temptation; they will be laughed at as Bible Christians; their virtue will be sorely tried. We warn them of danger, we try to strengthen them beforehand, by admonition and counsel. Over 150 of them have signed the pledge-cards of the social purity society, and nearly all have taken the total abstinence pledge.[36]

The founders of Spelman College believed that a strict, orderly, and Christian environment was the best one in which to educate its students. In their minds, this type of education would soon put Spelman on par with its northeastern women's college counterparts.[37]

By the time of the printing of the first issue of the *Spelman Messenger* in 1885, Spelman was boasting of its possession of a full-fledged academic curriculum likened to that "given in all the higher normal and academic schools of the North," with the progress of its students being "something wonderful."[38] The desire for validation or comparison of curricular rigor with northern seminaries and colleges is a pervasive theme during the late nineteenth and early twentieth centuries, particularly among southern women's colleges (Black and White alike).[39]

Spelman's students began to enjoy public recognition during the late 1800s. As students who had studied in the printing and nurse-training programs began to receive remunerative employment in their fields of study, and students, such as those in the nurse training department, became subject to thorough public examinations, Spelman's programs became better known and concomitantly, better respected.[40]

The curriculum described thus far existed without much change until 1891 when Malcolm MacVicar, Superintendent of Education for the ABHMS, endeavored to examine the "present academic work and future needs" of Spelman Seminary.[41] Following his examination of the institution's various courses of study, MacVicar made recommendations to reconfigure the current course of study, which were ultimately accepted by Packard and Giles. MacVicar recommended the organization of a collegiate department; an academic department with a thorough English course for prospective teachers or missionaries; a college preparatory (high school) course with foreign languages; a training school department with a normal course, a missionary training course; and an industrial course including sewing, dressmaking, and typesetting.[42] Until 1891, the Spelman curriculum had consisted of the following: an elementary course (the Model school); a scientific course yielding an academic diploma; a missionary training course (which did not yield a certificate until 1892); a nurse training course yielding a certificate; a normal course yielding an academic diploma; a higher normal course yielding an academic diploma; and an industrial course yielding a certificate.[43] MacVicar's recommendations meant an upgrading of all academic areas from merely classes of instruction to bona fide departments of study.

On June 2, 1891, Sophia B. Packard died of influenza, and Giles ascended to the presidency of Spelman Seminary. Of Packard's work on behalf of Black Southern girls, Spelman's fourth president, Florence Read, would later state:

> In ability and achievement, she deserves to stand in the same echelon of workers in unpopular causes as Mary Lyon, Emma Willard, Lucretia Mott, or Catherine Beecher. Like recognition might have come to her if her field of work had been almost anywhere in the world except in our own Southern states, where the beneficiaries were American Negroes, a people who have lived and learned and worked and suffered, and had their trial and joys *and* their achievements *overlooked*, sometimes *belittled*, more often *ignored*.[44]

Not long after her assumption of the presidency of Spelman, Giles began to focus her attention on strengthening the teacher-training component of the curriculum.[45] This direction was supported by MacVicar who had completed the study of Spelman's curriculum just that year; the conference presidents of the Home Mission Society Schools; Dr. Henry L. Morehouse of the ABHMS; Frederick T. Gates, Secretary of the Baptist Education Society and advisor to John D. Rockefeller; and the National Convention of Colored Baptists, which had held its annual meeting in Dallas, Texas on September 17, 1891.[46] In support of this expansion in normal training, the Slater Fund provided further grant monies to Spelman to support its normal work and the Model School, which was reorganized under a teacher who was a graduate of the Potsdam, New York Normal School. The normal training of Spelman was decidedly "northeastern" in form and scope. The course catalogues often stated that the methods employed in the normal department were those utilized in northeastern schools such as the Oswego, New York method.[47] Under the terms of the reorganization, the Atlanta Baptist Seminary and Spelman joined together in an arrangement wherein the former maintained a practice school for boys on its campus and the latter did the same for girls, while the male and female teachers-in-training at both institutions received instruction in normal studies at Spelman.[48]

During the Giles administration, the nurse-training department was enhanced and the medical care of students improved through the enlargement of its physical capacity by the linking of two buildings, thereafter called Everts Ward. This increase in capacity effectively provided an operating room, a surgical ward, a medical ward, classrooms, closets, bathrooms, and so on, for use by the nurse-training course students as well as their patients.[49]

Similar improvements and expansions of the physical plant and subsequently the curriculum of the institution yielded a multitude of commendations from educators intimately familiar with the school. For instance, H. L. Morehouse of the ABHMS said, on the occasion of the dedication of Giles Hall, that the school had evolved from "the germinal idea" of two Christian women of New England "to found for the colored young women of the South, a Christian school somewhat on the order of Mt. Holyoke Seminary . . . to a thoroughly graded institution with nurse training, missionary training," and now "this high grade normal school for more thorough preparation of teachers than is now afforded by any other institution of either race in the South."[50] Similarly, MacVicar, at the Annual Trustees Meeting of the

ABHMS in March of 1894, indicated the organization's intention to raise the standards of its institutions, and that "Atlanta Baptist Seminary and Spelman Seminary are among the schools named to do advanced work of as high an order as any college in the Southern states."[51] The trustees then authorized changes in the charters of both institutions, if necessary, to carry out this move toward higher education.[52]

A couple of years later the issue of the move toward collegiate status would be raised again by Rev. Dr. H. L. Morehouse in a letter to John D. Rockefeller. In this letter, Morehouse solicited a special financial gift for Spelman that would allow it to provide complete collegiate instruction:

> Atlanta is strategically located for a southern [sic] educational center; now located here are the two seminaries, Spelman for women and Atlanta Baptist Seminary for men; they should provide complete *college instruction* [emphasis in original] for both groups. To do so would require more buildings, teachers, assured income. The suggestion was made that there be constituted Spelman University, planned by Dr. MacVicar, President Sale, Miss Giles, and Miss Upton. For a beginning, the income at 5% on one million dollars would be needed; the sum of $200,000 in the next twelve months would give the program a good start. Such an income would enable the Baptist Mission Boards to deal constructively with other pressing needs. The hope was expressed that approval of the plan by Mr. Rockefeller might be announced at Spelman's fifteenth anniversary.[53]

Rev. Dr. Morehouse's proposal was not accepted by Rockefeller.

By 1895, the primary and intermediate departments comprised the practice school (formerly the model school) within the Normal Training Department.[54] The grammar and academic departments were separately housed. The "Academic Diploma" replaced the "Normal & Scientific Diploma" that had theretofore been granted. The Academic Course was revised so that instruction was no longer given in the methods and practice of teaching. Further, the Teachers Professional Course (or TPC) began to garner significant outside distinction. The Missionary Training Course was still in place, but was disbanded in 1906 due to a perceived lack of opportunity for American Blacks in foreign mission fields, including Africa. However, as a means of familiarizing Spelman students with the culture of Africa, a school museum was begun which served as host to valuable collections of African artifacts, particularly a collection of rare birds found in Africa.[55]

Beyond the academic training, training in domestic and other socialization skills was still very prevalent, as all Spelman students were expected to be adept at serving and cooking food and the proper way to do laundry work. Additionally, all Spelman students were still expected to perform the work of the boarding department (in shifts) and tend to the upkeep and care of themselves and their own rooms.[56] As before, the expectations of the possession of religion, virtue, piety, domesticity, and academic knowledge were still considered to be congruent with the stated aims of the seminary and of its founders:

> What the mass of the colored people need is leaders of their own race who shall live among them to help them onward and upward. Spelman's mission is to provide such leaders, so far as it can do it. This is the great aim of all the schools of the Home Mission Society. . . . The talented tenth man or woman of this type is needed more even than nine others with some knowledge of the use of the jack-plane, the saw and the blacksmith's forge, and very little else. The low grade common school of brief duration will not discover nor develop this talented tenth person. Here, if anywhere, the talented tenth woman will be brought out and will go forth to bless the rising race.[57]

By 1897, the Atlanta Baptist Seminary had become Atlanta Baptist College, and though Spelman did not at that time achieve collegiate status, its teachers of Latin, history, and English assisted in the instruction of the Atlanta Baptist College students.[58] In this same year, two Spelman students registered as freshmen in the Spelman College Department, although many of their upper-level courses were taken at the Atlanta Baptist College.

The turn of the century saw the erection of MacVicar Hospital on Spelman's campus, which, along with several other buildings erected on the campus during this period, was funded by John D. Rockefeller.[59] The hospital provided a training site for student nurses. It also served as the hospital for Spelman and Morehouse students as well as the public.[60] One drawback associated with the hospital was that it operated under a "closed staff" of only White physicians and surgeons. Because of its fine reputation of first-rate doctors and medical procedures, admission to MacVicar Hospital was considered an honor, though the segregated nature of its operation was contradictory to the racially inclusive values of Spelman Seminary. Although one Black doctor served on the staff for a short period of time, the hospital continued to effectively exclude Black doctors when outside [White] patients were cared for.

Black doctors in the city could have their Black patients admitted to MacVicar, but only through a White doctor.[61] This procedure continued until 1928 when some progressive White doctors on the staff were amenable to working with the Black doctors; but in 1928, nurse training of Spelman students was discontinued, thereby limiting the nurse training students' professional interaction with these Black doctors. It must also be noted however, that the "closed staff" of MacVicar Hospital was not supported by President Giles. However, this arrangement was in accordance with prevailing laws in the state of Georgia. Giles viewed the hospital as useful, despite the segregated set-up, as it gave student nurses the rare opportunity to practice their nursing skills on real patients with a variety of ailments.[62]

Despite the presence of debilitating social circumstances such as unequal treatment, Spelman students pressed forward with determination toward completion of their courses of study. In 1901, the first enrollees in the collegiate course completed their coursework and were awarded the Bachelor of Arts (AB) degree. These two students were the first college graduates of Spelman Seminary.[63] They returned the following academic year to pursue the Teacher's Professional Course.[64]

The latter years of the Giles administration, the early 1900s, coincided with the "cult of true womanhood,"[65] and a period of southern racial insurrection, including the Atlanta Riot of September 22, 1906. Both of these impacted the Seminary, the latter in more inconspicuous ways, as school was not in session during the time of the riots. No harm was reported as having been done to any of the Seminary teachers or students during the weeks that followed. However, MacVicar Hospital ascribed its decline in practice days to the anxiety and "unsettled feeling" caused by the riot.[66] The effects of the "cult of true womanhood" and socialization had already been in many respects pervasive at Spelman, but were clearly exemplified via the following letter from a former Spelman student: "When a girl comes to Spelman and returns home, everybody can see great improvement in her manners, housekeeping, and in every respect . . . One special thing Giles requires of her girls is quietness, which always shows the mark of a lady."[67]

The Giles administration is credited with having ushered in the early development of the institution as equal to other colleges through curricular modifications and improvements of physical plant resources that supported the curriculum, such as the addition of bricks and mortar. Giles died November 12, 1909 of pneumonia. Lucy Houghton Upton, who had served as Associate Principal and Dean under Giles, served as acting president of Spelman for the 1909–1910 academic year.[68]

The administrations of Sophia Packard and Harriet Giles were marked by religious fervor and an undying quest to fulfill godly missions to save an uneducated mass of people that they felt would otherwise have not had the opportunity to be educated. The foundation of the academic curriculum, the hidden curriculum, the extra-curriculum, and socialization during their presidencies was clearly reflected in the school's motto: "Our Whole School for Christ." However, beyond the school's religiosity, the curricular content of the school at the time also heavily reflected the pedagogy and subject matter being taught in northeastern women's academies and seminaries.

The increasingly strong curricular content of the institution, combined with the seemingly perpetual financial assistance from the philanthropic Rockefeller family, put Spelman on the path to becoming a fine college, not just among Black colleges, but White colleges as well. The efforts of the founders toward educating the Black women of the South were not initially intended to create the Spelman of 1909, nor to turn Spelman into a world-class institution, per se, but merely to create an educational environment for Black women, on par with the educational institutions they had attended, taught in, and served in as administrators. This humble goal would not be enough. The vision and passion of Sophia Packard and Harriet Giles, which brought Spelman from the basement school to a rising academic institution, would be a sustaining factor for the succeeding presidential administrations of the school.

Notes

1. Annual Report to the WABHMS from Packard and Giles, 1883, p. 14 in Spelman College Archives.

2. 1888 Annual Report of the Packard and Giles, April 11, 1888, no page given, in Spelman College Archives.

3. Read, *The Story of Spelman*, p. 57

4. "Norms of conduct" refers to etiquette or societal expectations of behavior.

5. A "Normal School" was the term used for an institution of teacher training. Derived from the French word, "normale," the normal school was one which trained secondary school graduates to become teachers.

6. For more in-depth discussion of the model school, see Read, *The Story of Spelman*, p. 72. See also handwritten letter from Sophia B. Packard and Hattie E. Giles to

Dr. H.L. Morehouse, April 16, 1883, p. 3, Packard Box, Personal Correspondence Folder, in Spelman Archives, which discusses the new educational endeavors of the school.

7. By 1882, the school had an enrollment of approximately 160 girls and women. See Annual Report to the WABHMS from Packard and Giles, 1882, no page given, in Spelman College Archives.

8. The name "principal" was used during the early Spelman years for Packard and Giles. This title was a holdover from the names given to heads of schools in New England. When Packard served as the head of a New England school, she was called the "preceptress," and her male counterpart the "preceptor." Packard and Giles would later both be identified as "presidents" of the seminary. The title "president," was used, by subsequent presidents, from the beginning of their respective administrations.

9. Read, *The Story of Spelman*, p. 70

10. Read, *The Story of Spelman*, p. 71. This course of action was also recommended because the ABHMS could not afford the mortgages of two different properties—the Atlanta Baptist Seminary and the Atlanta Female Baptist Seminary.

11. Guy-Sheftall, *Spelman: A Centennial Celebration*, p. 23.

12. Annual Report from Packard and Giles to the WABHMS, 1883, p. 14, in Spelman Archives [emphasis in original].

13. Although this figure sounds fairly large, one must remain cognizant that though approximately 300 pupils were on the rolls, they often stopped out for work in their home communities or other reasons. So this number may not have been an accurate reflection of the total number of students who showed up for school on a given day. In many of the early presidents' reports, the presidents speak of the effects of such external factors as the diminished price of cotton crop; the widespread proliferation of diseases such as "grippe," yellow fever, smallpox, or malaria; and the need for Spelman students to also teach in country schools as impediments to these students' continuous and uninterrupted enrollment at Spelman. For examples of such, see Tenth Annual Report of Spelman Seminary, April 4, 1891, p. 2; Principals' Annual Report, 1892–1893 in *Spelman Messenger*, April 1893, to Trustees from Giles and Upton, p. 1; April 1894— Annual Report of the Principals of Spelman Seminary (1893–1894) from Harriet Giles and Lucy Upton, p. 2; Annual Report of the Principals of Spelman Seminary (1894–1895) in *Spelman Messenger*, April 1895, from Giles and Upton, p. 1; and Annual Report of Spelman Seminary (1897–1898) in *Spelman Messenger*, March 1898, from Giles and Upton, pp. 3, 4. *Note*: The reports listed in the footnotes of this research as being located in the *Spelman Messenger*, do indeed exist in the *Messenger*. However, the page numbers I cite in this research are from the drafts of the reports which were printed prior to placing them in the *Messenger*. Thus, the page numbering will be different than the numbers listed in the *Messenger*, unless a volume and issue number are given to indicate that the information is excerpted from the *Spelman Messenger* itself.

14. Spelman Seminary—1886 Annual Report from S.B. Packard and H.E. Giles, Principals, in *The Home Mission Monthly*, p. 129, in Spelman Archives.

15. Spelman Seminary—1887 WABHMS Annual Report from S.B. Packard and H.E. Giles, Principals, in Spelman Archives.

16. Ibid.

17. Guy-Sheftall, *Spelman: A Centennial Celebration*, p. 25.

18. The Educational Society of the Atlanta Baptist Female Seminary was established June 20, 1881 by Rev. William Jefferson White of Augusta, as a means of involving the students themselves in the fundraising effort for their new school building.

19. This gift of $250.00 would be Rockefeller's first known gift to Negro education. See Read, p 64 and Guy-Sheftall, p. 22. This gift would be the first of a multitude of very significant gifts from the Rockefeller family's personal estates, the General Education Board, and the Spelman Fund. Rockefeller also was one of the first co-signers of the original charter's application for establishment of a corporation that was organized for the purpose of the "establishment and maintenance of an institution of learning for young colored women, in which also special attention was to be given to the formation of industrial habits and of Christian character." See Petition of Henry L. Morehouse (NY), Ellen A. Harwood (MA), and William J. White (GA) to Superior Court of Fulton County for renewal of Charter, April 23, 1912, p. a1, which lists names of original petitioners, in Spelman College Archives.

20. See Read, *The Story of Spelman*, pp. 80–83 and Guy-Sheftall, *Spelman: A Centennial Celebration*, p. 24.

21. Guy-Sheftall, *Spelman: A Centennial Celebration*, p. 23.

22. 1884 Annual Report to WABHMS from Packard and Giles, p. 10.

23. Norman Calvin Rothman, "Curriculum Formation in a Black College: A Study of Morris Brown College, 1881–1980," dissertation, Georgia State University, 1981, pp. 52, 53.

24. 1885 Annual Report to WABHMS from Packard and Giles, p. 15; Read, *The Story of Spelman*, p. 86, in Spelman Archives.

25. Spelman Seminary—1886 Annual Report from S.B. Packard and H.E. Giles, Principals, in *The Home Mission Monthly*, p. 129, in Spelman College Archives.

26. Read, *The Story of Spelman*, p. 88. See also 1885 Annual Report to WABHMS from Packard and Giles, p. 14, in Spelman College Archives. In the latter reference, the principals mention their having hired a "Southern lady of culture and refinement" to teach the course, as she graduated from the Conservatory in Cincinnati. Statements such as these demonstrate the reverence that was afforded scholars who attended northern schools during this period.

27. Spelman Seminary—1886 Annual Report from S.B. Packard and H.E. Giles, Principals, in *The Home Mission Monthly*, p. 129, in Spelman College Archives.

28. See handwritten letter from Sophia B. Packard and Hattie E. Giles to Dr. H.L. Morehouse, April 16, 1883, Packard Box, Personal Correspondence, pp. 3, 4, in Spelman College Archives.

29. 1885 Annual Report to WABHMS from Packard and Giles, p. 14, in Spelman College Archives.

30. 1885 Annual Report to the WABHMS from Packard and Giles, p. 15, in Spelman College Archives. See also Annual Circulars and Catalogues for 1886–1909 in Spelman College Archives.

31. See *Spelman Messengers* from 1885–1910 and all Annual Reports from Presidents Packard and Giles, in Spelman College Archives.

32. 1888 Annual Report to the WABHMS from the Packard and Giles, April 11, 1888, no page given, in Spelman College Archives.

33. See 1890 Annual Report of Spelman Seminary, no page number given, for discussion of "choice women of rare ability of experience" serving as teachers in the Seminary, in Spelman College Archives. This reference describes the care taken to select teachers who were considered pious and Christian.

34. Spelman Seminary Catalogue, 1888–1889, p. 38.

35. For examples of rules during the Packard/Giles administrations, see the Spelman Seminary Catalogues for the years 1886–1909, in Spelman College Archives.

36. 1889 WABHMS Annual Report from Packard and Giles, p. 15, in Spelman College Archives [emphasis in original].

37. Read, The Story of Spelman, p. 88.

38. *Spelman Messenger*, March 1885, in Spelman Archives. See also Read, *The Story of Spelman*, p. 88.

39. Corley, "Higher Education for Southern Women," p. 170.

40. 1889 WABHMS Annual Report from Packard and Giles, p. 17, in Spelman College Archives. See Annual Report of the Principals of Spelman Seminary (1895–1896), p. 8, in Spelman College Archives. See also Read, *The Story of Spelman*, p. 88.

41. Read, *The Story of Spelman*, p. 114.

42. Read, p. 114.

43. See Spelman Course Catalogues for the years 1881–1891 in Spelman College Archives.

44. Ibid., p. 122 [all emphases in original].

45. See Letter from Giles to Rev. Buttrick of the GEB, March 15, 1904, Box: Tapley, Folder: General Education Board (1903–1921), Spelman College Archives.

46. Read, *The Story of Spelman*, p. 124.

47. See "Normal" sections of Spelman Seminary Course Catalogues for years 1884–1909, in Spelman College Archives.

48. For description of initial agreement see *Twelfth Annual Circular and Catalogue of Spelman Seminary for Women and Girls, 189–93*, p. 18 in Spelman College Archives. See also Read, p. 125.

49. See Spelman Seminary Course Catalogue, 1891–1892 and Annual Report to ABHMS (1891–1892), in Spelman College Archives.

50. Read, *The Story of Spelman*, p. 127.

51. Ibid., p. 130.

52. Ibid. The charters were not changed to reflect this shift toward higher education at that time. The first official amendment of the charter toward this end did not occur until June 2, 1924 when the charter was changed to reflect the change of the school's name from Spelman Seminary to Spelman College. See p. x3[sic], "Petition of the Spelman Seminary to Superior Court of Fulton County," June 2, 1924 in Spelman College Archives. The second amendment of the charter toward this end, which di-

rectly spoke to the desire to move toward higher education, occurred on March 5, 1928. The charter was amended to include the following language: "#1. The object of this corporation is the establishment and maintenance of an institution of learning for young Negro women in which also special attention is to be given to the formation of industrial habits and of Christian character; and #2. For the accomplishment of these objects, the Board of Trustees will establish such departments, schools and courses of study as they shall deem proper and needful, with power to confer such literary and honorary degrees as are wont to be conferred by academic and collegiate institutions in the United States." See p. 8, "Petition of the Spelman College to Superior Court of Fulton County," March 5, 1928, all in Spelman College Archives.

53. See Read, *The Story of Spelman*, pp. 131, 132. See also letter from Rev. Dr. H. L. Morehouse to John D. Rockefeller, March 16, 1896, Giles Box, J. D. Rockefeller folder, in Spelman College Archives.

54. The name of the model school was changed by President Giles to more accurately reflect the purpose of the school—practice teaching for normal students.

55. See Tenth Annual Report of Spelman Seminary, April 4, 1891, p. 3, in Spelman College Archives.

56. See Spelman Catalogues, 1891–1909 and Annual Reports of the President, 1891–1909 in Spelman College Archives. See also Read, *The Story of Spelman*, pp. 130–134.

57. Rev. H.L. Morehouse, "The Worth of Spelman Seminary to the World," in *The Spelman Messenger*, 1896, v. 12, no. 8, p. 5, in Spelman College Archives. It is worthy of note, that within this quote Morehouse uses the term "talented tenth" to describe educated and intellectual Blacks; this usage of the term predates W.E.B. DuBois' public use of the term.

58. See Read, *The Story of Spelman*, p. 135 and Jones, *A Candle in the Dark*, pp. 59–65.

59. MacVicar Hospital replaced Everts Ward.

60. Morehouse students utilized MacVicar under payment arrangement from 1928 until well into the 1940s. See Jones, *Candle in the Dark*, pp. 138, 143, 160. See also Read, *The Story of Spelman*, p. 138.

61. Black students from Spelman and Morehouse however, were permitted to be treated in the hospital by the White doctors.

62. See Annual Report (1900–1901) to the Trustees of Spelman Seminary, in *Spelman Messenger*, March 1901, p.3; Annual Report to the Trustees of Spelman Seminary from Harriet Giles and Lucy Upton (1901–1902), in *Spelman Messenger*, April 1902, no page given; Annual Report (1902–1903) to the Trustees of Spelman Seminary, in *Spelman Messenger*, March 1903, p. 3; and Twenty-third Annual Report of Spelman Seminary (1903–1904), in *Spelman Messenger*, March 1904, p. 2 , all in Spelman College Archives.

63. These two students were Jane Anna Granderson and Claudia White (Harreld). The former alumna taught at Spelman from 1902 until her death in 1905. The latter remained associated with the institution (in a variety of capacities) until her death in 1952. For more information on these graduates, visit Spelman College Archives.

64. Annual Report (1900–1901) to the Trustees of Spelman Seminary, in Spelman Messenger, p. 2 and Annual Report (1901–1902) to the Trustees of Spelman Seminary, in Spelman Messenger, no page given, in Spelman College Archives. See also, Read, The Story of Spelman, p. 140. Recounting the success of these first two graduates, is a letter from Dean Edna Lamson to Mr. David G. Mullison, President of Hartshorn Memorial College, February 28, 1927, Tapley Box, Hooper Alexander Folder, in Spelman College Archives.

65. The cult of true womanhood defined a woman's responsibilities and station in life relative to other women, but particularly in relation to men. For more on this notion, see Solomon, *In the Company of Educated Women*, p. 95.

66. See Twenty-sixth Annual Report of the President of Spelman Seminary (1906–1907) to the Board of Trustees, in *Spelman Messenger*, p. 3 and Read, *The Story of Spelman*, p. 154. Practice days were the actual number of days the doctors tended to and treated patients.

67. Read, p. 143. See also Barbara Miller Solomon, *In the Company of Educated Women*, pp. 95–114 for discussion of women's collegiate experiences during this era. On p. 95 she notes three significant "generations" of women which emerged between the Civil War and World War I, who shared common collegiate experiences. Of relevance here, are the first two generations: the woman of the first generation (1860s–1880s) who defined herself as a "true woman"—pure and pious, generally, and usually obedient and domestic; and the college woman of the second generation (1890s–1900s) who, though still possessing many of the attributes of the first generation, had a more expansive spirit, and was more likely to dub herself a "new woman."

68. See Letter from Rev. Dr. H.L. Morehouse (Corresponding Secretary, ABHMS) to H. Lucy Upton, November 24, 1909, Tapley Box, Folder: ABHMS (1898–1919) in Spelman College Archives, re: the appointment of Upton to the acting position, and Rev. Morehouse's personal request, without direct consent of the ABHMS, asking Lucy Hale Tapley to serve as president based on the rules of the Board which requires the Dean to become president in the absence of the president herself.

4

NEW DIRECTIONS: TOWARD
COLLEGIATE STATUS

The Lucy Hale Tapley Administration (1910–1927)

Not many significant curricular changes accompanied Lucy Upton's ascendance to the position of acting president. The most noteworthy of her accomplishments as acting president were the expansion of the curriculum to include a regular course of study in music, and the establishment of the Granddaughters Club for students whose relatives had also been students at Spelman Seminary.[1]

A drastic change did, however, accompany the election to the presidency, by the Spelman Board of Trustees, of Lucy Hale Tapley in March of 1910. Spelman's third president subscribed to a heavily utilitarian curriculum, with academic components—a marked departure from the educational philosophies of the founding presidents who saw the need for Black women to be educated for missionary work, utilitarian purposes, and ethical and moral piety—all tempered with a sound version of liberal arts education. President Tapley's subscription to the more vocational aspects of education was consistent with the views of Booker T. Washington, who at one time had been embroiled in a fierce debate with W.E.B. DuBois over the purposes of higher education for Blacks.[2] The vocationalism of the Spelman curriculum did not disintegrate the progress made toward the realization of a strong academic curriculum; however, it did encourage the socialization of Spelman students for greater service in their homes, social lives, and church.

Tapley, for the six years prior to her presidency, served as head of the Teachers Professional Department at the Seminary, and came to the school in

1890 from West Brooksville, Maine, as a teacher of English and arithmetic. Tapley implemented very rigorous rules of conduct and dress, and required the strictest adherence to the rules:[3]

> As it is impossible to enumerate the many fads which arise from time to time and which violate the principles already indicated in this leaflet, we desire to urge upon all who are interested in this matter that they strictly observe the *spirit* as well as the *letter* of the rules, and thus avoid the embarrassment which must unavoidably result from any further attempt to follow fashion and inappropriate dressing. We have attempted to make plain our policy regarding the students' clothing and any question which may arise in the mind of any patron will be answered gladly from the office. Hall teachers are requested to take charge of all which violate our rules.
>
> We trust that the above will meet the hearty approval of all patrons. These rules will be carried out.
>
> L.H. Tapley, President, Spelman Seminary, Atlanta, Ga.[4]

Beyond changes in the student policies at Spelman, Tapley also invoked significant changes in the curricular content and the focus of the institution, which was in many ways a marked departure from the curriculum the school had followed under the three previous administrations. "In her first annual report to the trustees, she indicated that her intentions were to promote the spirit of the Founders and to emphasize moral and religious training. However, the most apparent shift in Tapley's administration from previous ones was the increase in industrial training (especially toward the production of teachers for rural schools)."[5]

This new emphasis on industrial education however, did not mean the complete dissolution of the academic departments at Spelman, and can therefore possibly be attributed to the clash between the two most pervasive sentiments of the period, which dealt with the purposes of Black higher education—training of the head vs. training of the hand. During this period, industrial (or practical) education as advocated by Booker T. Washington began to be stressed above the more intellectual education advocated by W.E.B. DuBois. Philanthropic organizations that had supported Black postsecondary education responded to this debate by way of their educational funding priorities. President Tapley, in effecting changes to the academic curriculum, continued to stress to Spelman faculty and the general public (via the *Spelman Messenger)* that these changes toward industrial education were appropriate, and that industrial education and academic education must complement one another, as they were, in her view, inextricably linked:[6]

> In order to equip as many young Negro women as possible for domestic and public efficiency, the work of our literary departments is re-enforced [sic] by that of the industrial departments, the work of the industrial departments is designed to arouse and stimulate the desire for real culture, and all the work, both the literary and industrial, is based upon religious culture and inseparably connected with it as the life-giving energizing force.[7]

President Tapley's curricular emphasis on vocational components may appear a bit contradictory to her maintenance of the academic curriculum of Spelman. Although direct evidence does not exist in the literature related to Spelman's history, or in the Spelman College Archives to this effect, we believe that Tapley's vocational emphasis, which was a noticeable departure from the vision of the Founders, had more to do with Spelman's need to access funds from private philanthropies whose focus had become vocational, than Tapley's adverse sentiment about the trajectory of the Spelman curriculum or the school as a whole.[8] To further support this notion, it should be noted that Tapley had been a member of the Spelman faculty for some time when she was named president, and had for all of those years supported not only the maintenance of a strong academic curriculum tempered with a racial uplift agenda at Spelman College, but also the advancement of the same. Thus, one can only assume that the public image of Spelman (which surely encompassed its curricular offerings) had to fit the expectations of society (as was always the case to some extent), but with more schools clamoring for limited funds, it was also important that the institution's curriculum conform to the tacit expectations and stated objectives of the private philanthropies that had helped to keep Spelman and similarly situated Black postsecondary institutions afloat.[9]

With the aforementioned in mind, we would argue that outside the public's eye, Tapley was working steadfastly toward the fulfillment of the vision long held by the Founders—that Spelman women and girls would be educated for professional aims as well as to uplift the Black race. This point is to some degree alluded to (and later made more explicit) in a letter from President Tapley to Major Robert J. Guinn, then Chairman of the Universities and

Colleges Committee of the National War Savings Committee (Atlanta). The letter asked Guinn whether he minded Tapley's presentation of his name to the Spelman Board of Trustees at the next annual meeting to fill a new board vacancy, as well as to serve on the Executive Committee of that board: "The duties are not arduous but we need local members who are in sympathy with our different lines of social uplift work for all peoples."[10]

Spelman's curriculum under Tapley consisted of work in all grades of academic instruction: high school, a normal school with its practice school of eight grades, home economics, and college. It offered a three-year course of academic instruction and practice in the MacVicar Hospital (nurse training), which continued to provide medical services to Spelman students and patients outside of the Spelman student body. High school graduates were offered a curriculum that trained teachers for high schools, elementary schools, and for teaching household arts subjects. Curricula also existed on the campus for those young women who did not plan to teach upon completion of their programs of study, but wished simply to complete an organized course of study leading to a degree. Although the seminary enrolled students for junior and senior high school courses, no diplomas were granted for less than two years of high school work done on the Spelman campus. A provision was also put into place that required applicants to be at least fourteen years old, and at least prepared to enter eighth grade, before their applications to enter the school as boarding students were considered.[11]

The Spelman curriculum in the Tapley years saw the addition of courses in "chicken culture," which, as best the authors could ascertain from descriptions contained in Spelman Seminary Course Catalogs, was a course that taught students the appropriate way to raise and prepare chickens for domestic cooking. Teacher training was also promoted, even among high school students.[12] Tapley's additions to the curriculum began to serve as true reflections of her belief that education should above all else be practical:

> Any course of study which fails to cultivate a taste and fitness for practical and efficient work in some part of the field of the world's needs is unpopular at Spelman and finds no place in our curriculum. Every course of study which makes women more womanly, more purposeful, more resourceful and more efficient is earnestly coveted.[13]

As the need for more trained teachers for rural schools emerged, Tapley saw a role for Spelman in the provision of qualified teachers for such service. She began to send Spelman students who had completed the normal course into rural areas, usually their home communities, serviced through the Anna T. Jeanes Fund or other such organizations that emphasized industrial and teacher training.[14] She saw the teacher as an educator, a missionary, and one who inculcated the industrial habits of life into the poor and unfortunate who had not been privileged enough to receive an education such as that provided at Spelman.[15] With this emphasis on industrial education, the emphasis of former Spelman administrations on better academic preparedness prior to entry waned in importance. This allowed "more average or even below average student's admittance to the Spelman courses." Tapley opined that "those . . . with the highest intellectual ability and interests were less likely to go back to their small home towns or rural areas."[16] The entrance requirements were soon made more rigid, however, so as to limit the escalating numbers of enrollees the school was then experiencing.[17] President Tapley often reiterated her intent to decrease registration in all areas due to steadily increasing enrollment and in anticipation of moving toward increases in college work.[18]

Tapley forged a lasting relationship with the International Sunday School Association, which advocated the training of qualified Sunday School teachers within the Black schools of the South. Spelman, along with a number of other Black schools of the period, offered Sunday School education and a diploma upon completion of the course, backed by the International Sunday School Association.[19] The affiliation with the International Sunday School Association was in keeping with Spelman and Tapley's ideals, similar to those of Packard and Giles, of training missionaries and educators. Spelman also remained faithful to its cause of converting Spelman students to Christianity.[20] President Tapley was especially proud of the Christian work being done by Spelman graduates who had traveled to Africa as missionaries. She often shared with her northern colleagues the work abroad of these Spelman alumnae, and encouraged their recognition in Home Mission publications.[21]

Under Tapley's leadership, the Spelman curriculum responded to the 1917 declaration of war on Germany. As a way of keeping Spelman students knowledgeable about the conflict overseas and the effects of the war on the United States, they were required to take courses that reflected the current state of events such as history and geography. Similarly, the students made great sacrifices in support of the war effort, by participating in "Wheatless & Heatless Days," purchasing war bonds, and giving gifts to the Red Cross.[22] Tapley stressed vocationalism and strict rules of conduct for Spelman students, in response to funding streams and the priorities of the funding organizations, as well as the fervor of the times.

During the Tapley administration, attention also began to be paid to the social life of the Spelman students. Tapley encouraged the entire Spelman community to better understand the importance and benefits of physical activity through greater participation:

> Real play was never needed more than now to keep the mind clear and vigorous for the sort of thinking which is essential in order that we may preserve a proper balance. Athletic games and sports, social hours, and wholesome entertainments are planned and encouraged. All games which demand good teamwork, concentration of the mind, control of the muscles, and generosity of treatment of opponents, have a real place in education. Play for play's sake is the end directly sought, but the permanent character training in it all is invaluable.[23]

In the midst of these many curricular changes and modifications, Tapley sought expansion of Spelman's facilities, which she believed would serve to enhance the educational level and offerings of the institution, particularly in the domestic arts and sciences. From 1917 to 1919, a number of physical plant improvements and expansions occurred on Spelman's campus; one was the erection of a home for the nurses of MacVicar Hospital, the second was a building that housed the home economics and household arts work.[24] The Dean of Spelman, Edith V. Brill, began to worry about the academic appropriateness of home economics as a viable course of study, based on her interaction with her colleagues in northern educational institutions. She asked a field agent of the General Education Board about rumors that home economics was not regarded as advanced work or on par with the highly regarded Teachers Professional Course.[25] The GEB Representative allayed her concerns:

> . . . Of course some of our friends do not believe in industrial work, and others take it as a necessary evil. The time has come when colored scholars are in position to do more academic work than has heretofore been possible. This is due of course, to a number of causes the improved economic condition of the colored people, the gradual improvement of public and private schools with the increased demands for teachers of a higher grade of preparation, and the opening up of new avenues of business, calling for more general, as well as, vocational training. Some people feel these changes very

keenly, and look to a school like Spelman to change very considerably its courses. I am sure you are feeling this pressure, and it is a difficult matter to decide what is best to do. You are constantly making improvements, and readjustments. I think we must make them as fast as conditions warrant, but no faster.

To my mind the outlook at Spelman has been towards the country, and towards the school and the home. I think this is the greatest field of service, because it is the greatest need, though we may not hear so much about it as about the newer things. I agree with you absolutely as to the type of well-balanced academic and industrial training, towards which you aim. Spelman graduates are making good as Home Economics teachers in our county training schools, and as county supervising industrial teachers. I only wish we had more of them.

I see no reason why the Home Economics course should not be recognized as of equal value with the other courses with the same entrance requirements, and the same quality of teaching. I have had the feeling that prejudice towards industrial work was gradually passing. The white normal schools and colleges in the South have put in Home Economics courses as well as other industries and in many rural high schools the teachers of vocational agriculture and Home Economics receive larger salaries than the other teachers, they being partly paid from Federal Funds under the Smith-Hughes Act.[26]

Thus, Tapley and Brill continued to improve the home economics curriculum accordingly, with Spelman students receiving professional certification in the home economics and normal fields, first in Georgia, and later in Alabama.[27]

By 1918, the State Department of Education of Georgia granted professional certificates to the graduates of the Teachers Professional Course.[28] By 1920, the graduates of the nurse-training department gained the privilege of examination for the state of Georgia certificate, which made them eligible for the Registered Nurse (RN) designation.[29] In 1922, the graduates of the Home Economics Department were granted the state certificate that enabled them to teach home economics.[30] Based on these accomplishments, President Tapley felt sure that once it developed a full college course, Spelman could also qualify for the professional college certificate, granted by the Georgia State Department of Education and endorsed by other states.[31] Thus, despite these significant gains, changes in course content (toward more collegiate-level work), faculty, and so on were still made in each of the above departments, seeking further improvement of the respective academic and industrial programs.[32]

In October 1922, Edna Lamson, who had also served as Dean during the Tapley administration, returned from a one-year sabbatical at Columbia University's Teacher College. During her time there, she received significant training in standardized testing and intelligence tests such as the Binet-Simon, the Stanford Revision of Binet-Simon, the Otis Group Intelligence Scale, the Thorndike McCall Reading Scale, the Ayres Spelling Scale, and a host of others.[33] Lamson shared with Tapley the fact that these tests were being administered in the finest northern schools, as well as her belief that administration of these tests to current and prospective Spelman students would assist in the division of students into the appropriate grade levels upon entrance into the school. Batteries of the various exams were soon administered to Spelman students, and results indicated that very few Spelman students were of "superior mental ability." In 1922–23, the exams showed that only twenty-six students, among all of the school's departments, were of "superior" or "very superior" ability. These data were subsequently used to create a new system of classification and promotion within the Seminary.[34] It appears that the new testing component at Spelman was widely accepted by Spelman faculty and students alike, as they, according to Tapley and Lamson, were "interested in comparing achievement at Spelman with that of schools at large, through results obtained through intelligence and educational tests."[35] Further, Spelman faculty and administration viewed testing as a means to readily identify potential leaders from among its ranks (based on high scores on the examination),

> Thus Spelman has twenty-six students who according to Terman's classification have superior intelligence—21 superior, 5 very superior. Since Spelman is essentially a training school for leaders, she must discover her pupils of unusual ability as early as possible that they may be given her best.[36]

Spelman students were always being socialized in some manner or another through their interactions with the teachers, administrators, or presidents on the Spelman College campus. This socialization was extended in great measure through the students' exposure to presentations from and conversations with local, national and world leaders who often visited the campus at the invitation of Spelman presidents. The consequences and impact of the students' ability to hear and see, firsthand, prominent and influential academic, political, and entertainment figures on their own campus cannot be underestimated or devalued. President Tapley's intentional exposure of Spelman students to these leaders as a co-curricular endeavor was therefore quite significant, as it transmitted to the students the tacit implication and belief that they had the potential to emulate the successes of these speakers, and it indicated that there was something important and meaningful about the work and societal contributions of these social and political figures.

The content of the speakers' addresses and presentations also underscored this notion; they encouraged the students to "carry the torch," so to speak, and not to just rely upon their educations to create change, but instead to utilize their educations to make a difference. Social agency, the right to achieve upward mobility, and the need to make a difference at home and abroad were all a part of the "privileges" being implied to Spelman students of this era. This unspoken conferral of "privilege" is the crux of the early Spelman student socialization—not privilege akin to an elitist construct, but privilege that confirmed to these students that they possessed inalienable rights to racial parity and equal opportunity. This is the legacy that Spelman students were a part of at every point in the institution's early history, which has transcended the years and helped to define the Spelman of the modern era.

Changes abounded during the Tapley administration, but none more important than those in the physical plant of the campus. Though vocational aspects in the curriculum remained, the expansion and modernization of Spelman's physical plant facilitated enhancement of both the academic and vocational course offerings of the institution.

President Tapley secured from the General Education Board funds to build a chapel and a science building. The latter served to alleviate Spelman's need to continue using the science facilities of Morehouse College for most of its collegiate work. This expansion of the campus physical resources and the addition of technical equipment in support of the curriculum were preliminary steps toward Spelman Seminary's becoming a full-fledged college. Collegiate status was sought once Spelman possessed the capacity to offer, on its own campus, all of the coursework required for the college degree.[37] Tapley spoke of this move,

> It seems to us that as though the time has come when Spelman should become a college and all of our college work be done on our own campus. Dr.

Buttrick [ABHMS official] does approve of this most heartily, in fact, he has been talking it for a couple of years. We have this year 81 students doing work above high school and we feel convinced that should we become a college we could very soon have not less than 150 students for the higher work. You know that when a step of as much importance as this would be to come [sic] before the Trustees, there should be as full a meeting as possible.[38]

A committee was appointed by the Spelman Board of Trustees to confer with the administration of Spelman Seminary about the proposed change, in form and function, of Spelman Seminary to Spelman College.[39]

During her 1923–24 Annual Report to the Board of Trustees, Tapley discussed the recent academic accomplishments of the institution:

The enrollment for collegiate courses is steadily increasing. Ninety-six graduates from various high schools made application for admission to collegiate courses for the year 1923–24. For some reason 7 of these applications did not arrive. Of the 89 applicants who enrolled, 82 are classified as college students; 7 are making up entrance units preparatory to college classification. Thirty-five college students are majoring in elementary education; 22 are majoring in home economics education; 25 are pursuing the liberal arts curriculum . . . In the year 1923–24, 536 as compared with 483 in 1922–23, of the student body are doing work of high school and college rank. A very significant and encouraging fact in the growth of higher education is the increasingly large percentage of seniors in high school who expect to continue their study in either a Junior or Senior college. . . .

The members of the freshman class who are pursuing the liberal arts curriculum, however, have had all their work on Spelman [sic] campus this year. There are in all 25 students enrolled for the A.B. degree. These students are pursuing a total of 110 courses. Of these 70 are given by Spelman faculty on Spelman [sic] campus. Upper class women go to Morehouse College for the remaining 40 courses.[40]

Impressed with these and previous accomplishments of the institution toward the strengthening and diversification of the curriculum, the Trustees of Spelman College passed a resolution that Spelman Seminary should become Spelman College on June 1, 1924.[41]

Miss Tapley and her administration responded quickly to the change to collegiate status through the continuous upgrading of the skills of the Spelman faculty, through sabbaticals and summer school training in the North.[42] For the first time in the institution's history, the faculty of the college was subdivided into instructional staff in the college and instructional staff in the high school, training school, piano, and other departments.[43] The staff of MacVicar Hospital continued to have the highest credentials and training, but unfortunately continued to exclude Black doctors.[44] Members of the academic faculty, Dean Lamson in particular, began to attend more meetings of professional associations and became a member of such associations as the Georgia State Teachers and Educational Association and the Student Interracial Study Group. Spelman also became one of the founding members of the Association of Negro Colleges and Secondary Schools; the Association of Colleges for Negro Youth; and the National Association of Collegiate Deans and Registrars in Negro Schools. Each of these organizations sought the general improvement of education for Black students and helped to increase academic standards.[45]

The first Spelman alumna was elected to the Board of Trustees in March, 1925. This same year, Tapley Hall was erected in honor of the president. This building was created for science studies and recitations. The facilities afforded separate laboratories for physics, biology, and chemistry for the college and high school students, a lecture room for both academic levels, as well as additional classrooms and offices. The building also featured first-rate scientific equipment.[46] The Georgia State Department of Education recognized Spelman as an "A" college, and the Spelman High School was rated in Class I by the state accrediting body.[47] The North Carolina State Department of Education, which had stricter standards than those of the state of Georgia, recognized Spelman by granting three years of credit for the Spelman degree course, and two years credit for the two-year course, toward a teaching certification in North Carolina.[48] Standardized testing soon became an important consideration.

The building of the Spelman Chapel, begun in 1923, was completed in 1927. The fourth president of Spelman, Florence Read, would later say that the chapel assisted in keeping "central in the life of the campus, the ultimate purpose of Christian education."[49] Sisters Chapel was erected in an effort to provide a centralized place for co-curricular endeavors such as speeches, presentations, colloquia, and other activities that students could benefit from, spiritually, intellectually, and socially. The building was named Sisters Chapel for John D. Rockefeller Jr.'s mother, Laura Spelman Rockefeller and her sister

Lucy Maria Rockefeller, whose estates funded the project. The dedication of the building took place on May 19, 1927, in the presence of such noteworthy Black persons as Mary McLeod Bethune, founder and President of Bethune Cookman College; Dr. John Hope, President of Morehouse College; and Marian Anderson, contralto opera singer.[50] John D. Rockefeller, Jr., in his remarks upon presentation of the building to the Chair of the Spelman Board of Trustees, told the trustees, students, friends, and faculty of Spelman, that the building was to be used for:

> the spiritual, intellectual, and social well-being of the College and of the people of this community. Neither the beauty of the building, its suitability to its uses, nor yet the cunning and skill with which it has been fashioned, is the measure of the value of the gift. Its value lies rather in the rich heritage of love, of faith, of hope, of confidence in the womanhood of the Negro race with which it is so richly endowed. In token of this gift, I hand you these keys. May the spirit of these sisters and the lofty ideals that they typify ever pervade this building and rest in benediction and inspiration upon all who enter its doors![51]

Tapley resigned as president of Spelman College on June 15, 1927 and was named President Emerita. Tapley is most remembered in the history of Spelman's early presidents as the one who led the institution in new directions by departing from the educational ideals of its founders. By some accounts, her heavily vocational curriculum led to Spelman's regression, as opposed to its progression toward becoming a women's college. Nevertheless, it cannot be disputed that Tapley's maintenance of an academic curriculum, in conjunction with the utilitarian components of the curriculum, as well as her efforts that led to the development and expansion of Spelman's physical plant, worked together to facilitate Spelman's achievement of collegiate status. Following President Tapley's resignation, Mount Holyoke–educated Florence Read (former Executive Secretary of the International Health Division of the Rockefeller Foundation and administrator at Reed College in Portland, Oregon) was elected president of Spelman College by the Board of Trustees.

Notes

1. Annual Report of Spelman Seminary, in *Spelman Messenger*, March 3, 1910 from Lucy Upton, Acting President, no page given, in Spelman College Archives. See also Spelman Seminary Course Catalogs, 1909 forward, in Spelman College Archives.

2. See Cedric Robinson, *Black Marxism: The Making of a Black Radical Tradition.* (Atlantic Heights, NJ: Zed Books, Ltd., 1983), pp. 266–278; W.E.B. DuBois, *Dusk of Dawn: An Essay Toward an Autobiography of a Race Concept.* (New Brunswick, NJ: Transaction Publishers, 1984), pp. 67–87; and W.E.B. DuBois, *The Souls of Black Folk.* (New York: Bantam Books, 1903, 1989), pp. 30–43, pp. 53–62.

3. See Spelman Seminary Course Catalogs, Regulations section, for the years 1911–1927 in Spelman College Archives.

4. It is probable that Tapley's strict application of a dress code policy which, theretofore had been only moderately regulated, resulted from the liberality with which women began to dress after the first decade of the 1900's, in conjunction with the emergence of the "flapper" period which enveloped the country during the 1920's. There is no doubt that these rules were attempts to thwart Spelman student's participation in dress that was considered lewd, lascivious, and non-Christian. Consult Spelman Seminary Catalogues, particularly 1920–27, p. 32, in Spelman College Archives re: the dress code regulation. See also Read, *The Story of Spelman*, p. 188 (all emphases in original). There were also occasions when Tapley found necessity to recommend that students not return to school due to disciplinary issues and general non-conformance with school policy. See letter from Tapley to Dr. Williams (parent of Spelman student), June 1, 1923, Tapley Box, Folder: Hooper Alexander, in Spelman College Archives, in which student is "uninvited" to return to school the following year, based on disorderly and non-conforming conduct.

5. Guy-Sheftall, *Spelman: A Centennial Celebration*, p. 42. See Read, *The Story of Spelman*, pp. 190–194. See also Annual Report of Spelman Seminary for the School Year 1910–1911, in *Spelman Messenger*, p. 1, in Spelman College Archives. The authors found no direct evidence to indicate that the Spelman Board of Trustees was in disagreement with the new curricular direction of the institution. As was stated in the introduction, often these types of changes coincided with funding considerations, particularly from funding sources such as the John F. Slater Fund and the Jeanes Fund, whose funding priorities were often more vocational/industrial in nature. Spelman complied with the funding criteria of these philanthropic organizations, despite the constant funding from the General Education Board which gave more to private educational entities with educational aims beyond industrial training.

6. There is evidence (though not direct) of the possible influence of Booker T. Washington's ideals on Tapley and the curriculum of the college at that time. However, we submit that this influence was more contrived than real based on the more important connection between industrial education on the Black college campus and their access to funds from private philanthropic organizations. See Tapley's school calendar, 1912–1913, no page number given, Tapley Box, no folder, in Spelman College Archives, for entry of December 13, 1912 wherein Mrs. Booker T. Washington addressed the assemblage of students. For information regarding Spelman's public image and support of industrial education, see also in this book, the number of lectures (1912–1919) given to the students by outside guests related to "useful work" and womanhood. See also correspondence which speaks to her dedication to the Anna T. Jeanes

work of rural teachers in teaching such things as canning and other non-academic lessons to rural students: Letter from Tapley to Mr. Henry Milam, Bartow County Super-
intendent of Education, November 1, 1915; Letter from Mr. Milam to Tapley, October
9, 1915; Letter from Tapley to Mr. Milam, December 14, 1915; Letter from W.B. Hill
(Jeanes Administrator) to Tapley, May 20, 1926, Box: Lucy Hale Tapley, Office of the
President (hereafter referred to as Tapley), Folder: Georgia Department of Education–
Jeanes Work (1916–1925) in Spelman College Archives. See also Letter from Tapley to
Harry S. Meyers, National Committee of Northern Baptist Laymen, August 16, 1919,
Box: Tapley, Folder: The General Board of Promotion of the Northern Baptist Con-
vention, Harry S. Meyers, all in Spelman College Archives.

7. Annual Report to Spelman Seminary (1913–1914), April 1914 in *Spelman Messenger*, p.1, in Spelman College Archives.

8. In examining the financial statements and donors lists of Spelman College, a
trend began to emerge wherein the curricular programs being funded were less general,
and philanthropic organizations began to earmark funds for certain academic (i.e. vocational) programs or courses of study such as home economics, rural teacher training,
etc. A trend also began to emerge wherein monetary donations began to come from
more diverse types of philanthropic organizations and individuals who did not necessarily specify the types of programs for which the money must be used. See Financial
Statement and Donor's Lists of Spelman Seminary for the following years: 1911–1912,
pp. 5–8, 17–23; 1915–1916, pp. 6–16; 1916–1917, pp. 1–4, 10–16; 1917–1918, pp. 1,2, 6–16;
1921–1922, pp. 1,2, 6–16; 1922–1923, pp. 1, 6–16; 1923–1924, pp. 3–6, 10–21; 1924–1925,
pp. 3–5, 10–23; and 1925–1926, pp. 3–5, 10–23, all located in Folder: Financial Statement & Donor List of Spelman Seminary, Box: L.H. Tapley, Office of the President
in Spelman College Archives.

9. This notion is also clearly elucidated in the case of Horace Mann Bond, who
was very astute in "controlling" his relationships with philanthropic organizations
toward his own benefit as well that of the organizations he represented. For further
discussion, see Wayne J. Urban, *Black Scholar: Horace Mann Bond, 1904–1972*, (Athens,
GA: University of Georgia Press, 1992), pp. 56, 64, 70, 72, 73.

10. The appointment of Major Guinn to the Spelman Board of Trustees and its
Executive Committee, would become a strategic move in the development of Spelman
during the Tapley years. Guinn assisted with many of the endeavors related to the
expansion of MacVicar Hospital, including its faculty development, as well as the war
effort. Tapley's interest in his serving on the Spelman Board of Trustees and its executive committee in 1915 becomes more evident in 1923 when he was appointed to the
committee to confer with the administration regarding the proposed change of Spelman Seminary to Spelman College. The authors can only venture to guess that to make
such a bold step as to propose the formal higher education (by way of a college education) for Black women, one had to have as many sympathetic supporters, who were
also well-respected and in "high-ranking positions," as one could possibly have. See the
following correspondence which supports these notions: Letter to Guinn from Tapley,
February 19, 1916; Letter to Tapley from R. Guinn, Chairman, Universities & Colleges

Committee (National War Savings Committee– Atlanta), December 17, 1917; Letter to R. Guinn from Tapley, June 19, 1919; Letter to R. Guinn from Tapley (assumed), June 6, 1923; and Letter from Major Robert J. Guinn, General Agent–New England Mutual Life Insurance Company, October 1, 1924. All correspondence located in Box: Lucy Hale Tapley, Office of the President, Folder: Trustee Letters–Miscellaneous, in Spelman College Archives.

11. See standard/generic letters sent to students desirous of attending Spelman from Tapley, no date on letters, Box: Tapley, Folder: GEB, Brierly, in Spelman College Archives. See also letter from Tapley to Mr. Arthur Lyman (International Sunday School Association), March 28, 1918, Box: Tapley, Folder: Correspondence Between Spelman & International Sunday School Association, in Spelman College Archives, regarding a 12-year-old student interested in attending Spelman. See also Spelman Seminary Course Catalogues, 1910–1927, in Spelman College Archives for admission criteria and coursework being offered.

12. Read, *The Spelman Story*, p. 190. See specifically, Annual Report of Spelman Seminary in *Spelman Messenger*, April 1914, p. 2.

13. Read, p. 191.

14. See Letter from Tapley to Mr. Henry Milam, Bartow County Superintendent of Education, November 1, 1915; Letter from Mr. Milam to Tapley, October 9, 1915; Letter from Tapley to Mr. Milam, December 14, 1915; Letter from W.B. Hill (Jeanes Administrator) to Tapley, May 20, 1926, Box: Tapley, Folder: Georgia Department of Education–Jeanes Work (1916–1925) in Spelman College Archives. See also Letter from Tapley to Harry S. Meyers, National Committee of Northern Baptist Laymen, August 16, 1919, Box: Tapley, Folder: The General Board of Promotion of the Northern Baptist Convention, Harry S. Meyers, in Spelman College Archives. See *Summary of Homemakers' Club Agents Season 1916*, January 1, 1917, Box: Tapley, Folder: Georgia Department of Education–Jeanes Work (1916–1925), in Spelman College Archives. See also Letter from Tapley to Mrs. Kathryn Westfall (WABHMS), October 29, 1918, and Letter from Tapley to Mrs. Westfall, June 14, 1918, Box: Tapley, Folder: Hooper Alexander, in Spelman College Archives, re: teaching endeavors of students in rural areas.

15. See Thirty-fourth Annual Report of the President to the Board of Trustees (1914–1915), April 1915, p. 1, in Spelman College Archives, for discussion of the role and work of teachers in the rural areas.

16. Read, *The Story of Spelman*, p. 193.

17. Annual Report of Spelman Seminary (1916–1917) in *Spelman Messenger*, p. 1, in Spelman College Archives. See also Letter from Tapley to Rev. Wallace Buttrick, ABHMS, October 21, 1921, Box: Tapley, Folder: ABHMS Charles White, in Spelman College Archives.

18. This notion was expressed within a letter from Tapley to Mr. D.G. Garabrant, Chairman of the Spelman Board of Trustees and the WABHMS Board, November 11, 1923, Box: Tapley, Folder: Mr. D.G. Garabrant, Spelman College Archives.

19. For thorough understanding of the relationship between Spelman and the International Sunday School Association, consult the following: Letter from F.H. Mills,

Chair Executive Committee, International Sunday School Association, to Lucy Tapley, September 12, 1911, Box: Tapley, Folder: Correspondence–International Sunday School Association; Letter from H.C. Lyman, Superintendent of Work Among the Negroes, International Sunday School Association, to Lucy Hale Tapley, October 1, 1914, Box: Tapley, Folder: Correspondence–International Sunday School Association; Letter from H.C. Lyman to Lucy Tapley, March 7, 1916, Box: Tapley, Folder: Correspondence–International SS Association; Letter from Lucy Tapley to H.C. Lyman, July 25, 1917, Box: Tapley, Folder: Correspondence–International S.S. Association; Letter to Lucy Tapley from H.C. Lyman, September 10, 1917, Box: Tapley, Folder: Correspondence–International S.S. Association; Letter from H.C. Lyman to Lucy Tapley, September 8, 1919, Box: Tapley, Folder: Correspondence–International S.S. Association; Receipt from International S.S. Association for donation from Spelman Seminary, June 1, 1920 for "Negro Summer Schools," Box: Tapley, Folder: Correspondence–International S.S. Association; Letter from Robert Cashman, Business Superintendent, International S.S. Association to Angie Kendall, Treasurer, Spelman Seminary, June 2, 1920, Box: Tapley, Folder: Correspondence–International Sunday School Association; Letter Lucy Tapley to H.C. Lyman, March 27, 1922, Box: Tapley, Folder: Correspondence–International Sunday School Association; Letter from H.C. Lyman to Lucy Tapley, March 24, 1922, Box: Tapley, Folder: Correspondence–International S.S. Association; Letter from Mabel E. Curtess, Department of Education, International S.S. Association to Lucy Tapley, March 21, 1922, Box: Tapley, Folder: Correspondence–International S.S. Association; Letter from Tapley to International Sunday School Association, March 16, 1922, Box: Tapley, Folder: Correspondence–International S.S. Association; Letter from H.C. Lyman to Lucy Tapley, March 15, 1921, Box: Tapley, Folder: Correspondence–International S.S. Association, all in Spelman College Archives.

20. Letter from Tapley to Mrs. George Coleman (Alice Coleman), WABHMS, October 23, 1913, Box: Tapley, Folder: Adair vs. Spelman, in Spelman College Archives. See also Annual Reports of President from 1910–1927, in Spelman College Archives.

21. See letter from Charles L. White, Assoc. Corresponding Secretary, WABHMS, to Tapley, April 5, 1910, Box: Tapley, Folder: ABHMS (1898–1919); Letter from Tapley to Mrs. Kathryn Westfall (WABHMS), October 29, 1918, Box: Tapley, Folder: Hooper Alexander; Letter from Tapley to Mr. Coe Hayne (ABHMS), January 17, 1922, Box: Tapley, Folder: Hooper Alexander; Letter from Tapley to Mr. Adams, November 1, 1922, Box: Tapley, Folder: WABHMS–Charles White; Letter from Tapley to Clara Norcutt (WABHMS Correspondence Secretary), November 10, 1922, Box: Tapley, Folder: Hooper Alexander; Letter from Clara Norcutt to Tapley, November 17, 1922, Box: Tapley, Folder: Hooper Alexander, all in Spelman College Archives.

22. See letter from Major R. Guinn, Chairman of the Universities and Colleges Committee and the National War Savings Committee to Tapley, December 17, 1917, Box: Tapley, Folder: Trustee Letters–Miscellaneous, in Spelman College Archives, re: government program to develop thrift, during war time, among American people, particularly college and university students. See also Annual Report of Spelman Seminary (1917–1918), in *Spelman Messenger*, p. 2, Spelman College Archives.

23. Annual Report of Spelman Seminary (1917–1918) in *Spelman Messenger*, April 1918, p. 2, Spelman College Archives.

24. Letter from Tapley to Jackson Davis, General Field Agent, General Education Board, March 5, 1917, Box: Tapley, Folder: GEB–Jackson Davis, in Spelman College Archives. See also Annual Report of Spelman Seminary, (1916–1917), in *Spelman Messenger*, April 1917, p. 1, in Spelman College Archives.

25. Letter from Edith V. Brill, Dean, Spelman College to Mr. Jackson Davis, GEB, April 21, 1921, Box: Tapley, Folder: GEB–Jackson Davis, in Spelman College Archives.

26. Letter to Edith Brill, Dean, Spelman Seminary from Jackson Davis, GEB, April 27, 1921, Box: Tapley, Folder: GEB–Jackson Davis, in Spelman College Archives.

27. Letters of request were submitted to both the Georgia Department of Education and the Alabama State Department of Education. The former was provisionally approved, pending a site visit from their high school supervisor, and advocated that Spelman apply for state accreditation for their high school course. The latter request was not granted, and required additional work to be done in reconfiguring the curriculum prior to awarding the professional certification. See letter to Edith V. Brill from Walter B. Hill, Special Supervisor, Georgia Department of Education, May 5, 1922, Box: Tapley, Folder: Georgia Department of Education–Jeanes Work (1916–1925) and Letter to Dr. John W. Abercrombie, State Department of Education, Alabama, from Ivol Spafford, Supervisor of Home Economics Education Alabama State Department of Education, January 5, 1927, Box: Tapley, Folder: ABHMS–Charles White; Letter from R.E. Tidwell, Superintendent, Alabama State Department of Education to Tapley, January 31, 1927, Box: Tapley, Folder: WABHMS–Charles White, all in Spelman College Archives. For letter of application for Professional Normal Certificate see letter from M.L. Brittain, Georgia State Superintendent of Schools, November 6, 1917, Box: Tapley, Folder: Georgia State Department of Education (1917–1927), in Spelman College Archives. This application was also provisionally approved, pending a site visit by a representative of the Department. Later, the Georgia State Superintendent of Schools granted the professional certificate. See Letter from M.L. Brittain, to Tapley, April 17, 1920, Box: Tapley, Folder: Georgia State Department of Education, 1917–1927, in Spelman College Archives.

28. 1923 Annual Report of Spelman Seminary (1922–1923) in *Spelman Messenger*, p. 4, in Spelman College Archives. See Letter from M.L. Brittain, to Tapley, April 17, 1920, Box: Tapley, Folder: Georgia State Department of Education, 1917–1927, in Spelman College Archives.

29. Letter from Tapley to John D. Rockefeller, October 21, 1922, Box: Tapley, Folder: GEB–John D. Rockefeller (1920–1924), Spelman College Archives. See also Annual Report of Spelman Seminary (1922–1923) in *Spelman Messenger*, April 1923, p. 4, Spelman College Archives.

30. Annual Report of Spelman Seminary (1922–1923) in *Spelman Messenger*, April 1923, p. 4, Spelman College Archives.

31. Ibid.

32. Ibid., p. 5

33. Read, *The Story of Spelman*, p. 196.

34. Annual Report of Spelman Seminary (1922–1923) in Spelman Messenger, April 1923, pp. 2–4, in Spelman College Archives.

35. Annual Report of Spelman Seminary (1922–1923) in *Spelman Messenger*, April 1923, p. 4, in Spelman College Archives.

36. Ibid.

37. Read, *The Story of Spelman*, p. 197.

38. Letter from Tapley to Mr. D.G. Garabrant (Chairman, Spelman and ABHMS Boards), January 26, 1923, Box: Tapley, Folder: Mr. D.G. Garabrant, Spelman College Archives.

39. Letter from "unknown" (assumed Tapley) to Major R. Guinn, June 6, 1923, Box: Tapley, Folder: Trustee Letters–Miscellaneous, Spelman College Archives.

40. 1924 Annual Report of Spelman Seminary (1923–1924) in Spelman College Archives.

41. See petition of Spelman College to Fulton County Superior Court, June 2, 1924, p. x3, in Spelman College Archives. See also letter from E.P. Johnson, Secretary to the Spelman Board of Trustees, to (presumably the Fulton County Superior Court–no addressee given), April 24, 1924, in Spelman College Archives, verifying that the Board voted on the motion of Major R.J. Guinn to change the school name, thereby supporting the Board's petition to amend the Spelman charter.

42. Letter to Tapley from W.W. Brierly, Chief Clerk, GEB, January 20, 1922, Box: Tapley, Folder: General Education Board–W.W. Brierly, in Spelman College Archives, requesting appropriation for next academic couple of years for teacher training in the North. For discussion of faculty studies in the North, see also the Annual Report of the President of Spelman Seminary (1925–26) in *Spelman Messenger*, May 1926, p. 2, Spelman College Archives.

43. See Read, *The Story of Spelman*, p. 202. For the division of the faculty, see also the Annual Report of the President of Spelman Seminary (1925–26) in *Spelman Messenger*, May 1926, p. 2, Spelman College Archives.

44. For example of this, see letter from Dr. James Baird, Jr. to Tapley, June 15, 1923, Box: Tapley, Folder: ABHMS–Charles White, Spelman College Archives.

45. See letter from Edna Lamson, Dean, Spelman Seminary, to Clara Norcutt, April 1, 1926, Box: Tapley, Folder: Hooper Alexander, Spelman College Archives. For announcement of Spelman's affiliation with the Association of Colleges for Negro Youth, see Annual Report of the President of Spelman Seminary (1925–26) in *Spelman Messenger*, May 1926, p. 2 Spelman College Archives.

46. For discussion of the use of the facilities, see Annual Report of the President of Spelman Seminary (1924–25) in *Spelman Messenger*, April 1925, pp. 1, 2 Spelman College Archives.

47. At the time, the "A" rating of the college indicated Spelman's adherence to a high standard of academic quality, thereby authorizing it to award baccalaureate degrees to its students. The Class I distinction authorized the high school to award the diploma, demonstrating the secondary school's compliance with established state and

regional guidelines for the secondary school curriculum. These ratings were given by the state accrediting body–the Southern Association of Colleges and Schools (SACS)—a private, non-profit, voluntary organization founded in 1895 in Atlanta, GA for the purpose of setting standards and improving education in the colleges and schools of the South.

48. For discussion of "A" rating, see Annual Report of the President of Spelman Seminary (1925–26) in *Spelman Messenger*, May 1926, p. 2, Spelman College Archives. See also letter from Edna Lamson to Mr. David G. Mullison, President–Hartshorn Memorial College, February 28, 1927, Box: Tapley, Folder: Hooper Alexander, Spelman College Archives.

49. Read, *The Story of Spelman*, p. 205.

50. For announcement of dedication, see 1927 Annual Report of Spelman Seminary (1926–1927), in *The Spelman Messenger*, p. 6, Spelman College Archives. See also Read, *The Story of Spelman*, p. 206.

51. Read, p. 206.

Sophia Packard and Harriet Giles, ca. 1885

Giles Hall, 1890

Basement classroom in Friendship Baptist Church, 1881

First graduating class of Spelman Seminary, 1887

Spelman Seminary campus in 1884—barracks formerly used as an encampment for Union soldiers

Spelman Seminary faculty, 1890

Graduates of the Missionary Training Department, 1893

Spelman Academic graduates, 1894

Graduates of the Teachers' Professional Course, 1898

Spelman students playing basketball on "the Oval," ca. 1901

Nurses' Training, College, English Normal (high school), Teacher Professional, and Music graduates, 1914

Spelman students in industrial arts class (no date)

Spelman Seminary sewing class, pre-1924

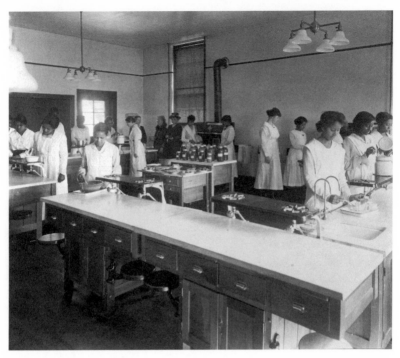

Spelman Seminary cooking class in Laura Spelman Hall, ca. 1917

A classroom in Giles Hall, probably a Teachers' Professional Course in progress, 1895

Lucy Hale Tapley, 1921

Spelman Granddaughters Club, 1926 (established by Interim President Lucy Houghton Upton)

Lucy Hale Tapley welcoming newly appointed president, Florence Read, July 1927

Florence Matilda Read, fourth president of Spelman College, 1927–1953

Presidents of the AUC schools and guests at the dedication of the AU Library, April 30, 1932

A production of "Dreamy Kid" by the AU-Spelman-Morehouse Players, 1920s

AU-Morehouse-Spelman Orchestra, ca. 1930

AU-Morehouse-Spelman College Chorus (Dr. Kemper Harreld, Director), ca. 1939, 1940s

Spelman College Glee Club, ca. 1952

Children playing at the Spelman nursery school, 1931

Children with tricycles and wagon at the Spelman nursery school, April 1931

GRADUATING CLASS OF SPELMAN COLLEGE, ATLANTA, GA. 1932

Graduates of Spelman College, class of 1932

5

ONWARD AND UPWARD— THE CREATION OF A LIBERAL ARTS INSTITUTION

The Florence Read Administration (1927–1953)

Upon assuming the presidency of Spelman College, Miss Florence Read was immediately entrusted, by the Spelman Board of Trustees, with the task of developing Spelman into a "very strong liberal arts college."[1] This new direction was incongruent with a normal-school emphasis; thus human, material, and capital resources were taken away from normal work (which had been the main focus of the Tapley administration) and directed toward the creation of a true liberal arts institution.[2] It must also be noted that the downward turn of the economy in 1929, which resulted in decreased job opportunities in teaching and other professions, in conjunction with immense decreases in funding from northern philanthropies (affected by the economic depression), also contributed to the change in trajectory away from normal work.[3]

In the academic year 1927–1928, Spelman consisted of a college, a senior high school, a junior high school, an elementary school, and a nurse-training department, yet funding for all five was limited.[4] At that time, majors could be chosen from among the following: biology, chemistry, education, English, French, history, political science, home economics, Latin, and mathematics.[5] Read had accepted the presidency of Spelman contingent upon the General Education Board's initiation of an endowment for the college.[6] The GEB agreed to these terms, and during the 1928–29 academic year, offered Spelman $1.5 million on the condition that Spelman raise an equal amount. The Laura

Spelman Rockefeller Memorial Fund was created with a $1 million gift from the Laura Spelman Rockefeller Estate, which was then donated to Spelman for the matching purposes associated with this endowment.[7] Mr. Julius Rosenwald personally donated $100,000, and another $100,000 was donated by the Julius Rosenwald Fund. The Women's American Baptist Home Mission Society donated $25,000, and other monetary gifts from sympathetic Black and White supporters of the institution trickled in to make up the difference, thereby eventually meeting the match requirement.[8] As income was being generated from the endowment, the General Education Board's annual fund donations to Spelman began to taper off and subsequently ceased altogether.

The northern mission societies and churches that had previously served as constant sources of financial support for private educational institutions such as Spelman were negatively impacted by the stock market crash of 1929 and the ensuing economic depression. Thus, external funding sources for Spelman began to essentially "dry up."[9] The Depression therefore had a profound impact upon the financial condition of Spelman College, particularly on its provision of services to its students. The financial situation negatively affected prospects for the continuation of the five departments of the college. Significant changes in the curricular offerings of Spelman were underway before the fiscal squeeze, as exemplified by the Board's May 20, 1927 decision to discontinue the elementary school in June 1928, as well as its vote that no new nurses be admitted to training at Spelman due to lack of capacity and the inability of MacVicar Hospital to keep up with modern methods of medical technology. Further, the December 15, 1927 decision to close the hospital to outside patients and to end the Nurse Training Course were caused by economic difficulties that preceded the Depression.[10] The suggestion to discontinue the hospital on Spelman's campus had actually been raised well before Read's administration, during the Tapley presidency, because of its decreased use by outside patients:

> I think this explanation may help you to see wherein there is a difference between a hospital which is a separate institution and a hospital which is only a department of an educational institution and which is really being maintained because of the nurse training department rather than because of the hospital side of the work.[11]

Thus, Tapley viewed maintenance of the hospital as an inappropriate use of the school's resources. MacVicar Hospital was, however, retained as an infirmary and college hospital for use by Spelman and Morehouse students.

The decision was made to continue the operation of Spelman High School, for the following reasons:

1. Few public high schools for Negroes were then in existence. In 1926, the whole state of Georgia maintained but two accredited high schools for 376,217 Negro children. In 1927, there were only six four-year accredited public high schools for Negroes in Georgia. Alabama and South Carolina had neither public nor private Negro high schools.
2. The Spelman High School and other academies of church-related colleges offered students better preparation for college.
3. About 60 percent of the Spelman High School students lived on the campus and thus benefited by training in and outside the classroom.
4. The number of college students, while steadily increasing, was small. There was a dearth of young Negro women with adequate preparation for college. Most of them had no opportunity even to complete high school.[12]

Despite the many reasons to support maintaining the high school, with the bulk of the limited funds available being allocated to the collegiate departments of the school, the Spelman High School was later discontinued in 1930.[13] The discontinuance of the Spelman high school would soon become inevitable, however, due to the establishment of an academic affiliation agreement with Morehouse College and Atlanta University in 1930, which established a laboratory high school to be conducted jointly by the three institutions. The downsizing and consolidation of academic units and levels at Spelman was indicative of the institution's move away from "quantity," in the way of attempting to provide a comprehensive education for its students, to an environment which emphasized the "quality" of the education its students received, particularly at the higher grade levels.

From 1928 onward, there was a decided change in the collegiate work of the institution:

> The declared aim of Spelman College was to provide, within a limited scope and with a relatively small number of students, as good educational facilities as were available in any college of liberal arts. The emphasis was to be on quality. . . . Accordingly, more college courses were provided in the humanities, in science and mathematics, in history and social science, philosophy and fine arts; and the college faculty was increased and strengthened.[14]

Read's presidency continued to usher in many changes toward a more academic institution, which contributed greatly to the ways in which Spelman students were being socialized. In the interest of creating a true liberal arts college, the library was fortified with additional volumes. The Spelman faculty continued to feature teachers from northeastern and midwestern colleges, including one African American faculty member. These men and women represented a myriad of academic areas including music, zoology, chemistry, Latin, history, English, drama, and the like, thereby contributing to Spelman's ability to deliver a high-quality liberal arts curriculum to its students.[15]

Cooperative teaching agreements were established with Morehouse College via faculty exchanges and joint appointments.[16] Elective courses for juniors and seniors on Spelman's and Morehouse's campuses afforded students the opportunity to take a wide variety of enriching courses and greatly enhanced the opportunity for socialization. A summer school was jointly operated by Morehouse and Spelman colleges with Atlanta University (AU) affiliation.[17] Spelman students began to receive a great many fellowships for graduate study in northern institutions via grants from philanthropic organizations such as the General Education Board and the Julius Rosenwald Fund. Spelman made other subtle, but no less important, changes in its curriculum, which had formerly been pervaded by domestic arts activities. For example, the college assumed responsibility for the school's laundry, replacing the students who had done the work in the past. Nevertheless, sufficient proficiency in the mechanics of doing laundry work still had to be exhibited by students at the end of the academic year.[18]

Spelman's extra-curriculum was significantly expanded during the Read administration with the ushering in of significant numbers and types of cultural events on the campus, particularly in the areas of art, music, and drama. Activities of this sort pervaded the curriculum of the Florence Read era. Nationally and internationally renowned musicians, actors, actresses, artists, and others began to perform regularly at Spelman or to exhibit their work on the Spelman campus. Dramatic performances on the Spelman campus began to play a significant role in curricular and extracurricular college life, which tremendously enhanced socialization opportunities across all AU campuses.[19] The president and administration of Spelman saw these cultural activities, which also included lectures, addresses, and chapel talks, as extremely important, because they "brought to Spelman students and teachers, mental stimulus and made connections with the world at large. . . . This has special value in a section where the students do not have free access to the cultural resources of the community."[20] The interaction with political and philanthropic speakers, actors, and others who visited the campus also demonstrated another mechanism for socializing Spelman students. The use of the speakers and the others who visited the campus could arguably have helped to make Read's dream of the complete liberal arts college seem more real. Students were now being socialized in a truer version of a liberal arts education, which provided a vehicle for the open expression of ideas and ideologies that were not necessarily Spelman driven.

With the many academic and non-academic resources available on the respective campuses of Spelman College, Morehouse College, and Atlanta University, it is no small wonder that the suggestion had surfaced, from time to time, that the three educational institutions for Black students work cooperatively toward the education of Black students. In an article written in January 1904, two years before his election to the presidency of Morehouse College, John Hope had expressed his dream that someday Black youngsters would not be bound or constrained in any way in their ability to attend a particular college based on denominational ties, but would instead be free to attend whichever school provided the best academic training. In Hope's words,

> When this time comes, the Atlanta schools, so close together and aiming at the same thing, the education of the Colored People will probably come to some agreement. Out of the community of interest will develop spheres of influence. In view of present tendencies in some, if not all, of these schools, is it Utopian to forecast the following division of labor? . . .

> With some such division of labor as this each school could make its peculiar demand and would have a better guarantee of progress and permanency. Without some such division, competition may result in an unseemly struggle for existence, causing untold detriment to defenseless students, honest in their eagerness for learning but inexperienced to discern between the real and shoddy in matters educational. . . .[21]

This notion was underscored once again during the National Interracial Conference held on December 16, 1928 in Washington, D.C.[22] There representatives of the large philanthropic organizations of the day gathered to discuss a better way of providing funding to Black, southern schools, particularly those in Atlanta, without "giving our little dots of money first to one college, then to another, in Atlanta."[23]

It was during this conference that Clark Foreman of the Phelps-Stokes Fund and formerly of the Commission on Interracial Cooperation suggested that a formal affiliation arrangement be made among Morehouse, Spelman, and Atlanta University, with the president of Spelman being retained, and Dr. John Hope taking over the presidency of Atlanta University. Upon return of the interested parties to Atlanta, a request was officially made of Dr. John Hope that he serve as president of Atlanta University. He agreed, but decided also to continue his service as the president of Morehouse College. This decision related primarily to his deep involvement in a capital campaign effort for Morehouse's endowment.[24]

An informal conference was convened of the Boards of Trustees of the three institutions—Morehouse, Spelman, Atlanta University—on May 25, 1929. The Boards of Morehouse and Spelman colleges designated their presidents as their representatives to the meeting. A plan was established during this meeting for the three institutions to become affiliated in a university plan, with graduate and professional work being done at Atlanta University and undergraduate studies being the focus of Spelman and Morehouse colleges. According to the proposed agreement, Spelman and Morehouse colleges would maintain their own separate trustee boards, officers, and management; the Atlanta University Board of Trustees would be reorganized to include three members nominated by Spelman College, three nominated by Morehouse College, and three existing Atlanta University Board members nominated by the Atlanta University Board; no freshman would be admitted into Atlanta University in September, 1929; and other Atlanta colleges for Blacks could enter the agreement at any time, with the approval of all three original schools.[25] On April 1, 1929, the Agreement of Affiliation or "Atlanta University Affiliation" was signed by President Read of Spelman, President Hope of Morehouse, and outgoing Atlanta University President Myron W. Adams. This historic agreement created the Atlanta University System, the first of its kind among Black institutions.[26]

With this new agreement of affiliation in place, changes with respect to curriculum development in all three schools ensued. In 1930, an agreement was reached specifying that all three schools would conduct, as a part of the work of the Department of Education, a coeducational laboratory school which would include K–12 grades. Spelman was to discontinue the operation of its high school and cooperate with Atlanta University in conducting its laboratory high school, and Spelman would lend the use of Giles Hall for the high school grades.[27] This was significant because Spelman was required to eliminate the normal school and secondary levels of education and fully acquiesce to "higher learning" and all of the accoutrements that accompanied this change. According to Read, "The laboratory school was to serve to give graduate students in the Department of Education more than training in teaching methods, but the opportunity to observe effective pedagogy and the ensuing results."[28] During this time, most Spelman High School students and Atlanta University Laboratory High School senior girls matriculated at Spelman College.[29]

During the 1929–30 academic year, fifteen undergraduate courses in biology, economics, English, French, Latin, and mathematics were offered by Atlanta University in cooperation with Spelman and Morehouse colleges.[30] These curricular offerings continued through the 1935–36 academic year. Atlanta University offered graduate coursework in economics, business administration, education, and English, as these areas were viewed as essential to the progress of Black communities.[31] Clarence A. Bacote became the first appointee to the graduate faculty in history in September of 1930.[32] Dr. Bacote taught the required sophomore history course at Spelman through the exchange arrangement with Atlanta University. This arrangement with Bacote, Atlanta University, and Spelman persisted for the next twenty-five years. Atlanta University undergraduate men and women, following the discontinuance of the institution's undergraduate course of study, finished their coursework at Morehouse and Spelman Colleges, respectively, and subsequently received their diplomas from Atlanta University during the graduation ceremonies in 1931 and 1932.[33]

The affiliation agreement served the three institutions well (as they began to receive recognition and formal accolades for the quality and types of academic courses offered on their campuses).[34] In December 1930, the Southern Association of Colleges and Schools (SACS) granted seven Black institutions, including Atlanta University, Spelman, and Morehouse Colleges admission to its approved list of colleges whose credits and degrees would then be acceptable among higher level academic institutions. Of the seven Black institutions on the approved list, only Fisk received an "A" rating. However, in December 1932, SACS gave an "A" rating to Atlanta University and its affiliated colleges, which included Spelman and Morehouse.[35] In 1930, Spelman College was elected to membership in the Association of American Colleges (AAC); it was one of only six Black institutions among the then four hundred member colleges.[36]

In June 1930, the General Education Board announced a gift of $450,000, thereby solidifying its intention to create a library for Atlanta University and the affiliated colleges. The library, named for Trevor Arnett of the General Education Board, was dedicated on April 30, 1932.[37] At the dedication ceremonies held in Sisters Chapel on Spelman's campus, students, faculty, and administrators alike heard this statement rendered by Mr. Dean Sage, Chair of Atlanta University's Board of Trustees:

> The keys will be symbolic of an open door to this stately building, this repository of accumulated learning—a wide way, beckoning to entrance and a welcome to all who "through knowledge seek wisdom". . . . Only through the storied knowledge of the Past can the Present hope to understand the great adventure of life, and so understanding, to solidify those foundations which the wisdom of experience has slowly fashioned and upon which the Future must build.

> I envision this library as the heart of a great center of cultural learning—an abiding home for that freedom of thought which denies prejudice, prompts the search for wisdom, and fights an eternal battle against the disorganization of ignorance and the deadness of materialism; an institution which shall give to America leadership measured in terms of men and women of the Negro race, a leadership fully competent, because of the advantages here gained, to match with the best leadership of the White race for the solution of those problems which the oneness of our country makes common to both.

> Mr. Arnett, to you and to the great foundation which you represent [the GEB] I tender the deepest and sincerest thanks of Atlanta University. Your magnificent gift is the keystone of our entire university structure, present and future. Permit me to say to you in words that are not my own, to express to you a thought that is within my heart. "Help thou thy brother's boat across. And, lo! Thine own has reached the shore."[38]

The formal and informal curricula of Spelman College were fortified greatly by the erection of the Atlanta University library whose very existence proliferated a body of knowledge (utilizing a variety of media) for Spelman students as well as students on the other campuses. The existence of the library also facilitated social interaction between and amongst Spelman students and students from the neighboring Atlanta University Center colleges. Beyond the purely academic education, cultural and artistic activities also began to come to the fore in the Spelman curriculum, against the backdrop of the New Negro Movement and the Harlem Renaissance.[39] From 1920 until about 1930, an unprecedented surge of creative activity burgeoned among African Americans in all fields of art. With its beginnings as a series of literary discussions in the lower and upper Manhattan sections of New York City, this African American cultural movement became known as the "New Negro Movement" and later the Harlem Renaissance. The Harlem Renaissance is the name given to this period within which a group of talented artists produced a significant body of literature in the prominent artistic genres of poetry, fiction, drama, painting, sculpture, dance, music, and essay. This movement encompassed more than just an increase in literary production among Blacks or a social revolt against racism; the Harlem Renaissance heralded the unique culture of African Americans and redefined African American modes and genres of expression. Thus, African Americans were encouraged to become the "New Negro," a term penned in 1925 by philosopher Alain LeRoy Locke.

> The foundations had been well laid. Now new curiosity was awakened. The New Negro described by Alain Locke and others stirred Negro students into more awareness of their lacks and their opportunities; and at the same time created within them a greater enthusiasm to enlarge their capacities, greater self-confidence, and a greater sense of responsibility to develop their latent abilities.[40]

This sentiment did not escape the minds and hearts of Spelman students. The administration responded in kind through the establishment of clubs and organizations that were characteristic of the artistic fervor of the period and greatly broadened and increased socialization opportunities. Spelman's new affiliation with the other AU institutions ushered in significant changes to the Spelman College environment:

> The extra-curricular life encouraged getting together on the basis of common interests, not at all on the snobbishness of sororities which were nonexistent [on Spelman's campus]. Instead, the English Club; the Biology Club; the music groups; the Pan American Club for students of Spanish and

Latin-American History; the French Club; the Dramatics organization which included University, Morehouse and Spelman students and took as its name the University Players; all these and other activities including tennis, basketball and track, demanded the best the students had to give outside the classroom. There was zest—and at times fatigue—but always growth.[41]

Similarly, courses in the fine arts grew in number and respect within the Spelman curriculum. Under President Read's leadership, courses for credit were offered in painting, sculpture, music (vocal and instrumental) and dramatics, and dance training was made available. Training in these formal academic courses also facilitated students' abilities to partake in extracurricular fine art activities such as the glee club, the quartet, the mixed chorus, and the orchestra or University Players. "Introduction to Fine Arts" was added to the curriculum in 1935.[42] This course introduced students to the myriad facets of the fine arts including music, dramatics, dance, painting, and sculpture—all in one course. Lectures, demonstration of techniques, exhibitions, musical programs, and student participation in the creation of works of art comprised the coursework of this new course. The Spelman campus saw the performances of well-known national and international plays by outside groups, as well as the University Players. This attention to the fine arts and the invitations to speakers of national and international renown (including some of the writers, poets, and artists of the Harlem Renaissance era) served as a great part of the legacy of the Florence Read administration.[43] According to President Read, "It was mainly the speakers, although occasionally also visitors who did not talk in public, who remained for a week or a day, or even for a meal, who made possible the atmosphere of a liberal arts college."[44]

In November of 1930, a nursery school was added to Spelman's campus with a grant from the Spelman Fund of New York.[45] The nursery was established to care for and teach the children in the facility, but also to serve as a laboratory for Atlanta University Center students who were engaged in studies of early childhood mental and physical growth, the preschool child, nursery school procedure, and behavior problems of children.[46] These were courses for which the students received credit. This nursery was the first such school among Black colleges, as well as among the eastern colleges (Black or White) for women.[47]

The curriculum of Spelman, as described in this chapter, generally persisted throughout all the years of President Read's tenure, with the exception of the World War II years. According to President Read, "Academically, the effort, during the war years was to continue the preparation and training of the students in the fundamental courses in the arts and sciences, and at the same time to relate as much as possible the long-range training to what was going on in the world."[48] Spelman students engaged in courses in a core curriculum, as well as in specialized courses in their field of choice. For the first two years of their collegiate lives at Spelman College, Spelman students took courses in English, history, and science. Foreign language was required for the Bachelor's Degree (two years of study in French, German, or Spanish). From 1936 forward, a three-credit-hour course in philosophy was required for the B.A. degree.[49] Beginning in 1940 (due to the war) every Spelman student was required to take a three-credit-hour course in political science, or a one-credit-hour course for two semesters called Political Orientation.[50] During their junior and senior years, the students embarked upon courses in their major subject areas, as well as engaging in elective courses. Home economics students at Spelman had fewer electives due to the rigid state board of education certification requirements, but the curriculum in this area was heavily laden with humanities courses. Students in this course of study received the Bachelor of Science (B.S.) degree.[51]

President Read continued her work to strengthen and diversify the faculty of Spelman College, which she felt was the key to the success of Spelman students: "Knowledge of and zest for the field of study, and enthusiasm to reveal knowledge to students were primarily considered in appraising a teacher's qualifications for appointment to the faculty. The possession of a Ph.D. was respected, but did not take precedence of [sic] the other qualifications."[52] Although Spelman had boasted an integrated, though only barely, faculty since 1885, according to President Read, under her leadership drastic changes to the racial and gender balance of the faculty were effected, particularly between 1926–1953.[53]

The curricular, physical plant, and faculty changes at Spelman from 1927 to 1953 were of great significance to Spelman College and its students. However, a Spelman alumna best summarized the influence of Miss Read's affinity for cultural and liberal arts education upon Spelman and Spelman students during the Read administration:

> Such confidence and such ability can be developed in part through study of biography, history, science and literature. But the study in library or labora-

tory needs to be supplemented by acquaintance with living men and women, who actually exemplify superior achievement in thought and action.

Familiarity with masterpieces in any field of human endeavor develops a person's ability to discriminate between the excellent and the mediocre, between good and bad. There are masterpieces in miniature, as well as in magnitude: quality and skill are what count, not the size of the undertaking.

Through association with persons of worth, through seeing great works of art in replica, through becoming acquainted with great drama and great music, and also, may it be said, through sitting under some first-rate teachers, Spelman students were encouraged to exert their minds; to emulate the best they saw or heard music, drama, the graphic arts, writing, to strive for achievement, mental and spiritual; and to achieve a spirit of genuine scholarship and a finer character.

Spelman College is proud of its founders, its co-workers, its benefactors, and likewise proud of its alumnae whose record of accomplishments tell a continuing story of grappling with difficulties of overcoming obstacles, and a marching forward toward the ideal of a better life for all people.[54]

Miss Florence Matilda Read, the fourth president of Spelman College, championed the cause of women's collegiate education. She advocated strongly for the independent education of Spelman women, tempered with progressive, as well as academically and socially beneficial affiliations with neighboring institutions such as Morehouse College and Atlanta University. President Read's leadership, which introduced a generation of Spelman students to the world around them through academic and social cultural programs, made the curriculum associated with her presidency the most forward-thinking and liberal of those implemented at the institution since its humble beginnings.

Notes

1. Read, *The Story of Spelman*, p. 210. See Catalog of Spelman College (1927–28), p. 10, in Spelman College Archives.
2. This move may serve as a signal that the Spelman Board of Trustees was not

happy with the direction that Tapley had taken the institution, despite the lack of evidence in the archives to this effect.

3. For discussion of economic crash and the New Deal, see Charles A. Beard and Mary Beard, *A Basic History of the United States,* (New York: Doubleday, Doran & Company, 1944), pp. 452–462.

4. See "Departments" in Catalog of Spelman College (1927–1928), pp. 50–55, in Spelman College Archives.

5. See Spelman Catalog (1927–28), p. 23, in Spelman College Archives.

6. Read, *The Story of Spelman*, p. 213.

7. For information on creation of Laura Spelman Rockefeller Memorial Fund, see Minutes of Executive Committee of Board of Trustees, May 10, 1929, Box: Manley Administration (hereafter Manley), Folder: Meeting—Minutes, Executive Committee (1927–1961), in Spelman College Archives.

8. See *Financial Statement and Donors' List of Spelman College for the school year 1928–1929*, pp. 11–17, in Spelman College Archives. See Annual Report of Spelman College (1928–1929), in Spelman College Archives. See also Read, *The Story of Spelman*, pp. 213, 214; Minutes of Executive Committee of Board of Trustees, July 12, 1929, Box: Manley Administration (hereafter Manley), Folder: Meeting—Minutes, Executive Committee (1927–1961), in Spelman College Archives; Letter from W.B. Harrell (Rosenwald Fund) to Florence Read, May 14, 1929, Box: Manley, Folder: Meeting—Minutes, Executive Committee (1927–1961), in Spelman College Archives; Letter from Julius Rosenwald to Florence Read, May 15, 1929, Box: Manley, Folder: Meeting—Minutes, Executive Committee (1927–1961), in Spelman College Archives.

9. Read, pp. 213, 214.

10. Read, p. 214. Regarding decision to close hospital and end nurse training course, see Catalog of Spelman College (1928–29), p. 10, in Spelman College Archives; See Minutes of Meeting of Executive Committee and of Informal Meeting of Southern Trustees, December 15, 1927, p. 2, Box: Manley, Folder: Meeting—Minutes, Executive Committee (1927–1961) in Spelman College Archives; Spelman College Report of the President, March 9, 1928, p. 7, Box: President Report (1928–43) & Miscellaneous Administrative Reports.

11. See letter from Tapley to R. Guinn, June 19, 1919 in Box: Tapley, Folder: Trustee Letters—Miscellaneous.

12. Read, *The Story of Spelman*, p. 215.

13. Ibid.

14. Ibid. See Catalog of Spelman College (1932–33), p. 75 re: merger of high school with AU laboratory school. This merger was meant to slowly, but surely, de-emphasize K–12 education at the institution, and therefore shift its curricular direction away from a secondary education to a more postsecondary emphasis.

15. Catalog of Spelman College (1929–1930), pp. 14–21, in Spelman College Archives.

16. See Catalog of Spelman College (1928–1929), p. 10, in Spelman College Archives.

17. See Catalog of Spelman College (1927–1928), p. 55 in Spelman College Archives, re: origin and content of the summer school. See also Report of the President of Spelman College, March 9, 1928, p. 9, Box: President Reports (1928–43) Miscellaneous Administrative Reports in Spelman College Archives.

18. Catalog of Spelman College (1927–1928), p. 45 in Spelman College Archives.

19. Read, *The Story of Spelman*, p. 220. For example, the Harmon Foundation sponsored yearly exhibits on Spelman's campus in 1928 and 1929 of paintings and sculptures, all by Black artists. The director of the High Museum of Art, which was closed to Blacks during the period, gave a lecture at Spelman on the second year's exhibit.

20. Read, *The Story of Spelman*, p. 223, 224. See Catalogues of Spelman College (1927–1953), Sections: Special Lectures & Concerts, College Preachers, Chapel Speakers, in Spelman College Archives.

21. Jones, *A Candle in the Dark*, p. 264. See also Read, *The Story of Spelman*, pp. 229–234.

22. It is the opinion of the authors of this book that Hope's dream, initially expressed in 1904, did not come to fruition during the intervening years between 1904 and 1928 because of the desire of the respective Atlanta colleges that Black students maintain their own identities. Also, as many of these institutions were founded and/or under the auspices of different religious denominations or missionary societies, no doubt reaching a consensus on the form and function of any type of cooperative educational agreement would have been difficult. Atlanta University was founded by the American Missionary Society; Spelman and Morehouse Colleges were founded by the American Baptist Home Mission Society; and Morris Brown College was founded by the African Methodist Episcopal Church. Spelman and Morehouse Colleges however, had always, since early on in their respective histories, to some degree shared academic facilities, faculty, etc. For more discussion of the founding of these and other Black colleges, see Albert N. Whiting, *Guardians of the Flame: Historically Black Colleges Yesterday, Today, and Tomorrow* (Washington, D.C.: American Association of State Colleges and Universities, 1991), pp. 16–20.

23. Ridgely Torrence, *The Story of John Hope* (New York: MacMillan Company, 1948), p. 296; Clarence Bacote, *The Story of Atlanta University, A Century of Service (1865–1965)*, (Princeton, New Jersey: Princeton University Press, 1969), p. 262; Jones, *A Candle in the Dark*, p. 116. For story of the discussion in Washington, D.C. , see also Read, *The Story of Spelman*, p. 230.

24. Jones, *A Candle in the Dark*, p. 117; Bacote, *The Story of Atlanta University*, p. 265; Read, *The Story of Spelman*, pp. 232, 233.

25. Jones, *A Candle in the Dark*, p. 119; Bacote, *The Story of Atlanta University*, p. 267; Read, *The Story of Spelman*, p. 233.

26. Bacote, *The Story of Atlanta University*, p. 269 and Read, *The Story of Spelman*, p. 235. Clark College, Morris Brown College, and Gammon Theological Seminary, later joined the arrangement, effectively creating the Atlanta University Center. See Jones, pp. 119, 120 and Read, p. 236; Donald J. Cowling, J. Curtis Dixon, Charles H. Thompson, Malcolm Wallace, "A Study of Cooperation in the Atlanta University

Center," December 1, 1946, pp. 3, 4; Catalog of Spelman College (1929–1930), p. 11, all in Spelman College Archives.

27. Donald J. Cowling, J. Curtis Dixon, Charles H. Thompson, Malcolm Wallace, "A Study of Cooperation in the Atlanta University Center," December 1, 1946, p. 7; Catalog of Spelman College (1932–1933), p. 75; Minutes of Executive Committee of Board of Trustees, February 20, 1930, Box: Manley Administration, Folder: Meetings—Minutes, Executive Committee (1927–61), all in Spelman College Archives.

28. Read, p. 236.

29. Ibid.

30. Catalog of Spelman College (1929–1930), pp. 29–45, in Spelman College Archives.

31. Read, p. 238.

32. Catalog of Spelman College (1932–1933), p. 21, in Spelman College Archives.

33. Read, p. 239. Bacote, *The Story of Atlanta University*, p. 281. See Catalog of Spelman College (1932–1933), p. 85, in Spelman College Archives.

34. After Morris Brown College moved to the Atlanta University vicinity in 1932, and Clark College in 1941, the exchange of students and teachers across the five campuses escalated, as well as the offerings of the formal curriculum, and the nature of extracurricular activities, thereby exposing Spelman students to fuller depth and breadth in a liberal arts college experience. See Read, p. 238. See also Jones, *A Candle in the Dark*, p. 119. For details of the move of Morris Brown & Clark Colleges, see Cowling, "A Study of Cooperation," pp. 11, 12. For exchange of teachers, see Cowling, "A Study of Cooperation," p. 13.

35. Read, *The Story of Spelman*, p. 240

36. Ibid, p. 241.

37. See Cowling, "A Study of Cooperation," pp. 8, 14, in Spelman College Archives.

38. Read, *The Story of Spelman*, p. 246, 247.

39. For discussion of modes of expression during this period, of W.E.B DuBois and author and playwright, Richard Wright, see Robinson, *Black Marxism: The Making of a Black Radical Tradition*, pp. 251–348 and 416–435. See also DuBois, *Dusk of Dawn*, pp. 268–326. Further, see Raymond Wolters, *The New Negro on Campus: Black College Rebellions of the 1920s* (Princeton, NJ: Princeton University Press, 1975). For information about other significant individuals in this movement such as: Langston Hughes, Zora Neale Hurston, Claude McKay, Jean Toomer, Carl Van Vechten, Countee Cullen, Angelina Grimke, James Weldon Johnson, Marion Vera Cuthbert, Ida B. Wells-Barnett, Palmer Hayden, Lois Mailou Jones, et al., visit: Paul P. Reuben, "Chapter 9: Harlem Renaissance—An Introduction," *PAL: Perspectives in American Literature—A Research and Reference Guide*. URL:http://www.csustan.edu/english/reuben/pal/chap9/9intro.html (May 19, 1999) or see Nathan I. Huggins, *Harlem Renaissance* (New York: Oxford University Press, 1971).

40. Read, p. 249.

41. Read, p. 250.

42. See Catalog of Spelman College (1935–1936), p. 32, in Spelman College Archives.

43. See Read, pp. 254–264.

44. Read, p. 323.

45. See Catalog of Spelman College (1932–1933), p. 10, in Spelman College Archives.

46. See Catalog of Spelman College (1932–1933), pp. 38, 39, 59, in Spelman College Archives.

47. Read, p. 273.

48. Read, p. 300.

49. See Catalog of Spelman College (1936–37), p. 65 and (1937–1938), p. 65, both in Spelman College Archives.

50. See Catalog of Spelman College (1940–41), p. 48, in Spelman College Archives.

51. See Catalog of Spelman College 1936–1953, under "Courses of Instruction," "Home Economics" sections, in Spelman College Archives. See also Annual Reports of the President for the same years, in the Spelman College Archives.

52. Read, *The Story of Spelman*, p. 306.

53. See Read, p. 310. For an example of diversification of faculty, see also Spelman College Report of the President, April 23, 1953, p. I, which references the way in which "the presence of a distinguished Chinese scholar, Professor John Wong-Quincey, and his wife, has added in a solid way to our [Spelman's] cultural life." See also Catalog of Spelman College (1931–1953) which demonstrates, via affiliation with Morehouse and AU, diversity of faculty, and Spelman College Report of the President, 1926–1953, all in Spelman College Archives.

54. Read, *The Story of Spelman*, pp. 368, 369.

6

THE SOCIALIZATION OF SPELMAN STUDENTS

According to Robert K. Merton, socialization is defined as a process through which individuals acquire the values, norms, knowledge, and skills needed to exist in a given society.[1] As stated in chapter 1, we believe that the socialization process of Black women at historically Black women's colleges (Spelman and Bennett Colleges) are very different from the socialization experienced by women attending coeducational HBCUs, PWWCs, and other institutions. Different methods of socialization and an array of socializing agents contribute to the comprehensive education of Spelman students. The backgrounds of Spelman students vary with regard to academic background, personal issues, economic status, and family structure. In addition, the societal norms of the time period which this book spans, 1881–1953, will be different depending upon the concerns, values, and educational experiences of that generation.

In 1972, Burton Clark introduced the concept of "organizational saga" to help explain how a college's founding mission influences college culture.[2] Examining the college culture can help one to better understand the role that the Spelman college culture has on the socialization of students. *Ethos*, taken from the Greek word meaning "habit," is another term that is widely used to explain the belief system shared among administration, faculty, staff, and students. Authors George Kuh and John Hall suggest that ethos is shared by a core set of educational values that are also manifested in the school's mission and philosophy and that these values were communicated and reinforced through implicit, daily messages and interactions by the college community.[3]

According to social-psychological theory, the early stages of socialization are especially important because attitudes, values, and beliefs tend to stabilize in young adulthood and become less likely to change as persons grow older.[4] Role modeling and mentorship also help new students understand the informal norms of the school. However, for the socialization process to be successful, members of the Spelman community, including students, faculty, administrators, and alumnae must work together as socializing agents to quickly become a part of the organizational culture of Spelman, either knowingly or unknowingly. To do this, Spelman students need to understand and believe in the mission and philosophy of the institution, as well as the importance of the cultural structure of the school. Spelman College has clear institutional values and expectations, which are learned both formally and informally and served as an influential component of the socialization process. John A. Clausen underscores this notion in his statement that:

> As an underlying basis for social control, socialization efforts are designed to lead new members to adhere to the norms of the larger society or of the particular group into which he is being incorporated and to commit him to its future.[5]

In reviewing the historical data from 1881 to 1953 (including transcripts of interviews with faculty and staff, published articles, and a variety of Spelman archival documents) along with a number of recent interviews of Spelmanites graduating between 1977 and 1985, several themes emerged that we have divided into three subgroups we have identified as: *training of the heads* (nurturing academic and intellectual environment), *training of the hands* (activism, civic engagement, leadership, and community service), and *training of the hearts* (Christian character, sisterhood, mentoring, and Black female social consciousness) of Spelman students.

In this chapter, we examine how institutional values or ideals shape the socialization of Spelman students and how they are transmitted through the internal environment to the student body. We begin with a bird's-eye view of life as a Spelmanite in the early years and explore the socialization of students using these three major themes as a framework, interspersed with quotes from Spelman alumnae, and concluding with comments from former Spelman College presidents. An interesting perspective on the socializing effects of the Spelman experience are summarized by a 1977 Spelman graduate:

> At Spelman, you get a well-rounded experience. Period. Bar none. I couldn't say it would be academic over a social environment. It's there. It's what you

make of it. It can go either way. Being situated where it is [Atlanta and the AUC], I think that it being a women's college, you eventually have to think about being a woman. It's an experience that would be difficult to put into words.

Life as a Spelmanite in the Early Years

In the 1885 issue of *The Spelman Messenger*, the administration describes a student's daily routine in a typical week on the Spelman College campus:

Every day of the week is filled full, from six in the morning to nine at night, Satan finds few idle hands to supply with mischief in the institution.

The day begins with the rising bell at six, the devotion bell at half past and breakfast at seven. The girls are busy before and after breakfast till school time, with their room work and the work in the kitchen, for the boarders take regular turns in doing the entire housework of the establishment.

At a quarter before nine, all are expected to be in school. The first hour is spent in devotional exercises, led by the Principal; then come recitations which last till two, with a short recess and lunch at noon.

Immediately after school, those taking music go to the music room, those whose turn it is to wash, to the laundry, and others to the sewing room, and the remainder to the study hall, excepting those who are taking lessons in type-setting and consequently go to the printing office.

Dinner comes at four and at half-past five the girls have a prayer meeting by themselves, followed by general devotions in the chapel at six. The evening is spent in study, preparatory to the next day's lessons.

Tuesday morning, Dr. Hicks gives a lecture in Physiology, Hygiene and Anatomy. Later in the day, Ms. Grover has the entire school in a class in Phonics.

On Wednesday, the first hour is devoted to vocal music in charge of Professor Kruger.

Thursday, before recitations, Mrs. Albert gives a brief but entertaining lecture on Natural Philosophy, accompanied by experiments. Occasionally, other teachers give similar lectures on different topics.

Particular attention is given every day to the teaching of Writing, and Drawing is also regularly taught.

On each Friday, a half hour is devoted to the reading of compositions by the pupils before the other students, who are expected to make any criticisms they can.

Saturday is general cleaning day, stoves are blacked, floors washed and faces too, and everything is made clean and bright for the Sabbath.[6]

According to the same issue of *The Spelman Messenger*, "The Alphabet of Health" was generously posted all around the Spelman College campus and printed in numerous student and college documents to indoctrinate students into the college's culture:

> A—s soon as you're up shake blanket and sheet;
> B—etter be without shoes than sit with wet feet;
> C—hildren, if healthy, are active, not still;
> D—amp beds and damp clothes will both make you ill;
> E—at slowly, and always chew your food well;
> F—reshen the air in the house where you dwell;
> G—arments must never be made too tight;
> H—omes should be healthy, airy and light;
> I—f you wish to be well, as you do, I've no doubt;
> J—ust open the window before you go out;
> K—eep your rooms always tidy and clean;
> L—et dust on the furniture never be seen;
> M—uch illness is caused by the want of pure air;
> N—ow open the windows be ever your care;
> O—ld rags and old rubbish should never be kept;
> P—eople should see that their floors are well swept;
> Q—uick movements in children are healthy and right;
> R—emember, the young cannot thrive without light;
> S—ee that the cistern is clean to the brim;
> T—ake care that your dress is all tidy and trim;
> U—se your nose to find if there be a bad drain;
> V—ery sad are the fevers that come in its train;
> W—alk as much as you can without feeling fatigued;
> X—erxes could walk full many a league;
> Y—our health is your wealth, which your wisdom must keep;
> Z—eal will help a good cause, and the good you will reap.[7]

Albert Manley, who served as president of Spelman College from 1953 to 1976, contended in his 1995 book that as a general rule during his presidency, all Spelman students lived on campus, but a few exceptions were made in special circumstances.[8] Except for Abby Aldrich Rockefeller dormitory, there were no single-student-room dormitories. Visiting the city was not encouraged, and was only allowed with written permission of student's parents and upon receipt of an invitation by the hostess. When off campus or during social activities on the shared Atlanta University Center campus, students were closely chaperoned by a faculty member, with an elaborate sign-in and sign-out system. Calling hours, when men would visit the young Spelmanites, were severely limited and closely chaperoned. Faculty always knew where each student was at all times. Life as a Spelmanite was structured and rigid, focusing on Christian character, manners, responsibility, discipline, and developing well-rounded women.

Training the Heads

In Manley's 1995 book, *A Legacy Continues: The Manley Years at Spelman College, 1953–1976,* he describes five important themes of his educational philosophy. First, Manley points out the distinct and important role of Black colleges within the United States and abroad. Second, he discusses the importance of gaining an international perspective on human problems, which he contends should be done through a variety of rich educational experiences at the undergraduate level, both inside and outside the classroom. Manley's third major argument is that there needs to be a greater appreciation for the ways in which learning can take place, whether it be in the classroom, around campus, in one's community, nationally or internationally. His fourth theme underscores the necessity for an understanding of the need to address the special problems and opportunities confronting women today. These women's issues, he explains, should be expressed in the context of both the Black community and America as a whole. Finally, Manley discusses his appreciation of the role that interdisciplinary studies can play in the exploration of human problems. Manley's educational perspectives are still quite consistent with the present day Spelman philosophy, with the exception that learning has become a bit more student driven, which is clearly a sign of the times.[9]

In Johnnetta Cole's 1994 book, *Conversations: Straight Talk with America's*

Sister President, she discusses the need for "pillars of a Worldcentric education." Cole describes *Worldcentric* as:

> . . . an education that not only teaches us about the world, but also prepares us to live purposefully in it. Such an education is structured, first and foremost, on the principle of social awareness and responsibility . . . the responsibility that emerges from a deeply instilled sense of community based on exchange and solidarity with others. The kind of responsibility develops only in an educational setting that insists on dialogue—cultural, intellectual, personal—within the rich diversity of humanity.[10]

This type of education, Cole contends, is built on:

> . . . social awareness and responsibility, knowledge of and respect for human diversity, and participatory learning.[11]

Such an education, she continues:

> . . . would help create an environment in which creativity, imagination, and intellectual curiosity flourish.[12]

Research on women's colleges has consistently reported that alumnae from women's colleges are more focused on education, involved in more leadership activities, and self-reportedly more self-confident.[13] Other scholars suggest that the effects of socialization are very strong and provide students with perspectives, orientations, and mindsets that often guide their academic and professional lives in the future.[14]

For example, one Spelman alumna fondly recounted her relationship with a Spelman faculty member:

> . . . This faculty member really took a personal interest in me as a freshman. It was her interest that molded me into what I'm doing today.

To further illustrate this point, in Alexander Astin's 1993 study, he reported that the climate of women's colleges tends to be more favorable and warm, which often results in women students having higher levels of self-confidence and greater involvement inside and outside the classroom.[15] Other scholars have reported that students in women's colleges experience greater satisfaction in their undergraduate careers, subsequently greater alumnae participation and higher occupational aspirations.[16]

In the January 1996 issue of the U.S. Catholic magazine, *Sounding Board*, Feigl argues that Christian women's colleges provide safe venues for women to intellectually explore the world around them:

> We who teach young women know that it is a time when they may push their horizons outward, accepting the sometimes scary fact that they have much to give and that much will be expected of them. Or they may hunker down in a closed, safe mental space that offers few risks or demands—and no real challenge. It is their decision to make, but we offer a supportive setting that encourages them to reach for their best. We offer a place where they can learn to take intellectual risks, practice leadership skills, and succeed often enough to get the hang of it.[17]

Similarly, Elizabeth Langdon, in her study of the persistence of affective outcomes of women's college alumnae, found that alumnae from women's colleges were more knowledgeable about diversity issues, were involved in a greater number of leadership activities, focused more on academic achievement, were committed more deeply to social change, and reported more positive relationship with faculty.[18]

Former Spelman President Albert Manley stated in his 1995 book that Spelman students regularly enjoyed hearing lectures from well-known persons such as poet Langston Hughes; Haile Selassie (Emperor of Ethiopia), the five Rockefeller brothers (John D., III, Nelson, Laurance, Winthrop, and David, whose grandfather and father made significant contributions to Spelman); the late Patricia Harris, U.S. Secretary of Health, Education and Welfare during the Carter administration; author Alex Haley; Nobel Laureate Martin Luther King, Jr.; former U.S. Secretary of State Henry Kissinger; and numerous others. In fact, in recent years, Spelman alumnae have reported having Bill Cosby read to the students regularly in the Marian Wright Edelman Childcare Center on Spelman's campus.

Several alumnae we interviewed explained the significance of lectures and interactions with notable Black professional role models:

> Shirley Chisholm was in residence [on campus] while I was at Spelman. It was great because we had small sessions with her; actually she was in my dorm. We would have social group with her and talk about whatever the

political agenda was at that time or we would just chit chat. It was nice to be able to sit down and just talk to someone you thought was untouchable. She was in residence for, I think a semester. We had a lot of interaction with her. Just to talk to her and know who she was.

We also had people like Nikki Giovanni. These types of people were very impressionable for me. To be from a small town and be involved and get to know and meet some people that I thought I couldn't touch.

I was in a class with Bill Cosby's daughter and Bernice King. So we had a lot of social things going on because Bernice was my classmate. We actually lived next door to each other. So I think those kind of things, just being there and seeing Coretta Scott King there, made a very positive impression. I remember we had to take this reading class, whether we needed it or not, from Dr. King's sister. So I think we all took it because she was his sister.

This tradition of bringing scholars, community advocates, and other famous figures to campus continues to be enjoyed, not just by the Spelman College community, but by the entire Atlanta University Center. These unique opportunities allow and encourage intellectual dialogue that nourishes the mind, spirit, and soul of every willing participant.

Training the Hands

According to Beverly Guy-Sheftall, one of Spelman's consistent priorities has been the training of Black women for leadership roles in their communities and the nation at large, despite the institution's earlier mission of training teachers.[19] Former President Donald Stewart confirmed this assertion in his inaugural address at Spelman in 1976:

> . . . Spelman and institutions like it provide a unique environment which is supportive of . . . female leadership roles in our society . . . Coed schools . . . tend to be male dominated. It is the presence of high-status women faculty and administrators in women's colleges that help develop strong identities and positive self-images on the part of female students.[20]

In 1937, ten years into her presidential administration, Florence Read authored an article in *Opportunity* magazine, describing the role of a women's college in Negro education.

. . . . One learns to lead by leading. In the same way, the young woman who has had full opportunity to develop her dramatic talents, to appreciate and understand good music and literature, and to engage freely in games and sports will carry back with her a full measure of her talents to her people, and if she is worth her salt, will in one way or another share her gifts and enthusiasm with those [with] whom she lives and works.[21]

Spelman College has always instilled the value of giving back to one's community and to society in general.

Beyond the contributions to the community, Spelman women are historically typified by the familial bonds and connections they experience while at the institution. Several Spelman alumnae we interviewed discussed the meaning of sisterhood in relationship to the Spelman College undergraduate educational experience:

> I think that family feeling and sisterhood is one of the biggest things that I love about Spelman.

> It's just a family. I really think of Spelman as a family. No matter where I go, when I greet people, there is a Spelman alumni association and somebody knows someone. It is a beautiful thing.

Another 1985 Spelman graduate elaborated on this notion by describing the Spelman bond as:

> . . . that Sisterhood thing. We really believed in that, so even till this day, when I meet Spelman people I don't even know, I tell them I went to Spelman and you just become friends. I know that positions are made available that way. It's not spoke[n] about, but it's just something that you feel you have to do. I know I do that here. If there's a Spelman student needing a position over another person. If I can pull them in, I do it. It's just something that you feel you're a part of. A family that you have and want to take care of.

The nurturing environment Spelmanites enjoy created a sense of self-discipline and often a strong desire to participate actively in causes that further the needs of others and make a difference, particularly in the lives of other women and those without a voice. Florence Read believed strongly that a Spelman woman had a responsibility not only to develop her talent to the best of her ability, but also to use that ability to improve the lives of those around her. Toward this end, one Spelman graduate we interviewed had this to say:

> Spelman helped to define us, in that we do what we want to do more. We want to give back. That doesn't mean we don't want to make as much money as we possibly can, but to give something of quality back. Because if any of us think about our motto, it's our whole school for Christ, I think that it says something about service and service to others. So I think that for the Spelman woman, regardless as to what occupation you've chosen to pursue, you have a responsibility to give back. It was just an expectation and you just lived up to the expectation.

Read further believed that only when a young student gave back could she reach her full potential. In her words,

> It is not enough that a woman shall become a self-contained, economically independent, and completely rounded individual. Neither is it sufficient that she shall have developed her taste for the good things of life and acquired skills in the arts. If the college has succeeded in its purpose, she will be not only willing but eager to share her gifts and use her newly acquired skills to better the lives of all those within her reach to her influence. And by that strange paradox which is the profoundest truth yet discovered or revealed, it is thus that her own life will reach its richest fulfillment.[22]

In support of Read's contention, Cole stated in her 1994 book:

> What should motivate large numbers of African American women to become personally and consistently involved in helping their sisters and brothers is a combination of compassion and enlightened self-interest.[23]

Over thirty years after the conclusion of Read's presidential administration, Johnnetta Cole took over the presidency of Spelman College. Prior to her arrival in 1987, Spelman students protested over the hiring of her predecessor, Dr. Donald Stewart, because, consistent with the historical leadership of the College as well as the students' socialization that women were empowered to serve in the highest of leadership positions, they felt a woman should serve as the leader of the women's historically Black college. Dr. Cole articulated in her book, *Conversations,* that African American women needed to be empowered. Empowerment, she contends, can only occur when:

. . . history and circumstances are acknowledged and analyzed, an education that *conditions* us to know ourselves. People without knowledge of who they are, cannot successfully participate in determining the direction in which they wish to go.[24]

She continued:

An education grounded in a social responsibility for making the world a better place, hinges directly and completely on a deep, studied, and ongoing education about the complexities of human diversity and culture in all the neighborhoods of our nation.[25]

It is important to note that most Black colleges and HBCUs view academic excellence and service to the community as "inextricably intertwined." One Spelmanite explained:

Spelman instills more of a confidence builder in young ladies. A lot of people say that we're snooty or snotty. I don't think that Spelman creates that image. The students come there the way they are and they build upon their positives within. People see it that way. They encourage you to become more than employed. You have a duty to reach back and pull someone up. That is your charge. I think that it is instilled in us year after year in everything that we do and the exposure, the people that they bring in, the social justice and social service is part. Regardless of what your career options are, you still have that obligation. I think there's an indoctrination that goes on there. I don't know how to explain that, but you do have a sense of the fact that you have to give back. That's part of your being. You had this opportunity, so it's your charge and now you must give back.

This cohesive link helps to establish and perpetuate an appreciation of the relationship between the curriculum, the nation, and the world.

The self-discipline and leadership skills that Spelman College inculcates in its students are more than just a notion and desire. Research has shown that in general, women were more likely to secure leadership positions, participate in student government, develop higher aspirations, and graduate if they attended a women's college.[26]

One Spelman 1985 graduate explains how her entire family was changed as a result of her experiences at Spelman College:

I never knew my parents were poor. I never knew that we didn't have things and I never felt it until I got to Spelman. Spelman just opened a whole new world for me. I think it was the best place for me, being from a small town. The choice was made by a high school teacher. I'm a first generation college student. My mom didn't even want me to go, my dad didn't care. My mom didn't know anybody who had gone to college, so she didn't want me to leave home. She didn't want me to go to Spelman either. She grew up picking cotton and she believed white is right. She truly believed that. She believed she needed to go to the white doctor, because the black doctors weren't good enough. When I went to Spelman and she watched me transcend, she started changing. My mother had all these pictures on the wall of just white people. She no longer does that anymore. I think we all grew up when I went there. It just opened up a new world for my whole family.

In the most recent decades, the applications for admission to Spelman College have steadily and significantly increased, resulting in greater competition for students and admission of more academically prepared students. In fact, Spelman College eliminated remedial studies in the late 1990s, because most entering students are so well prepared academically. As one Spelman alumna said:

I think I have a very strong foundation professionally from Spelman. Academically, you're very well-prepared from Spelman once you leave. I don't know if we're prepared in the sense of life experiences, but we were prepared academically.

Spelman College has proudly graduated many of America's female leaders and continues to receive the highest rankings among liberal arts colleges, regardless of race and gender specification.

Training the Hearts

Other than the academic curriculum, one of Spelman College's most revered shared experiences, as discussed earlier, is that of sisterhood. The term *sister* at Spelman College denotes a common term of endearment for students, faculty, administrators, and alumni. The value of sisterhood and community at Spelman has been encouraged through a nurturing environment and common experiences, such as formal mentoring between upper and lower classmates, students and faculty, and students and alumnae. Sisterhood also extended to the dorm mothers, as described below by another 1977 Spelman alumna:

> We felt very safe. We had the gates, we had the security, and we had dorm mothers. The old traditional dorm mothers, not like what they have now. When I was a freshman, we had an older lady in the dorm that did dorm checks. So you had to go and get permission to do things. It was totally different from what is there now. I think we were the last class that had to do that while I was there. Even after freshman year and sophomore year, we still had curfews. But junior year and senior year, there were no more curfews. Whenever you were on campus, you had to check in with the resident director, the dorm mother. You had to let her know where you were, when you were in trouble [late after curfew, a boy in your dorm, skipping class, inappropriate behavior] or something like that. When you got in trouble, it was like you were on house arrest or something. The only way you could go out was if you went to lunch and classes.

Several Spelman alumnae articulated that the relationships that exist among and between sisters on campus are strong, with each sister being responsible for helping the other through mentoring, academic assistance, resources, and community activity. Each sister, whether she is a student, faculty, administrator, or alumna, has a sincere and vested interest in the success of one another. Formally, Spelman College conducts a ceremony, typically during freshman orientation week, for the induction of new students into the sisterhood. This demonstration of sincere interest and love from fellow Spelmanites continues throughout academic and professional careers and into retirement.

During the presidency of Johnnetta Cole, two-thirds of Spelman faculty were women and three-quarters were Black. The impact of majority African American or majority African American female faculty on students, Cole argued in her 1994 book, was noticeable because students could see themselves mirrored through male and female faculty role models who looked like them.[27] A 1977 Spelman alumna underscored this notion in her description of her relationship with one of the male Spelman faculty:

> The department chair was Dr. Warren Newsome. To me, he was the epitome of intelligence and class. He was very reserved and seemed to be an old man, but I don't know how old. His relationship with the students was more like, a wise old professor, a father, or grandfatherly type, but he de-

manded excellence. He was very clear in what the objectives were and what we had to do to achieve good grades. He knew what he knew. It was no joke. He pressed you academically. If you wanted to talk about something, he would sit and listen. Bottom line was, if you thought he was going to listen to you cry and moan to get something changed, that wasn't going to happen.

The Spelman alumnae we interviewed consistently reported that the faculty they encountered at the institution were very supportive of students:

The faculty were always friendly, accommodating, open and willing to help. Of course, there were a few that we didn't know where they were coming from, but for the most part, they were engaging and helpful.

Several others said:

I spent a lot of time in a couple of faculty's houses. They extended their homes to us or had social functions for us that were outside of Spelman. So you really got into just understanding that it extended beyond just the gates of Spelman. In fact, my faculty advisor has been my children's godmother, so the relationships have continued to grow over years.

The faculty members are really close knit at Morehouse, Clark and Spelman. They do a lot of things together and so they bring the students together in different venues. It is a benefit because they pool their resources, although they're [the AUC schools] very separate.

One aspect of the socialization process, was the opportunity to cross-enroll within the AUC [Atlanta University Center]. I guess there were so many hours you had to take at Spelman, but then the whole campus was open. So you could take classes at Morehouse, Morris Brown or Clark. By having classes on any of those campuses, you met other students and got into a whole other social network. It opened up new possibilities and experiences. It wasn't just Spelman, but part of the AUC.

The whole environment was open, so while I attended Spelman, I was a student of AUC. I took classes everywhere. There wasn't anywhere that was closed to me. By virtue of the fact that many folks partied together, it didn't matter whether you went to Clark, Morehouse, Spelman, even the ITC. It didn't matter, because my junior year, I stayed over in the apartments by

ITC. They had opened them up to all AUC students. It was a very open, very fluid environment and very supportive environment.

There were clear classroom expectations, because if you missed so many classes or whatever, you were disciplined. There were expectations for behavior. We still had curfew and it was basically put out there that you did not want to do anything that would embarrass yourself or your family. So it kept us pretty much in line.

Within this warm and nurturing environment, according to Johnnetta Cole, students could rest assured that their future was within reach if they performed to their fullest potential and took full advantage of the opportunities Spelman College had to offer.

Spelman may not be a paradise, but it is an environment where individuals are encouraged and empowered to be a positive "somebody" in their walk through life.[28]

Spelman College has been grounded in the Christian tradition using religious principles as its foundation, since the missionaries founded the institution in 1881. Several of the Spelman alumnae recounted their memories of the importance of religion and religious symbols during their educational experience at Spelman. A campus building that serves as the central representation of the Christ-centered nature of the institution is Sisters Chapel, the historical location of religious services, convocations, lectures, concerts, and the like. One Spelman alumna reminisced about Sisters Chapel and its significance:

I remember the whole idea of chapel was important. We had to take religion class for a whole semester. It was discussed at length during freshman orientation. And we had numerous activities and workshops to orient you to college life and get you thinking about what direction you really wanted to go in. But more or less, most activities centered around chapel.

I remember doing the march. They would always do the march around the time of King's birthday, even before it was a holiday. We would go from Ebenezer down to the Capital and they used to do it with a donkey drawn cart. It was just that commemoration and most of the students took part in that. There were various things in the chapel to commemorate certain events, but a lot of it was just really pushing the social consciousness issues.

The Sisters Chapel was only one such example of the tangible resources that contributed to the socialization of Spelman students. It is important to remember that such tangible and intangible resources were part and parcel of the early socialization of Spelman women, particularly since the the first four presidents wanted not only to encourage the students' regular and fervent religious participation, but also to provide a location where local and world leaders could share their experiences with the students, thereby effectively fostering racial uplift.

Missionaries like Packard and Giles felt it was their Christian duty to establish institutions such as Spelman to teach moral development, social and cultural refinement, and educational and religious instruction to the Black students they served. President Read, in a 1937 article, stated:

> It is the duty of the college not only to train the mind to the highest point of usefulness, but it is even more important, to develop an attitude to life that will mean growth in college after college, and ability to stand the strain and stress of life. It is in that respect, as much as the curriculum, that the women's college is a special responsibility. Every person needs an inner source of strength, a power of endurance, and the ability to hold one's place. But women are in a special sense, the keepers of social standards, and the guardians of spiritual values. Unless the women of any race have high standards of personal and family and community life, those standards will slump and social life will decline. Much attention is given to manners and much attention is given to character in the women's colleges.[29]

In support of this contention, more recent research by Joeri Sebrechts has shown that there are four factors that help to create a positive learning environment for women. The first factor he identifies is the provision of successful role models for female students with an emphasis on mentoring.[30] Spelman College perpetuates this version of sisterhood by way of mentorship the first week students are on campus. This ritual continues and often even strengthens over time and later throughout the Spelman woman's career. One 1977 Spelman alumna reported that she regularly meets with fellow Spelmanites in her home:

> Matter of fact, some people that I was friends with in the dorm freshman year, still get together. We have a reunion every year. They come to my house for four or five days and we just kind of chill out and hang with each

other . . . It is just more of the opportunity to meet a diverse group of Black folks and to watch them grow in their own right. As my parents would say, put some things out there for you and expect you to live up to it. It was just great!

Role modeling and mentoring of this type provided by senior students, faculty, and administrators have been shown to affect student academic achievement positively.[31] The second of Sebrechts's four factors is the fostering of diverse and challenging leadership opportunities for students. These types of opportunities are continually encouraged and offered to all Spelmanites through numerous activities both on and off campus and continuing even after graduation.[32]

The third factor that helps to create a positive learning environment for students, according to Sebrechts, is the expansion of the curricular opportunities for women by encouraging their participation in male-dominated fields, such as math, sciences, and engineering.[33] In the late nineteenth century, Spelman college students were relegated, not unlike other Black women in colleges across the country, to fields of study such as home economics, teaching, and nursing. By the twentieth century, however, there was a shift in the types of courses these women undertook and the professions they were encouraged to enter, as Black women began academic training for positions as writers, doctors, lawyers, scientists, and other non-traditional fields for women at the time.

However, while the curriculum changed, the structured environment that reinforced ladylike behavior, social graces, and manners did not. As previously stated, the codes of behavior outlined within *The Blue Book: A Decorum Guide for Spelman Women,* were strictly adhered to and required strict rituals and traditions including proper dress, behavior, regular participation in chapel, convocation, and other required events. There were also the "unwritten and unspoken rules" of behavior that defined the expectations of female students both academically and socially and were reinforced through informal norms and behaviors.

Despite the contradiction in social norms and expectations with rigorous non-traditional curricular engagement, Spelman students flourished in traditional and non-traditional fields.

Joeri Sebrechts's last factor for consideration by institutions that foster a positive learning environment is the recognition of the need for gender differences and gender reflection in the learning material and curriculum.[34] Toward this end, Spelman College, as well as most historical and contemporary women's colleges, tended to highlight the achievements of women in the curriculum as a means of providing same-sex reflections for the purposes of passive inspiration and role modeling. Historically, as a means of reflecting successful female role models in the curriculum, this emphasis, in turn, inspired female students to pursue positions of leadership in their respective fields of study. Finally, the faculty, administrators, and rigorous curricula of Spelman College have historically worked in concert to encourage its students' participation in male-dominated professions. This type of encouragement, coupled with the fervent belief in the students' success, has resulted in Spelman's continuous demonstration of the net effect of social factors and gender differences in the learning environment, upon the production of successful Black, female, college graduates.

Summary

As Florence Read clearly articulated in her 1937 article, women's colleges have a three-fold function:

> To develop to the full the ability of each student to face the practical problems of life and to help solve the problems most effectively. To help each student to cultivate her creative and imaginative powers to the full to the end that her life may be rich, happy, and socially useful. And to enable each student to grow spiritually in the same degree that she grows intellectually and culturally. Unless there is this three-fold development, college is a failure. It is not enough that a woman shall be healthy and strong, and trained to earn her living. Nor is it sufficient that she be a cultivated, well-read, alert, and socially intelligent individual. The growth must be three-fold, in body, mind and spirit.[35]

In her 1994 book, *Conversations*, Johnnetta Cole addressed the function of the women's college as well as the secrets to Spelman College's success:

> First, Spelman women have their basic necessities cared for, live in a relatively safe environment, and are not haunted on campus by racism and sexism, and as a result can turn their attention to their studies. Second, the women and men of the Spelman faculty are seriously committed to the edu-

cation of these young women. Third, at Spelman, students see individuals who look like them serving as the president of the college, a professor of biology, or economics, the president of the student body, editor of a newspaper and captain of the basketball team. Fourth, at Spelman, there is no assumption that Black folks don't like math and women cannot do science . . . There is no assumption that women are just not as bright as men and will never understand economics as easily as men do. On the contrary, the assumption is that Spelman women will excel in all of their studies . . . and they do. Fifth, Spelman women are required to take a course in African American Studies or Women's Studies before they graduate. But, perhaps more importantly, the realities of African Americans and women are mainstreamed into the entire curriculum. Sixth, it is as if a family, indeed a community, comes to Spelman behind each student . . . If I had to summarize the lessons that the Spelman experience has taught me about the education of Black folks, it would be this: In an atmosphere relatively free of racism and sexism, where teachers care and expect the very best, parents and kinfolk are involved, and the curriculum and those around the students reflect in positive ways who the students are—there are no limits to what individuals can learn and who they can become.[36]

Former Spelman presidents Read and Cole both clearly believed that the mind, body, and spirit of students must be fed and nurtured in college, else the college will fail. Our contention is very similar. Spelman College is successful because the college successfully trains the heads, hands, and hearts of every Spelman College student who performs to her fullest potential and takes full advantage of the opportunities Spelman College has to offer.

Notes

1. See Merton, Robert K. *Social Theory and Social Structure.* Glencoe, Ill: Free Press, 1957.

2. For more information see Clark, Burton. "The Organizational Saga in Higher Education." *Administrative Science Quarterly,* 17, pp. 178–184.

3. Kuh, George D. and John E. Hall. "In the Blue Tradition: The Spelman Archives." No. 113, Vol. 2: 8–15 *Spelman Messenger,* Atlanta, Georgia: Spelman College.

4. For more information on this concept, see Glenn, Norval. "Values, Attitudes and Beliefs" in *Constancy and Chance in Human Development,* edited by O.G. Brim, Jr. and J. Kagan. Cambridge: Cambridge University Press, pp. 596–640.

5. Clausen, John A. *Socialization and Society.* Boston, MA: Little, Brown, and Company, p. 6.

6. *Spelman Messenger.* Atlanta, Georgia: Spelman Seminary, 1885, p. 17.

7. Ibid.

8. Manley, Albert. *A Legacy Continues: The Manley Years at Spelman College, 1953–1976.* Lanham, MD: University Press of America, 1995.

9. For more thorough discussion, see Manley, Albert. *A Legacy Continues: The Manley Years at Spelman College, 1953–1976.* Lanham, MD: University Press of America, 1995.

10. Cole, Johnnetta. *Conversations: Straight Talk with America's Sister President.* New York: Doubleday, 1996, pp. 170–171.

11. Ibid., p. 174.

12. Ibid.

13. Examples of such research include: Astin, Alexander. *What Matters in College? Four Critical Years Revisited.* San Francisco: Jossey-Bass, 1993; Feigl, Diane. "Women's Colleges Still Make Sense," *Sounding Board, U.S. Catholic Magazine,* January, 13–18; and Langdon, Elizabeth. "A Study of the Persistence of Affective Outcomes of Women's College Alumnae," Dissertation, University of California, Los Angeles, 1997.

14. See Clark, Shirley and Mary Corcoran. "Perspectives on the Professional Socialization of Women Faculty: A Case of Accumulative Disadvantage," *Journal of Higher Education,* Vol. 57, No. 1: 20–43; and Trow, Meirion. *Teachers and Students: Aspects of American Higher Education; A Volume of Essays Sponsored by the Carnegie Commission on Higher Education.* New York: McGraw-Hill, 1977.

15. Astin, *What Matters in College?.*

16. For information on alumnae participation, see Langdon, 1997. For discussion on higher occupational aspirations, see Astin, Helen S. and Laura Kent, "The Development of Relatedness and Autonomy in the College Years" In *Men and Women Learning Together: A Study of College Students in the Late 70s.* Providence, RI: Brown University Press, 1980.

17. Feigl, "Women's Colleges Still Make Sense," p. 14.

18. Langdon, A *Study of the Persistence of Affective Outcomes of College Alumnae.*

19. Guy-Sheftall, Beverly. "Black Women and Higher Education: Spelman and Bennett Colleges Revisited," *Journal of Negro Education* Vol. 51, No. 3, pp. 278–287.

20. Stewart, Donald. Spelman Inaugural Speech, November 1976, Spelman College Archives.

21. Read, Florence. "The Place of the Women's College in the Pattern of Negro Education," *Opportunity,* 15 (September 1937), p. 270.

22. Ibid.

23. Cole, p. 152.

24. Ibid, p. 169.

25. Ibid, p. 171.

26. See Astin, *What Matters in College? Four Critical Years Revisited.*

27. For discussion of faculty composition during the Cole administration, see Cole, *Conversations: Straight Talk with America's Sister President.*

28. Ibid, p. 47.

29. Read, p. 268.

30. See Sebrechts, Joeri. "Cultivating Scientists at Women's Colleges." *Initiatives*, No. 55, Vol. 2: 45–51.

31. Pascarella, Ernest. "College Environmental Influences in Student Educational Aspirations." *Journal of Higher Education*, No. 56, pp. 640–663.

32. Sebrechts, "Cultivating Scientists at Women's Colleges."

33. Ibid.

34. Ibid.

35. Read, pp. 268–269.

36. Cole, p. 191.

7

CONCLUSION

To say the least, during the first seventy-two years of its existence Spelman College evolved greatly from the anachronistic basement school in Friendship Baptist Church to the burgeoning liberal arts institution of 1953. The first five presidents of Spelman College sought to educate its student body of Black women by training their heads, hands, and hearts for work in the community at large; the limited public and private places available for their employment; and, of course, the home. In so doing, Spelman not only contributed academically and socially to the women who graced its halls, but was also successful in extending its reach to the homes, towns, cities, communities, and race from which its graduates emanated. Such was the initial and lasting desire of the founders of Spelman College.

Each of Spelman's presidents left an indelible mark upon the institution, as well as on the women and girls who attended the institution. Every advancement and progression, whether in the form of curricular changes or expansion and modernization of physical plant, initiated by these academic leaders served to create the Spelman legacy which encompassed education for practical, professional, and personal uses, but also education toward racial uplift.

It is important that any reader of this book or any other literature related to the history of Spelman College recognize that the first four presidents of Spelman College had a difficult task to accomplish against seemingly insurmountable odds—the education of Black women and girls—particularly during a time when the pervading sentiment was that these women and girls did not deserve to be nor were they capable of being educated. Yet these academic leaders persevered not only to accomplish the goals initiated by the founders, but to exceed them as well. These women took up the banner to educate the women of the so-called "despised" race, and endeavored to do so despite their isolation and verbal castigation from many of their White contemporaries for attempting to do so. These women also relinquished their personal and social lives, and in many cases, much of their livelihood, to labor in the vineyard we know as Spelman College. This was no ordinary feat.

This work has shown that the purposes and goals of the Spelman College curriculum changed significantly over time, based on the vocational opportunities available to Black women during specified periods; the beliefs held by the president at the helm of the institution; societal expectations of Black women's education; and the expectations and/or requirements of philanthropic entities that financially supported the institution. These curricular changes are consistent with what the Carnegie Foundation for the Advancement of Teaching has termed the "eternal points of tension" with respect to the aims of the college curriculum.[1] For instance, Spelman struggled during the Packard, Giles, and Tapley administrations with the tension of whether or not the curriculum should focus on scholarship or training. During all presidential administrations studied in this book, however, the crafters of the school's curriculum struggled with whether or not the curriculum should focus its attention on the past, present, or the future; whether or not the curriculum should encourage and support socialization into the dominant culture or alienation from it; as well as whether improvements to the curriculum should focus on its breadth or its depth.[2]

Curriculum theorists provide many options for examining curricular development, particularly in Black and women's institutions. Though the curriculum of Spelman during its first seventy-two years did not fit neatly into any particular periodic paradigm, the paradigms set forth in the research of Elizabeth Barber Young and Florence Fleming Corley come closest to describing the curricular development of Spelman College.[3] Their curricular paradigms both include characterizations of various periods of the mid- to late nineteenth century as well as the early twentieth century. These periods, though they do not directly coincide with the presidential administrations of Spelman College, overlap with the presidential administrations and provide an apt description of Spelman's curricular development.

Generally, Young posits that between the years of 1881 and 1886 the ornamental branches of the women's college were sustained, but that during the period from 1886 to 1927 noticeable changes in the curriculum and functioning of women's colleges began to take place. Such changes included the establishment of definite entrance and graduation requirements for the bachelor of arts degree and direction of women's college students away from preparatory, irregular, and special courses into more academic channels. Spelman's curricular history followed the actions described in both of the above periodic breakdowns, however what Young terms the "ornamental branches" of the women's college were actually, in the case of Spelman, not necessarily "ornamental" at all, but instead considered necessities in a Black woman's college such as Spelman where the most rudimentary skills had to be conveyed, particularly during the earliest years following the college's founding.

Florence Fleming Corley's curricular paradigm, of the two mentioned above, most closely approximates an accurate depiction of the curriculum of Spelman College during the tenures of its first four presidents. Translating Corley's periodic divisions into the division utilized in this book—the Spelman presidential administrations—one can more easily see that Spelman's curriculum pretty much followed the trajectory described in Corley's work.[4] During the period 1881 to 1901 (Packard administration) hygiene and physiology courses were standard fare for Spelman students as well as most women's colleges of the period, though other women's colleges by 1881 had begun to place less emphasis on such courses. Spelman, out of necessity, however, during the earliest years of this period focused mainly on the training of the hand by equipping its students, many of whom had not long since been away from slavery, with training in household basics and etiquette for "finishing." As the public began to display dissatisfaction with the finishing school idea, classical languages such as Latin and other courses such as higher mathematics, natural science, and philosophy all began to receive heavy emphasis in the Spelman College curriculum. The courses at Spelman during this period also sought to prepare women for their roles as wives and mothers. For instance, the Bible was taught, required, and central to the entire Spelman curriculum, and adherence to a pious lifestyle was of utmost importance.[5]

Toward this end, Spelman students were taught using religious principles and were expected to go forth into their respective communities to work as missionaries, but never necessarily to become members of the clergy. This expectation was a product of [White] societal beliefs not only of Black women's racial inferiority but most importantly [Black and White] societal beliefs about women's gender inferiority. During this same period (1881–1909) education for White women in the South began to fall behind that of their White counterparts in the Northeast; however, in many ways the education of Spelman women kept up with their southern women's college counterparts.

During the early part of the Packard presidential administration (1881–1886), courses such as mathematics emerged as required courses for graduation, while the so-called "ornamental subjects" of music, art, and elocution, often considered classes for refinement of students, became specialized and vocational areas of study at Spelman, along with domestic science, nursing, and missionary training.

During the Giles administration (1901–1909) and the first ten years of the Tapley administration (1910–1920), Spelman still held fast to a traditional or classical curriculum that emphasized ancient languages, literature, math, natural science, and philosophy. Vocational and professional courses emerged as departments within the institution as pressure mounted from society in general and philanthropic organizations specifically for the training of Black females to assume professional positions as teachers, nurses, and domestic workers. Domestic studies and domestic arts courses remained critical to the Spelman curriculum as these courses were considered well correlated with life activities.[6] Of course, normal training remained paramount during both the Giles and Tapley administrations; however, the methodology and pedagogy used to instruct the students as well as the expectations of the students enrolled in this course of study increased in sophistication over the years.

During the latter portion of the Tapley administration (1920–1927) and the early years of the Florence Read administration, the curriculum of Spelman again overlapped with Corley's assessment of this period—one that supported the maintenance of traditional courses, concomitant with the offering of significant numbers and varied types of elective courses. English and modern languages emerged during this period within the Spelman curriculum, while courses such as philosophy still held a strong position within the curriculum as well. From 1927 to 1953 (the Read administration), industrial coursework, long a mainstay within the Spelman curriculum, was de-emphasized. It was during this period that significant numbers of elective courses began to be offered at Spelman. While these elective course offerings were novel in the case of Spelman, they had pretty much become institutionalized in the women's colleges of the Northeast by this time. Cultural and artistic studies flourished at Spelman under President Read's leadership, along with courses in physical education. Business courses for Spelman women would not become popular, however, until much later.

Beyond Spelman's close adherence to Young and Corley's periodic assessments of curricular evolution, Spelman's curriculum also closely fits the Carnegie Foundation for the Advancement of Teaching's definition of curriculum that not only encompasses the formal curriculum, but also the hidden and extra curricula. Over the course of the first seventy-two years of Spelman's existence, recreational, social, and cultural activities such as speeches, talks, and lectures given by local, regional, national, and international leaders and religious figures contributed significantly to a great portion of the education that these young women received.

During the Packard and Giles administrations, the extracurricular activities of the school were equal in importance to the formal curricular components. As the school's motto was "Our Whole School for Christ," the extra- and hidden curricula surely had to reflect this sentiment as well. Thus, social clubs and groups organized during this period, often at the direction of the school's academic leadership, boasted activities that paralleled and enhanced the formal curriculum through their emphasis on attributes such as temperance, purity, piety, and religious zeal. During the Tapley administration, while the aforementioned extra- and hidden curricular components were still strongly emphasized, the formal academic curriculum began to take precedence among the school's priorities. Not many significant developments or changes took place among Spelman's extracurricular activities during the Tapley administration.

The Read administration ushered in a new era at Spelman College, not just with respect to the formal curriculum, but also with respect to the extra- and hidden curricula as well. The clubs and student organizations of Spelman, under the Read administration, reflected more than ever the ambitions, ideas, and interests of the student body, with less focus being placed outwardly on the maintenance of chastity, purity, and religious zeal. Though the school's motto remained the same, the extra- and hidden curricular components of the formal curriculum focused attention more on the creation of well-rounded citizens who had extensive exposure to the arts, music, literature, and diverse cultures. Though not formally described in the course catalogs of the institution, participation in extracurricular clubs and organizations, attendance at speeches and lectures given by prominent and less well-known individuals, and other activities all assisted in the proliferation of the hidden curriculum that played as paramount a role as the other curricular components, in training the heads, the hands, and the hearts of Spelman's students.

Each of the presidents of Spelman College wielded tremendous influence over the school's curriculum and the socialization of students, and in turn, what was communicated to Spelman students—academically, socially, spiritually, and otherwise. They inculcated their culture, values and beliefs in these women, via a formal academic and social system, for use in a world whose values and beliefs looked more like those of the White women presidents than the African American students of Spelman.[7] The use of higher educational environments to impart societal expectations and values is still happening today, but in a less formal context—awareness of this is the true value of the early curricular history of Spelman. The formal, hidden, and extracurriculum of Spelman College, orchestrated by its White presidents, administration, and predominantly White faculty, combined to socialize the Black Spelman students as well as provide them with useful skills for professional endeavors.[8] The combination of these curricular types to educate students encapsulates the purpose of higher education not only in historically Black institutions, but also in majority institutions—to prepare students for citizenship in the larger world.[9]

The examination of the formal curriculum, as well as the unintended consequences of learning at Spelman College, is a very interesting endeavor. This study utilized the evolution of the academic, social, and other curricula of the institution as the lens through which to examine the evolution of the institution itself and its progression over its first seven decades in existence. There are so many other angles, however, that could have been used to examine this subject. With this said, there are definitely opportunities for further study, particularly with respect to curriculum formation. Worthy of note are two research directions in particular: the effects of philanthropic giving to Spelman, during the first four presidencies, on Spelman's curricular formation and development, and a study of the post-1953 curriculum and the internal and external factors (e.g., the civil rights movement) that impinged upon its development. Further, biographies of the presidents under examination in this book and successive presidents, which included significant "firsts," such as the first male president of Spelman College, the first Black president of Spelman College, the first Black female president of Spelman College, and the first alumna president of the institution, would also make for interesting points of departure for an examination of the Spelman of yesterday, today, and tomorrow.

Notes

1. Carnegie Foundation for the Advancement of Teaching, *Missions*, pp. 1, 2.

2. Ibid.

3. For description of curricular periodic paradigms of both authors, see: Elizabeth Barber Young, *A Study of the Curricula* . . . pp. 195, 196 and Florence Fleming Corley, "Higher Education for Southern Women," pp. 158–163.

4. Corley's periodization states that during the first period, 1836–1861, the American public showed dissatisfaction with the finishing school idea. During her second period, 1861–1886, education in the South lagged behind that of their northern counterparts; the mathematics requirement fluctuated in colleges for women; religion still played a major part in the women's college curriculum; and ornamental subjects were mainstays in the women's college curriculum. During Corley's third period, 1900–1920, Black and White southeastern women's colleges attempted to emulate the curriculum of their White counterparts, and women's college curricula became more correlated with life activities.

5. It is important to note that while religious education had always been a critical component within the women's college, its function within the curriculum was not equivalent to that of the men's college wherein men were being prepared to serve as clergy persons.

6. These courses remained in most coeducational and women's colleges of the South, but began to dissipate in those colleges of the Northeast.

7. See Lawrence Stenhouse, *Culture and Education*, p. 56 for discussion of liberal arts education for acculturation.

8. See discussion of Harold Taylor's three curricular philosophies in Jeanne Noble, *The Negro Woman's College Education*, p. 11. See specifically the instrumentalist curricular philosophy.

9. For discussion of education for citizenship see Louis Franklin Snow, *The College Curriculum*, p. 12.

EPILOGUE

The Spelman Legacy Continues

Beverly Daniel Tatum

Spelman College is an institution with a distinguished history and a clear mission—a mission that spans generations of Black women, from the early days as a fledgling school in the basement of Friendship Baptist Church to our contemporary existence as an institution ranked as one of the top one hundred liberal arts colleges in the United States. As the ninth president, a role I assumed in 2002, I stand on the shoulders of not only the first four presidents, white women whose contributions and curricular vision are so ably chronicled in these pages, but also on the shoulders of the first four Black leaders (two men and two women) whose presidential leadership brought Spelman College through the second half of the twentieth century, a period of tremendous growth and expansion.

I write this epilogue in 2004, fifty years after the 1954 *Brown v. Board of Education* Supreme Court decision. This was a pivotal year in Spelman's history, not only because Spelman College had made the transition from the leadership of white women to the modern era of Black presidential leadership just one year before, but also because 1954 marked the end of legalized segregation in the United States and the beginning of a new chapter in American higher education. Though it was not instant, the 1954 decision opened new doors of educational opportunity for Black students in ways that initially challenged and ultimately strengthened the college. Like many historically Black institutions, Spelman faced new competition for its students from those predominantly white colleges and universities that had previously excluded them. But, in fact, increased competition spurred important improvements at Spelman College. The post-*Brown* initiatives of each of four presidents—Albert

Manley, Donald Stewart, Johnnetta Betsch Cole, and Audrey Forbes Manley—helped build Spelman's competitive edge. During those years, professors were actively encouraged to increase their research and publication efforts, and new resources for scholarships were created. Successful fundraising efforts to increase the endowment provided increased financial stability and fueled campus construction of new residence halls and academic buildings, creating an environment that now attracts over four thousand talented young women annually, competing for 525 spaces in our first-year class.

Spelman's current strength is not only the result of wise leadership during the last half of the twentieth century, but it is also fueled by an enduring and compelling mission that is propelling us forward into the twenty-first century. Read again that mission statement:

> *An outstanding historically Black college for women, Spelman promotes academic excellence in the liberal arts, and develops the intellectual, ethical, and leadership potential of its students. Spelman seeks to empower the total person, who appreciates the many cultures of the world and commits to positive social change.*

It is that mission that drew me to Spelman College in 2002, and that guides my vision for its future. At the heart of this mission is the notion of leadership—a holistic understanding of leadership development that includes mind, body, and spirit—an understanding of leadership that includes the cultivation of wisdom and an understanding of social justice. The technological advances of the twenty-first century will provide unanticipated opportunities for all of our students. They will have access to ample information, but will they possess the wisdom to use it for the common good? At Spelman College, we want the answer to be yes. We seek to develop a clear sense of collective responsibility and ethical leadership to prepare our students for wise stewardship of their world. *It is our heritage and our calling.*

As global conflict escalates, conflict that will disproportionately affect communities of color who send their young people to the front lines, and whose needs will be neglected as the cost of war rises, the voices of Black women are needed now more than ever. Our mission calls us to be intentional about the cultivation of their leadership.

Lee Bolman and Terrence Deal, authors of *Leading with Soul*, describe the crisis of leadership facing our nation. They write,

To prevail in the face of violence, homelessness, malaise, and the many other spiritual challenges of modern life, we need a vision of leadership rooted in the enduring sense of human wisdom, spirit and heart. We need a new generation of seekers . . . How will we develop the seekers we need? To begin with we need a revolution in how we think about leadership and how we develop leaders. Most management and leadership development programs ignore or demean spirit. They desperately need an infusion of spiritful forms such as poetry, literature, music, art, theater, history, philosophy, and dance.[1]

They do not use the words "liberal arts"—but their meaning is clear. We need the arts and humanities—along with the logic of math and science and the insights of social science—to foster the reflection, the integration, and the action that leads to wisdom, and we need to foster critical dialogue in and out of the classroom, dialogue that ultimately leads to constructive action—and social transformation.

Spelman ALIVE

What does this mission mean for Spelman College in practical terms? How will we focus our institutional energy over the coming years? We have a five-point plan consonant with our mission:

1. Continual striving for *academic excellence*—through the recruitment and retention of the next generation of faculty committed to the residential liberal arts college model of excellence in teaching, continual growth in scholarship, and shared responsibility for service—and through the recruitment and retention of strong students, continually seeking to improve our capacity to provide financial support so that there will be no economic barriers for the best and the brightest to come to Spelman.

2. Maintaining our focus on *leadership development* through civic engagement and community service—with the establishment of a leadership center as one avenue to bring together a number of leadership-related initiatives into a synergistic whole.

3. Improving our *environment*—on campus and off—by attending to our infrastructure (renovating buildings and improving technology), as well as working with our community partners to enhance our neigh-

borhood and create new opportunities for the residents of the West End of Atlanta, a historically Black and underserved community.

4. Increasing our *visibility*—so that the accomplishments of our students, our faculty and staff, and our alumnae—are apparent to everyone. We do not want to hide our light under a bushel—we want to be a beacon in higher education. We *have* been in the past, and we want that light to shine even more brightly in the future.

5. And finally, we want to be a model of *exemplary customer service*. The Spelman College motto, "Our whole school for Christ," hearkens to our nineteenth century founding by Christian missionaries, but it has twenty-first century relevance. It is relevant today not because we are an exclusively Christian community. Indeed we acknowledge and appreciate the religious diversity of our academic community. However, our motto still has relevance because at the core of Christian teachings is the principle of "hospitality"—welcoming the stranger, treating others the way you would want to be treated. At Spelman College our definition of excellence should include a pervasive sense of hospitality and generosity of spirit for each other and everyone who passes through our gates.

These five components, Academic excellence, Leadership development, Improving our environment, Visibility of our achievements, and Exemplary Customer Service, are easily remembered by the acronym, ALIVE. "Spelman ALIVE"—strong, vital, and productive well into the twenty-first century, is the goal for this administration. In 1903, Atlanta University Professor Dr. W. E. B. DuBois published his classic text, *The Souls of Black Folk.* In the introduction he wrote, "The problem of the twentieth century is the problem of the color line." Will it be the problem of the twenty-first century? Or will it be something else—the degradation of our environment, the threat of nuclear war, or the growing gap between those who have access to resources, irrespective of color, and those who do not?

We do not know what the future holds, but we do know Spelman women will help shape the future. We want to be sure that they are ready and that Spelman remains ALIVE—a strong and vital learning community.

The curricular implications of this vision are still unfolding. We know that increasingly the cutting edge of scholarly production is interdisciplinary in nature, crossing traditional academic boundaries. There is evidence of this developing trend at Spelman College, seen through the recent establishment of such programs of study as International Relations, Environmental Studies, Neuroscience, and the development of a Women's Health concentration within Women's Studies.

However, the most visible manifestation of the Tatum administration's curricular and extracurricular influence is the creation of the Center for Leadership and Civic Engagement, affectionately known as Spelman LEADS, officially launched in October 2003.

Spelman LEADS: The Center for Leadership and Civic Engagement at Spelman

Since its founding Spelman College has been committed to preparing its students to lead their communities and to make a difference in the world. At the core of the Spelman College mission is the notion of leadership—a holistic understanding of leadership development that includes mind, body, and spirit—an understanding of leadership that includes the cultivation of wisdom and an understanding of social responsibility. We have been cultivating leaders for more than 122 years—through the speaking, writing, and critical thinking we demand in the classroom every day; through the mentoring that occurs between faculty and students in offices and laboratories; through the guidance that staff throughout the college provide to students outside of the classroom; through late night conversations between older and younger students; through the wisdom shared by our alumnae with their Spelman sisters; and through the confidence gained from community service opportunities. Developing leaders is what we do and have been doing. *It is our heritage and our calling.*

Yet the challenges of the twenty-first century demand a new emphasis on leadership development. The world is changing rapidly—technological advances, shrinking natural resources, changing demographics, global conflict, and economic uncertainty—all call for a new understanding of leadership. Leadership in the twenty-first century will require an informed global vision, prophetic voices, inclusive values and courageous action.

The success of Spelman alumnae attests to the past effectiveness of our curriculum and extracurricular environment; however, the creation of a leadership center at Spelman allows for a more powerful expression of this core dimension of our mission. The Center for Leadership and Civic Engagement is intended to bring together many disparate and emerging initiatives into a synergistic whole that will be a resource not only for Spelman women but also for constituents beyond our gates (e.g., alumnae, community members, corporate supporters, members of other educational institutions). The potential engagement between these constituents and our students in the context of the Center for Leadership and Civic Engagement represents a powerful enhancement of the Spelman educational experience.

The Center for Leadership and Civic Engagement has been conceived as an entity that will serve as an umbrella organization with five main spokes, linking both curricular and co-curricular initiatives. The five areas of emphasis include Leadership Development, Economic Empowerment, Advocacy through the Arts, Dialogue across Difference, and Service Learning and Civic Engagement (LEADS). Each of these areas is briefly outlined here, recognizing that ongoing input from faculty, staff and students as well as other constituents will further shape this vision in important ways.

Leadership Development

Led by an Executive Director with scholarly expertise and experience in leadership development, the Center could eventually offer some credit-bearing courses in the interdisciplinary field of Leadership Studies (e.g., Leadership and the Liberal Arts; Ethics of Leadership in the Information Age) as well as non-credit bearing programs like those currently offered at Spelman—the "Women of Excellence in Leadership" Series (coordinated through the Office of Student Affairs) and Spelman Women Empowered through Professional Training (SWEPT), a career exploration seminar offered through the Career Development Center. From its inception, the Center has offered a "Leaders on Leadership" speaker series, offering students the opportunity to explore the intellectual, ethical, and spiritual dimensions of leadership, broadly defined to include both common and uncommon examples of leadership in both the private and public sector. The series is intended to allow a structured opportunity for alumnae, corporate partners, community members, and others to engage actively in meaningful interaction with Spelman students.

Spelman LEADS is envisioned to include a *Global Peace Initiative*, a programmatic emphasis on the understanding of global issues with a particular focus on the role of women as peacemakers. As the premier educator of Black women, Spelman College is uniquely situated to provide this focus. Atlanta, the cradle of the Civil Rights movement and the home of two Nobel Peace Prize winners—Rev. Dr. Martin Luther King, Jr. and President Jimmy Carter—provides an appropriate setting in which Spelman College students can explore conflict resolution across the African Diaspora and beyond. As global conflict escalates, the voices of women of color need to be strengthened. Through an emphasis on the peacemaking of women, the opportunity for Spelman College students to see themselves as potential change agents can be increased. Curricular linkages between the Leadership Center's Global Peace Initiative and our International Relations Program could be easily forged and would be mutually enhancing.

Economic Empowerment

The Center also offers the opportunity to bring together synergistically two desired areas of activity—the economic development of the West End community and the financial preparation of Spelman students. For example, members of the Economics Department are seeking ways to involve Spelman students in assisting women in the local community to develop their own small businesses. Students engaged in such a proposed project would certainly deepen their understanding of the processes involved in starting a business and community development. This and other similar projects can bring a real-life relevance to the classroom experience.

In addition, the Center could provide non-credit-bearing courses (weekend or evening workshops) to address issues of financial management for students. Many women (including alumnae) are seeking opportunities to develop their confidence in this area. Learning to make wise decisions about the use of one's resources is an important dimension of leadership development that is being incorporated into the programs of the Center, creating a mechanism not only for economic development but also for intergenerational interaction between alumnae, students, and other members of the community.

Advocacy through the Arts

The arts have long been an important dimension of Black cultural expression—providing an avenue for social protest and critique. Some of the most important African American artists of the twentieth century found their way to Spelman College. We seek to revitalize this tradition for the twenty-first century, creating a venue for cutting-edge interdisciplinary exploration of important social issues through the arts. Currently the endowed Cosby Scholars program provides an opportunity to bring noteworthy artists to campus for a year or two in residence. An arts initiative as part of the Leadership Center is intended to create a structure for such events as a lecture series, media presentations, and short-term residencies, exposing the entire campus and the surrounding community to new artistic visions of our collective future.

Dialogue across Difference

In order to be an effective leader in the twenty-first century, one must be able to interact effectively with people whose experience and perspectives are different from one's own. The art of dialogue—the ability to engage in meaningful conversation about difficult social issues in a context of mutual respect—is an essential leadership skill that can be acquired if given an opportunity to practice. At Spelman College, we have begun developing a dialogue project, based on the model developed at the University of Michigan, which gives students an opportunity to participate in peer-led dialogue groups conducted over the course of a semester, focusing on important social issues related to socioeconomic status, religious identity, sexual orientation, or gender. The experience of participating in these dialogues is a powerful learning opportunity for the participants, but it is an especially effective leadership development tool for the students who are learning to facilitate the dialogues. The Dialogue Project also creates a link between the curricular and co-curricular experiences of students. Those students who learn how to engage in meaningful dialogue about difficult social issues often become more actively involved in classroom discussions as a result of their experience.

Service Learning and Civic Engagement

Spelman College has a long-held commitment to community service, and many students are involved in volunteer work in the local community through the Office of Community Service or as part of the Bonner Scholars Program. In addition, some course offerings involve students in service learning projects as part of the course experience. For example, students participating in a sociology course on research methods have been engaged in surveying local residents about their attitudes toward and usage of a local medical clinic, using the experience as a way of not only understanding survey research methods but also of providing valuable information to the director of the clinic about how to improve service delivery to the community. The Center's focus on service learning is intended to create a space on campus where faculty could be provided assistance in developing community-based learning opportunities for their students, and such opportunities could be expanded. In addition, bringing the various community service opportunities together under the umbrella of the Leadership Center will allow for improved coordination and increased impact.

Each of these five programmatic emphases allows the opportunity for the development of powerful pedagogy and fruitful research. Program documentation and ongoing evaluation will not only provide valuable data for use at Spelman College but will also create the possibility of dissemination through presentations and publications to other institutions. The development of the leadership potential of Spelman College women has always been part of the Spelman College experience; however, by marshalling our resources in a coordinated way as described here, our efforts will have greater synergy and effectiveness as a result.

The value of a liberal arts education is in its capacity to develop critical thinking across the disciplines and imbue students with the ability to solve complex problems and communicate ideas effectively. At Spelman College we continue to embrace this model of education for our students. However, the broad programmatic approach of Spelman LEADS, anchored within the liberal arts tradition, will provide students the opportunity to reflect on the contemporary dilemmas of leadership and deepen their own leadership preparation inside the classroom as well as outside it.

As illustrated by the emergence of the new Center for Leadership and Civic Engagement, the Spelman legacy of education of the head, hand, and heart is ongoing. For more than 120 years, Spelman College has had a special mission: to empower women to fully use their talents to succeed and to better the world. The establishment of the Center for Leadership and Civic Engagement is the perfect expression of our mission. As we build on our tradition of excellence, we are shaping the future—continuing the Spelman legacy—one leader at a time.

Note

1. Bolman, Lee G., & Deal, Terrence E. (2001). *Leading with Soul: An Uncommon Journey of Spirit.* San Francisco: Jossey-Bass, p. 173.

BIBLIOGRAPHY

Secondary Sources

Anderson, James D. *The Education of Blacks in the South, 1860–1935.* Chapel Hill, NC: University of North Carolina Press, 1988.

Astin, Alexander. *What Matters in College? Four Critical Years Revisited.* San Francisco, CA: Jossey-Bass, 1993.

Astin, Helen S. and Laura Kent. "The Development of Relatedness and Autonomy in the College Years." In *Men and Women Learning Together: A Study of College Students in the Late 70s.* Providence, RI: Brown University Press, 1980.

Bacote, Clarence A. *The Story of Atlanta University: A Century of Service, 1865–1965.* Atlanta University Press, 1969.

Barzun, Jacques and Henry F. Graff. *The Modern Researcher.* Orlando, FL: Harcourt Brace Jovanovich, 1985.

Beard, Charles A. and Mary A. Beard. *A Basic History of the United States.* New York: Doubleday, Doran, 1944.

Bell-Scott, Patricia, "Black Women's Higher Education: Our Legacy." *SAGE: A Scholarly Journal on Black Women* 1 (Spring 1984): 8–11.

Bernard, H. Russell. *Research Methods in Anthropology: Qualitative and Quantitative Approaches.* Walnut Creek, CA: AltaMira Press, 1995.

Carnegie Foundation for the Advancement of Teaching. *Missions of the College Curriculum.* San Francisco, California: Jossey-Bass, 1977.

Clark, Burton "The Organizational Saga in Higher Education." *Administrative Science Quarterly* 17 (1972): 178–184.

Clark, Shirley and Mary Corcoran. "Perspectives on the Professional Socialization of Women Faculty: A Case of Accumulative Disadvantage." *Journal of Higher Education* 57, 1 (1986): 20–43.

Clausen, John A. *Socialization and Society.* Boston, MA: Little, Brown, and Company, 1968.

Cole, Johnetta B. *Conversations: Straight Talk with America's Sister President.* Anchor Books: New York, 1994.

Corley, Florence Fleming. Higher Education for Southern Women: Four Church-Related Women's Colleges in Georgia: Agnes Scott, Shorter, Spelman, and Wesleyan, 1900–1920. Doctoral Dissertation, College of Education, Georgia State University, 1985.

Cowling, Donald J., and J. Curtis Dixon, Charles H. Thompson, Malcolm Wallace, *A Study of Cooperation in the Atlanta University Center,* Atlanta, Georgia, December 1, 1946.

Cross-Brazzell, Johnetta. "Bricks Without Straw: Missionary-Sponsored Black Higher Education in the Post-Emancipation Era." *Journal of Higher Education* Vol. 63, No. 1 January/February 1992.

Cross-Brazzell, Johnetta. *Education As a Tool of Socialization: Agnes-Scott Institute and Spelman Seminary, 1881–1910.* Doctoral Dissertation, University of Michigan, 1991.

Davies, Emily. *The Higher Education of Women.* New York: AMS Press, 1973.

Denzin, Norman K., and Yvonna S. Lincoln, eds. *Handbook of Qualitative Research.* Thousand Oaks, CA: Sage, 1994.

Derbigny, Irving A. *General Education in the Negro College.* Stanford University, California: Stanford University Press, 1947.

DuBois, W.E.B. *The Autobiography of W.E.B. DuBois.* International Publishers, New York, 1968.

DuBois, W.E.B. *Dusk of Dawn: An Essay Toward an Autobiography of a Race Concept.* New Brunswick, NJ: Transaction Publishers, 1984.

DuBois, W.E.B. *The Souls of Black Folk.* New York: Bantam Books, 1903, 1989.

Farnham, Christie Ann. *The Education of the Southern Belle: Higher Education and Student Socialization in the Antebellum South.* New York: New York University Press, 1994.

Feigl, Diane. "Women's Colleges Still Make Sense." *Sounding Board, U.S. Catholic Magazine* (January 1996): 13–18.

Fleming, Jacqueline. "Black Women in Black and White College Environments: The Making of a Matriarch." In *ASHE Reader on Racial and Ethnic Diversity in Higher Education,* edited by Caroline Sotello Viernes Turner. Needham Heights, MA: Simon & Schuster Custom Publishing, 1996.

Fontana, Andrea and James H. Frey. "Interviewing: The Art of Science." In *Handbook of Qualitative Research,* edited by Norman K. Denzin and Yvonna S. Lincoln. Thousand Oaks, California: Sage, 1994.

Fraser, Barry J. "An Historical Look at Curriculum Evaluation." In *Curriculum History Conference Presentations from the Society for the Study of Curriculum History,* edited by Craig Kridel. Lanham, MD: University Press of America, 1989.

Frazier, E. Franklin. *Black Bourgeoisie.* New York: The Free Press, 1957.

Gatewood, Willard B. *Aristocrats of Color in the South.* Bloomington, IN: University Press, 1990.

Giddings, Paula. *When and Where I Enter: The Impact of Black Women on Race and Sex in America.* New York: William Morrow, 1984.

Glenn, Norval. "Values, Attitudes and Beliefs." In *Constancy and Chance in Human Development,* edited by O.G. Brim, Jr. and J. Kagan. Cambridge, MA: Harvard University Press, 1980.

Gordon, Lynn D. *Gender and Higher Education in the Progressive Era*. New Haven, CT: Yale University, 1990.

Gregory, Sheila T. *Black Women in The Academy: The Secrets to Success and Achievement*. Lanham, MD: University Press of America, Inc., 1995.

Guy-Sheftall, Beverly. "Black Women and Higher Education: Spelman and Bennett Colleges Revisited." In *Journal of Negro Education* 51 (Summer 1982): 278–87.

Guy-Sheftall, Beverly and Patricia Bell-Scott. "Finding A Way: Black Women Students and the Academy." In C. S. Pearson, D. L. Shavlik and J. G. Touchton (Eds.), *Educating the majority: Women challenge tradition in higher education*. New York: Macmillan, 1989.

Guy-Sheftall, Beverly. "A Conversation with Willa P. Player." In *SAGE: A Scholarly Journal on Black Women* 1 (Spring 1984): 16–19.

Guy-Sheftall, Beverly. *Spelman: A Centennial Celebration*. Atlanta, GA: Spelman College, 1981.

Harris, Patricia Roberts. "Achieving Equality for Women." In *Women in Higher Education,* edited by Todd W. Furniss and Patricia Alberg Graham. Washington, D.C.: American Council on Education, 1974.

Harvard Committee. *General Elections in a Free Society*. Cambridge, MA: Harvard University Press, 1945.

Hodder, Ian. "The Interpretation of Documents and Material Culture." In *Handbook of Qualitative Research*, edited by Norman K. Denzin and Yvonna S. Lincoln. Thousand Oaks, California: Sage, 1994.

Horowitz, Helen Lefkowitz. Alma Mater: Design and Experience in the Women's Colleges from Their Nineteenth Century Beginnings to the 1930s. New York: Alfred A. Knopf, 1984.

Huggins, Nathan I. *Harlem Renaissance*. New York: Oxford University Press, 1971.

Jones, Edward A. *A Candle in the Dark: A History of Morehouse College*. Valley Forge, PA: Judson Press, 1976.

Kaestle, Carl F. "Recent Methodological Developments in the History of American Education." In *Contemporary Methods for Research in Education*, edited by Richard M. Yaeger. Washington, DC: American Educational Research Association, 1997.

Kimball, Bruce A. "Curriculum History: The Problems in Writing About Higher Education." In *Curriculum History: Conference Presentations from the Society for the Study of Curriculum History*, edited by Craig Kridel. Lanham, MD: University Press of America, 1989.

Kridel, Craig, ed. *Curriculum History: Conference Presentations from the Society for the Study of Curriculum History*. Lanham, MD: University Press of America, 1989.

Kuh, George D. and John E. Hall. "Cultural Perspectives in Student Affairs." In G. D. Kuh (Ed), *Cultural Perspectives in Student Affairs Work*, (pp. 1–20). Baltimore, MD: American College Personnel Association, 1993.

Kuh, George D. and John E. Hall. "In the Blue Tradition: The Spelman Archives." *Spelman Messenger 113*, 2 *(1993): 8–15.*

Kuh, George D. and E. Whitt. "The Invisible Tapestry: Culture in American Colleges and Universities." *ASHE-ERIC Higher Education Report, No. 1.* Washington, D.C.: ERIC Clearinghouse on Higher Education, 1988.

Langdon, Elizabeth A *Study of the Persistence of Affective Outcomes of Women's College Alumnae.* Doctoral Dissertation, University of California, Los Angeles, 1997.

Manley, Albert. *A Legacy Continues: The Manley Years at Spelman College, 1953–1976.* Lanham, MD: University Press of America, Inc., 1995.

Manning, K. *Ritual, Ceremonies, and Cultural Meaning in Higher Education.* Westport, CT: Bergin and Garvey, 2000.

Manning, K. "Properties of Institutional Culture." In G. D. Kuh (Ed), *Cultural Perspectives in Student Affairs Work,* (p. 21–36). Baltimore, MD: American College Personnel Association, 1993.

Maxwell, Joseph A., "Designing a Qualitative Study." In *Handbook of Applied Social Research Methods,* edited by Leonard Bickman and Debra J. Rog. Thousand Oaks, California: Sage, 1998.

McMillen, Sally G. *Southern Women—Black and White in the Old South.* Arlington Heights, Illinois: Harlan Davidson, no date.

Merton, Robert K. *Social Theory and Social Structure.* Glencoe, IL: Free Press, 1957.

Newcomer, Mabel. *A Century of Higher Education for American Women.* New York: Harper & Brothers, 1959.

Noble, Jeanne. *The Negro Woman's College Education.* New York: Garland, 1987.

Novick, Peter. *That Noble Dream: The "Objectivity Question" and the American Historical Profession.* New York: Cambridge University Press, 1988.

Pascarella, Ernest T. "College Environmental Influences in Student Educational Aspirations." *Journal of Higher Education Vol. 56 (1984): 640–663.*

Perkins, Linda M. "The Education of Black Women in the Nineteenth Century." In *Women and Higher Education in American History,* edited by John Mack Faragher and Florence Howe. New York: W.W. Norton, 1988.

Perkins, Linda M. "The Impact of the Cult of True Womanhood on the Education of Black Women." In *ASHE Reader on the History of Higher Education,* edited by Lester F. Goodchild and Harold S. Weschsler. Needham Heights, MA: Ginn, 1989.

Read, Florence. "The Place of the Women's College in the Pattern of Negro Education." *Opportunity,* 15 (September 1937): 267–270.

Read, Florence. *The Story of Spelman College.* Princeton, NJ: Princeton University Press, 1961.

Rice, J. K. and A. Hemmings. "Women's Colleges and Women Achievers: An Update." *Signs: Journal of Women in Culture and Society,* 13(3): 546–559, (1988).

Robinson, Cedric. *Black Marxism: The Making of the Black Radical Tradition.* Atlantic Heights, NJ: Zed Books, 1983.

Roebuck, J.B. and K.S. Murty, *Historically Black Colleges and Universities: Their Place In American Higher Education*. Westport, CT: Praeger, 1993.

Reinharz, Shulamit. *Feminist Methods in Social Research*. New York: Oxford University Press, 1995.

Reuben, Paul P. "Chapter 9: Harlem Renaissance—An Introduction." *PAL: Perspectives in American Literature—A Research and Reference Guide*. URL: http://www .csustan.edu/english/reuben/pal/chap9/9intro.html (May 19, 1999)

Ridgely, Torrence. *The Story of John Hope*. New York: MacMillan, 1948.

Rudolph, Frederick. *Curriculum: A History of the American Undergraduate Course of Study Since 1636*. San Francisco: Jossey-Bass, 1977.

Sebrechts, Joeri. "Cultivating Scientists at Women's Colleges." *Initiatives*, 55 (2): 45–51 (1993).

Schwandt, Thomas A. "Constructivist, Interpretist Approaches to Human Inquiry." In *Handbook of Qualitative Research*, edited by Norman K. Denzin and Yvonna S. Lincoln. Thousand Oaks, California: Sage, 1994.

Shaw, Stephanie. *What A Woman Ought To Be and To Do: Black Professional Women Workers During The Jim Crow Era*. Chicago, Illinois: University of Chicago Press, 1996.

Sicherman, Barbara. "The Invisible Woman: The Case for Women's Studies." In *Women in Higher Education*, edited by W. Todd Furniss and Patricia Albjerg Graham. Washington, D.C.: American Council on Education, 1974.

Smith, D. "Women's Colleges and Coed Colleges: Is There a Difference for Women?" *Journal of Higher Education*, 61(2): 181–197, (1989).

Snow, Louis Franklin. *The College Curriculum in the United States*. New York: Teachers College, Columbia University, 1907.

Solomon, Barbara Miller. *In the Company of Educated Women*. New Haven, CT: Yale University Press, 1985.

Spelman College. *Spelman College Annual Report, 1998–1999: Measuring Up to the Mission*. Atlanta, GA: Spelman College, 1998.

Spelman Messenger. Published by Spelman Seminary, 1885–1924; by Spelman College in subsequent years. Atlanta, GA: Spelman College, Various Years.

Stampp, Kenneth. *The Peculiar Institution: Slavery in the Ante-Bellum South*. New York: Vintage Books, 1956.

Stenhouse, Lawrence. *Culture and Education*. New York: Weybright and Talley, 1967.

Tidball, M. E., Smith, D. G., Tidball, C. S., and L. E. Wolf-Wendel. *Taking Women Seriously*. Phoenix, AZ: Oryx, 1999.

Tidball, M.E. "The Search for Talented Women." *Change*, 6: 51–52, 64 (1974).

Trow, Meirion. *Teachers and Students: Aspects of American Higher Education*. A volume of essays sponsored by the Carnegie Commission on Higher Education. New York: McGraw-Hill, 1975.

Tuchman, Gaye. "Historical Social Science: Methodologies, Methods, and Meanings." In *Handbook of Qualitative Research* edited by Norman K. Denzin and Yvonna S. Lincoln. Thousand Oaks, California: Sage, 1994.

Veysey, Laurence R. *The Emergence of the American University*. Chicago, Illinois: University of Chicago Press, 1965.

Wegener, Charles. *Liberal Education and the Modern University*. Chicago, Illinois: University of Chicago Press, 1978.

Weschler, Harold S. "An Academic Gresham's Law: Group Repulsion as a Theme in American Higher Education." In *ASHE Reader on the History of Higher Education* edited by Lester F. Goodchild and Harold S. Weschler. Needham Heights, MA: Ginn, 1989.

Whiting, Albert N. *Guardians of the Flame: Historically Black Colleges; Yesterday, Today, and Tomorrow*. Washington, D.C.: American Association of State Colleges and Universities, 1991.

Willie, Charles V. and Ronald R. Edmonds, eds. *Black Colleges in America: Challenge, Development, Survival*. New York: Teachers College Press, 1978.

Wolf, L. E. *Models of excellence: The Baccalaureate Origins of Successful European American Women, African American Women, and Latinas*. Doctoral dissertation, The Claremont Graduate School, Claremont, CA., 1995.

Wolf-Wendel, L. E. "Models of Excellence: The Baccalaureate Origins of Successful European American Women, African American Women, and Latinas." *Journal of Higher Education*, 69(2): 141–183, 1998.

Wolters, Raymond. *The New Negro on Campus: Black College Rebellions of the 1920s*. Princeton, NJ: Princeton University Press, 1975.

Yin, Robert K. "The Abridged Version of Case Study Research: Design and Method." In *Handbook of Applied Social Research Methods*, edited by Leonard Bickman and Debra J. Rog. Thousand Oaks, California: Sage, 1998.

Young, Elizabeth Barber. *A Study of the Curricula of Seven Selected Women's Colleges of the Southern States*. New York: Teacher's College, Columbia University, 1932.

Primary Sources Found in the Following Collections:

Spelman College Archives, Spelman College, Atlanta, Georgia
Special Collections, Woodruff Library, Atlanta, Georgia.

APPENDIX A

Statistical Table, No. 1

1896–7	Teachers		40
"	Students	Total Enrollment (sic)	549
"	"	Boarders	267
"	"	Normal Training	21
"	"	Missionary Training	5
"	"	Elective	10
"	"	College Preparatory	5
"	"	Academic	51
"	"	English Preparatory	456
"	"	Nurse Training	38
"	"	Printing	20
"	"	Dress-making	34
"	"	Sewing	290
"	"	Advanced Industrial	20
"	"	Instrumental Music	73

Source: Sixteenth Annual Report of the Principals of Spelman Seminary (1896-1897), in Spelman College Archives.

APPENDIX B

Statistical Table, No. 2
1896-97

Total Enrollment,	
Boarders and Day-Scholars	9327
Boarders	4102
Day-Scholars	5225
Approximate Number of Different pupils, Day-Scholars	2500
Number of Different Pupils, Boarders	2081
Number of Boarders in attendance	
1 year	1162
2 years	448
3 "	204
4 "	110
5 "	60
6 "	37
7 "	27
8 "	14
9 "	10
10 "	9
Students from Africa	4
" " Central America	2
" " South America	3
" " Jamaica	2
Number of Communities represented	576
" " States "	21
Per cent of Communities in Georgia	63
Per cent of Communities in States Touching Ga.	27
Per cent Other Regions	10
Homes influenced by Boarders (Approximate)	2,000
Members of Families influenced by Boarders (approximate)	10,000
Members of Communities influenced by Boarders (approximate)	200,000
Persons influenced by Day-scholars (approximate)	40,000
Total Number influenced by Students (approximate)	250,000

Source: Sixteenth Annual Report of the Principals of Spelman Seminary (1896–1897), in Spelman College Archives.

APPENDIX C

To the Board of Trustees,

Gentlemen:

There have been enrolled in Spelman Seminary for the school year 1906-1907: 670 students, 309 day-pupils and 361 boarders. They are thus classified by departments:

College	9
Teachers Professional	29
Christian Workers	10
High School	119
Normal practice school	472
Nurse training	13
Dressmaking only	11
Music only	7

In special classes the numbers are as follows:

Agriculture	134
Basketry	72
Cooking	144
Dressmaking	42
Millinary	35
Music, instrumental	89
" Vocal	521
Nature study	260
Printing	28
Sewing	460

300 Students are residents of Atlanta, 271 are from other cities or from towns, and 99 from the country.

Source: Twenty-sixth Annual Report of the President of Spelman College (1906–1907), in Spelman College Archives.

APPENDIX D

1920–1921
Spelman Seminary
Atlanta, Georgia

RATES FOR BOARDERS.

Entrance fee, payable, annually,	$5.00
Tuition for the year,	*20.00
Board, including room, per month,	14.00
Exceptions.	
Home Economics, advanced, per month	$9.00
Nurse Training department	No charge

RATES FOR DAY-PUPILS.

Entrance fee, payable annually,	$1.00
Grades 1 and 2 are excepted.	
Tuition per year	
Grades 1 and 2,	*$6.00
Grades 3, 4, and 5,	*8.00
Grades 6, 7, and 8, and Dressmakers,	*16.00
High School,	*20.00
College,	*25.00

BOOKS AND MATERIALS.

The approximate amount needed is as follows	
Primary department,	
Grade 2	$1.50
Grades 3 to 5	$5.00
Night school,	$2.25
Grammar department,	$7.00
Teachers Professional department,	
First year,	$7.00
Second year,	$6.00
High School department,	$7.00 to $10.00
Home Economics, adv'd, cost of sew'g mat'l not incl'd,	$6.25 to $7.50
Home Economics, el'ry, " " " " "	$6.50 to $7.50
Dressmaking dept., deposit for material for 1st year,	*$20.00
" " " " " " 2nd year,	*$30.00
Millinery dept., deposit for material for 1st year,	$5.00
" " " " " " 2nd year,	*$11.00

EXTRA FEES.

Lessons on piano, per month, preparatory	$3.25
Deposit for sheet music and materials: At beginning	$3.00
At mid term,	$3.00
Whatever remains of this deposit at end of year will be refunded.	
High School laboratory fee,	$1.00
College laboratory fee, (paid at Morehouse College)	
Chemistry II,	$3.00
Physics,	$2.00

GRADUATION FEES.

College, Teachers Prof'l and Adv. Home Econ departments,	$5.00
High School and Nurse Training departments	$2.50
Industrial departments	$1.00

Source: Catalogue of Spelman Seminary (1920-1921), in Spelman College Archives.

APPENDIX E

March, 1921		March, 1926	
STUDENT ENROLLMENT		STUDENT ENROLLMENT	
College, 4-year course	14	College, 4-year course	56
Freshman	8	Freshman	28
Sophomore	3	Sophomore	11
Junior	1	Junior	11
Senior	2	Senior	6
College, 2-year course	47	College, 2-year course	30
(T P & G E Courses)			
Freshman	18	Freshman	17
T P	7	E E	10
H E	11	H A	7
Sophomore	29	Sophomore	13
T P	25	E E	7
H E	4	H A	6
Total College enrollment	61	Total College enrollment	86
High School		High School	
Senior	155	Senior	160
Grade 12	40	Grade 12	51
Grade 11	56	Grade 11	58
Grade 10	59	Grade 10	51
High School		High School	
Junior	238	Junior	129
Grade 9	70	Grade 9	70
Grade 8	73	Grade 8	37
Grade 7	86	Grade 7	22
Total High School enrollment	393	Total High School enrollment	289
(Junior and Senior)		(Junior and Senior)	
Elementary School		Elementary School	
Grade 6	72	Grade 6	19
Grade 5	65	Grade 5	17
Grade 4	55	Grade 4	25
Grade 3	52	Grade 3	16
Grade 2	44	Grade 2	22
Grade 1	41	Grade 1	20

Total, Grades 1–6 329

Nurse Training 33

Special 6

Dressmakers 30

Total student enrollment of
   Spelman Seminary 852

Total, Grades 1–6 119

Nurse Training 19

Unclassified and Special 4

Extension 13

Total student enrollment of
   Spelman College 517

Total extension students 13

Source: Catalog of Spelman Seminary (May 1926), in Spelman College Archives.

APPENDIX F

October 2, 1927	President John Hope, Morehouse, College, Atlanta.
October 9, 1927	Doctor E.R. Carter, Friendship Baptist Church, Atlanta.
October 16, 1927	Professor John R. Van Pelt, Gammon Theological Seminary, Atlanta.
October 23, 1927	Mr. John Pinkett, Director of Agencies of the National Benefit Insurance Company, Atlanta.
October 30, 1927	Reverend W.M, Seay, West End Baptist Church, Atlanta.
November 6, 1927	Reverend J. Sprole Lyons, First Presbyterian Church, Atlanta.
November 13, 1927	Reverend C.N. Perry, Liberty Baptist Church, Atlanta.
November 20, 1927	Professor C.W. Daniel, First Baptist Church, Atlanta.
November 27, 1927	Professor Charles D. Hubert, Morehouse College, Atlanta.
December 4, 1927	Dr. Will W. Alexander, Dir. of Commission on Interracial Cooperation, Atlanta.
December 11, 1927	Bishop Robert E. Jones, Bishop of the Methodist Episcopal Church, New Orleans, Louisiana.
December 18, 1927	Reverend D.D. Martin, Gammon Theological Seminary, Atlanta.
December 25, 1927	President John Hope, Morehouse College, Atlanta.
January 1, 1928	President M.S. Davage, Clark University, Atlanta.
January 8, 1928	Reverend D.D. Crawfor, Executive Secretary of the General Missionary Baptist Convention of Georgia, Atlanta.
January 15, 1928	Reverend W.J. Faulkner, First Congregational Church, Atlanta.
January 22, 1928	Professor L.O. Lewis, Professor of Philosophy and Theology, Morehouse College, Atlanta.
January 29, 1928	Mr. D.G. Bickers, Associate Editor of the Savannah News, Savannah, Georgia.
February 12, 1928	Professor Willis J. King, Gammon Theological Seminary, Atlanta.
February 19, 1928	Professor S.H. Archer, Dean of Morehouse College, Atlanta.

February 26, 1928	Mr. Louie D. Newton, Editor of the Christian Index, Atlanta.
March 4, 1928	Professor W.A. Smart, Emory University.
March 11, 1928	Doctor Robert Brooks, Gammon Theological Seminary, Atlanta.
March 18, 1928	Reverend J.M. Nabrit, Pres., General Missionary Baptist Convention of Georgia.
March 25, 1928	Miss Mary McDowell, Head Resident, The University of Chicago Settlement, Chicago, Illinois.
April 1, 1928	Mr. R.W. Riley, President of the Young Men's Christian Association, Morehouse College, Atlanta, Georgia.
April 8, 1928	Doctor Franklin N. Parker, Dean of the Candler School of Theology, Emory University, Atlanta.
April 15, 1928	Reverend Carter Helm Jones, Second Baptist Church, Atlanta.
April 22, 1928	Reverend L.A. Pinkston, Beulah Baptist Church, Atlanta.
April 29, 1928	Doctor J.H. Lewis, President of Morris Brown University, Atlanta.
May 6, 1928	Doctor Hugh H. Harris, Professor of Sociology, Emory University, Atlanta.
May 13, 1928	Reverend Luther Rice Christie, Ponce de Leon Avenue Baptist Church, Atlanta.
May 20, 1928	Reverend C.L. Fisher, 16th Street Baptist Church, Birmingham, Alabama.
May 27, 1928	Reverend Franklin Halsted Clapp, President-elect of Gammon Theological Seminary, Atlanta.
June 3, 1928	Major Robert R. Moton, Principal of Tuskegee Normal and Industrial Institute, Tuskegee Institute, Alabama.

Source: Catalog of Spelman College (1927-1928), pp. 41, 42 in Spelman College Archives.

APPENDIX G

SPELMAN COLLEGE
DRESS
(1927–28)

A student's wardrobe should include clothes and shoes suitable for out-of-doors activities and for general wear in a moderate climate. Elaborate or extensive wardrobes are not in keeping with the standards and ideals of Spelman College.

The regulation gymnasium outfit consists of black bloomers, white middy blouse with white collar and short sleeves, black ties, black cotton, lisle or woolen stockings, and high white sneakers.

Each student should be provided with a raincoat, umbrella, and overshoes or rubbers.

Students taking courses in foods and cookery are required to have at least two white aprons and two white caps.

Each student should have one white wash dress, simply made, to be worn on special occasions when uniformity is desired. At least two dark aprons are needed.

Source: Catalog of Spelman College (1927-1928), p. 45, in Spelman College Archives.

APPENDIX H

SPECIAL LECTURES AND CONCERTS, 1927–1928

September 27, 1927	Mr. and Mrs. Jan Gordon
	Reproduction of Primitive Music on Guitar and Spanish Lute.
October 21, 1927	Miss Opal DeLong and her Accordion Girls.
November 4, 1927	Miss Marguerite Avery, Dramatic Soprano
	Recital under the auspices of the Atlanta Spelman Club.
November 11, 1927	Miss Cora Wilson Stewart
	Lecture—"The Moonlight Schools of Kentucky."
December 9, 1927	STUDENT PIANO RECITAL
December 14, 1927	SPECIAL ASSEMBLY
	Dr. Trevor Arnett, President of the Board of Trustees Spelman College
	Dr. M.L. Duggan, State Superintendent of Education in Georgia.
	Mr. H.J. Thorkelson, Secretary of the General Education Board
	Mr. Walter B. Hhill, State Supervisor of Negro Schools in Georgia
	Dr. Joseph Stewart, Professor of Secondary Education in the University of Georgia
	Mr. Jackson Davis, Field Agent of the General Education Board
	Mr. Leo Favrot, Field Agent of the General Education Board
	Mr. B.C. Caldwell, Assistant Director of the Jeanes and Slater Funds
	Mr. Emery Jackson, Architect, of New York City
December 14, 1927	Russian Cossack Chorus
December 21, 1927	Christmas Carol Concert
January 2, 1928	Mr. Jesse O. Thomas, Field Secretary of the National Urban League
	"The Third Emancipation of the American Negro."
	(Emancipation Day Program under the auspices of the Wheatley-Fauset Literary Club.)
February 3, 1928	"Adam and Eva"
	Presented by the Campus Mirror Staff.

February 7, 1928	Rabbi Stephen Wise, of the Free Synagogue of New York.
March 4, 1928	Dr. Roy Akagi, National Secretary of the Japanese Student Movement
	Talk before the Interracial Forum.
March 16, 1928	STUDENT PIANO AND VIOLIN RECITAL
March 22, 1928	Dr. E.J. Sanders of the Georgia State Board of Health
	Address to the Atlanta Association for the Advancement of Science
March 23, 1928	MOREHOUSE BENEFIT CONCERT
March 29, 1928	Mr. and Mrs. Julius Rosenwald.
April 6, 1928	OPERETTA
	Junior High School.
April 11, 1928	Mrs Mary McLeod Bethune, President of Bethune Cookman College
	Founders Day Address.
April 21, 1928	"The Old Peabody Pew"
	High School Class of 1928

Source: Catalog of Spelman College (1927-1928), pp. 43, 44 in Spelman College Archives.

APPENDIX I

AIMS AND IDEALS

It is the aim of Spelman College to provide, within a limited scope and with a relatively small number of students, as good educational facilities as are available in any college of liberal arts. To that end, emphasis is placed on courses in fundamental subjects in the humanities, science, and languages. Attitude toward life is considered of more importance than the mere acquisition of knowledge. Knowledge must be lighted with imagination if the student is to relate her learning to the facts and realities of life. Added knowledge should go hand in hand with practical application of knowledge; straight, courageous thinking with honesty, clean living, thorough-going mastery of the task in hand, kindness and helpfulness to one's neighbors on the campus or in the community.

Source: Spelman College Course Catalog (1928–1929), in Spelman College Archives.

APPENDIX J

1928–1929
REQUIREMENTS FOR DEGREES

The requirement for the degree of Bachelor of Arts Consists of one hundred and twenty semester hours of credit, together with eight hours of work in physical education. The unit of time Is the semester hour; that is, one class appointment a week for one semester.The usual schedule consists of fifteen hours for each semester, exclusive of the requirement in physical education. The Work of the senior year must be taken in residence.

It is the aim of the College that every graduate should possess a command of written and spoken English, the ability to read at sight at least one foreign language, some familiarity with the past experiences and achievements of the human race in the fields of history and science and, most important of all, the ability to think with clarity and precision.

Every candidate for the degree of Bachelor of Arts is required to do intensive work in two fields, choosing a major and a minor subject, and must satisfy the requirements of courses of study approved by the faculty for her particular need.

The degree of Bachelor of Science is given to students who fulfill the requirements of the Home Economics curriculum. For a major in this field, the courses are for the most part prescribed by the state departments of education. Liberal arts courses are emphasized in the freshman and sophomore years, and the work of the junior and senior years consists mainly of professional courses and courses in related arts and sciences. One hundred and twenty semester hours of credit and eight hours of work in physical education are required for the degree.

Source: Catalog of Spelman College (1928-1929), in Spelman College Archives.

APPENDIX K

CATALOG
OF
SPELMAN COLLEGE
1929–1930

GENERAL CURRICULUM

Freshman
Biology 11–12
English 11–12
History 11–12
Home Economics 11–12
Speech 11–12
One Elective
Physical Education

Sophomore
Education 21–22
English 21–22
History 21–22
OR
Bible 21–22
Two Electives
Physical Education

Junior
Education 31
Education 32 or 36
History 21–22
OR
Bible 21–22
Major Subject
Two Electives
Physical Education

Senior
Major Subject
Electives
Physical Education

HOME ECONOMICS CURRICULUM

Freshman
Applied Art 11–12
Biology 11–12
Chemistry 11–12 or 11A–12A
English 11–12
Home Economics 13–14
Speech 11–12
Physical Education

Sophomore
Applied Art 26
Chemistry 24
Education 21–22
English 21–22
Home Economics 23 and 24
Home Economics 25
Physics 32

Junior	Senior
Biology 32	Education 35
Economics 21–22	Education 42
Education 31	Home Economics 44
Home Economics 31	Home Economics 45 and 46
Home Economics 33 and 34	Sociology 33–34
Sociology 31–32	Electives
Physical Education	Physical Education

Source: Catalog of Spelman College (1929-1930), in Spelman College Archives.

APPENDIX L

SPELMAN COLLEGE
SPECIAL LECTURES, CONCERTS,
ENTERTAINMENTS
1935–1936

Oct. 29	Scientific motion picture films shown by Donald Bean, head of the University of Chicago Press
Nov. 7	Kryl Symphony Band
Nov. 8	Lecture by Dr. W. E. B. DuBois, "The Furture of the Darker Races"
Nov. 20	Lecture by John Langdon- Davies, "Europe on the Verge"
Nov. 22–23	University Players presented "Fashion"
Nov. 29	President Roosevelt visited the Atlanta University Athletic Field
Dec. 9–14	Conference on Vocational Guidance and Education for Negroes held at Atlanta University by the National Occupational Conference
Dec. 11	Spelman, Morehouse, Atlanta University Concert in Howe Hall
Dec. 19	Ninth Annual Christmas Carol Concert
Jan. 4	Student Musical Recital
Jan. 24–25	University Players presented "The Cherry Orchard"
Feb. 8	College Mid-year Party
Feb. 14	Concert by Marian Anderson
Feb. 25	Memorial Service for Dr. Hope, arranged by Morehouse students in Sale Hall Chapel
Mar. 5	Assembly: Address by Reverend W. J. Faulkner
Mar. 9	Dr. George Opdyke talked to the Fine Arts Group
Mar. 13	Fine Arts Class Demonstration
Mar. 17	Lecture by Louis Untermeyer, " Critic's Half Holiday"
Mar. 26	All University Assembly: Address by John R. Mott
Mar. 26–27	University Players presented " Much Ado About Nothing"
Apr. 10	Spelman Glee Club and Orchestra Concert
Apr. 11	Spelman Founders Day: Address by Miss Mary van Kleeck on " National Economic Backgrounds for Interracial Cooperation"
Apr. 17–18	University Players presented three original Negro plays
Apr. 24	Ninth Annual Atlanta-Morehouse-Spelman Concert, dedicated to Kemper Harreld, Director
May 1	Concert by the Harreld String Quartet
May 3	Virgil Fox in Organ Concert

Source: Catalog of Spelman College (1935-1936), in Spelman College Archives.

APPENDIX M

SPELMAN COLLEGE
CHAPEL SPEAKERS
1935–1936

Oct. 1 — Dr. Channing H. Tobias, Senior Secretary, Colored Work Department, National Council Y.M.C.A.

Oct. 31 — Mrs. David D. Jones, Bennett College, Greensboro, North Carolina

Nov. 15 — Miss Lan Ching Chou, Principal Girls High School, Nanchang, China

Nov. 19 — Mrs. Claudia White Harreld, Spelman alumna

Nov. 25 — Reverend George W. Rhoad, a missionary in Ethiopia

Dec. 6 — Miss Edythe Tate, Spelman alumna, now at Payne College

Dec. 9 — Dr. Franklin J. Keller, Director of the National Occupational Conference

Dec. 10 — President J.B. Watson of Arkansas A. & M. College
President John W. Davis of West Virginia State College

Dec. 11 — Miss Fannie Williams Principal, Valena C. Jones School, New Orleans

Dec. 12 — Mrs. Josephine Holmes, New York State Employment Service

Dec. 13 — Dr. Rufus E. Clement, President of Louisville Municipal College for Negroes
Mr. Max J. Bond, Supervisor of Negro Training, Tennessee Valley Authority

Jan. 3 — Miss Josephine Harreld, Spelman alumna, now studying at Radcliffe College

Jan. 24 — Miss Margaret Eldridge, Missionary, Belgian Congo, Africa

Feb. 5 — Mr. John Bennett, Student Christian Movement

Feb. 10 — Mr. H. S. Murphy, Journalist, Atlanta

Feb. 14 — Mr. James O. Slade, Professor of Sociology, Morris Brown College

Feb. 21 — Reverend W. J. Faulkner, College Minister, Fisk University

Feb. 25 — Mr. Tage Palm of the Division of Self-help Co-operatives, FERA

Feb. 26 — Dr. M. C. Winternitz, Professor of Pathology, Yale University Medical School

Mar. 2–5	Reverend W. J. Faulkner
Mar. 9–10	Dr. John Knox, Professor of Religion, Fisk University.
Mar. 23	Miss Ruby Lucas, Atlanta School of Social Work
Mar. 25	Dr. Channing H. Tobias
Apr. 2	Mr. Victor E. King, Member of Yale University Seminar of Race Relations
Apr. 3	Mr. O. E. Emmanuelson, Member of Yale University Seminar of Race Relations
Apr. 7–10	Mr. Donald Grant, Scotland, formerly Secretary of the Student Movement in Great Britian, lecturing in this country under the auspices of the Institute of International Education of New York City
Apr. 14	The Reverend Canon L. A. Lennon, Nigeria, West Africa
Apr. 15	Mr. William D. Carter, graduate student at the Institute for Research in Social Science, University of North Carolina
Apr. 16	Dr. Rufus E. Clement
Apr. 20	Mrs. Ethel McGhee Davis, former Dean of Spelman College
Apr. 27	Mr. J.C. Dixon, Supervisor Negro Education, State Department of Education, Georgia
	Mr. Trevor Arnett, President of the General Education Board

Source: Catalog of Spelman College (1935-1936), in Spelman College Archives

APPENDIX N

SPELMAN
COLLEGE PREACHERS
1935–1936

Sept. 9   President S. H. Archer, Morehouse College

Oct. 6   Dr. C. D. Hubert, Director of the School of Religion, Morehouse College

Oct. 13   Dr. R. A. Schermerhorn, Professor of Philosophy, Clark University

Oct. 20   Reverend E. M. Hurley, Pastor of Warren Memorial Church

Oct. 27   Dr. W. A. Smart, Emory University

Nov. 3   Dr. Willis J. King, President of Gammon Theological Seminary

Nov. 10   Service of Special Music

Nov. 17   Reverend J. M. Nabrit, Pastor of Mt. Olive Baptist Church

Nov. 24   Reverend Henry C. Bowden, Rector of St. Paul's Episcopal Church

Dec. 1   Dr. Lavens Thomas II, Professor of Religious Education, Emory University

Dec. 8   Reverend C.L. Hill, Dean of the Theological School and Professor of Philosophy at Morris Brown College

Dec. 15   Service of Special Christmas Music

Jan. 5   Toyohiko Kagawa

Jan. 12   Service of ritual with Reverend Lloyd O. Lewis as leader

Jan. 19   Dr. Clarence R. Stauffer, Pastor of First Christian Church

Jan. 26   Dr. M. S. Davage, President of Clark University

Feb. 2   Professor Orville L. Davis, Secretary of the Stewart Foundation, Gammon Theological Seminary

Feb. 9   Dr. M. Ashby Jones

Feb. 16   Professor John H. Lovell, Professor of Practical Theology, Gammon Theological Seminary

Mar. 1   Mr. R. E. Eleazer, Educational Director of the Commission on Interracial Co-operation

Mar. 8   Reverend John Knox, Professor of Religion, Fisk University

Mar. 15   Reverend Buell Gorden Gallagher, President of Talladega College

Mar. 22   Reverend John C. Wright, Pastor of First Congregational Church, Atlanta

Apr. 5	Dr. William A. Fountain, Jr., President of Morris Brown College
Apr. 12	Dr. Charles D. Hubert, Director of the School of Religion, Morehouse College; Special Easter Music
Apr. 19	Reverend Herman L. Turner, Pastor of the Covenant Presbyterian Church
Apr. 26	Reverend Nat. G. Long, Pastor of Glenn Memorial M. E. Church, Emory University

Source: Catalog of Spelman College (1935–1936), in Spelman College Archives.

APPENDIX O

SPELMAN COLLEGE
1938–1939

GENERAL CURRICULUM

Freshman
Biology 101–102
English 101–102
History 111–112
Home Economics 101–102
Speech 101–102
One Elective
Physical Education

Sophomore
Education 204
English 211–212
History 211–212
or
Bible 211, 202
Psychology 201
Two Electives

Junior
History 211–212
or
Bible 211, 202
Major Subject
Two Electives
Physical Education

Senior
Major Subject
Electives
Physical Education

HOME ECONOMICS CURRICULUM

Freshman
Applied Art 101, 106
Biology 101–102
English 101–102
History 111–112
Home Economics 101, 122
Speech 101, 104
Physical Education

Sophomore
Applied Art 204
Chemistry 101–102
English 211–212
Home Economics 111, 112
Home Economics 209, 221
Physics 340
Physical Education

Junior
Biology 339
Chemistry 239
Economics 201–202
Education 204
Home Economics 312, 316
Psychology 201
Sociology 301
Physical Education

Senior
Education 300, 400
Education U405, U408
Home Economics 323,
    431–432
Sociology 315
Physical Education

Source: Catalog of Spelman College (1929-1930), in Spelman College Archives.

INDEX

A

ABHMS, *see* American Baptist Home Mission Society

Academic, xiv, iv, 1, 6–8, 10, 13–17, 20, 22–28, 31–33, 35–36, 40, 44–46, 48, 53, 58, 63, 67–70, 72, 74, 75, 77, 81, 83–93, 96, 100, 117, 119, 120–121, 123, 125–126, 128, 130, 133–134, 138–139, 143, 145, 149, 155, 157, 159–160, 164–166; curriculum, 3, 8, 10, 16, 19, 39–40, 43, 45, 49, 71, 77, 83, 85, 94, 144, 159; diploma, 72, 74

Academies, 1, 11, 28, 35, 51, 57, 77, 119

Accreditation, 8, 99

Accrediting agencies, 8

Acculturation, 35, 41, 47, 161, 17, 26

Activism, 32, 134

Adams, Myron, 98, 122

Administrators, 14, 17, 40, 77, 90, 124, 134, 140, 144, 149–150

Admissions, 23, 26, 32

Africa, 67, 69, 74, 87

African American Studies, 151

Agreement of Affiliation; Atlanta University Affiliation, 119–120, 122–123, 125, 128, 132

Agriculture, 46, 89

Alphabet of Health, 25, 136, 167–169

Alumnae, 15, 87, 128, 134, 138–139, 141, 145–148, 152, 166

Alumnae Arch, 22

AMA, *see* American Missionary Association

American Baptist Home Mission Society (ABHMS), 4–5, 64–65, 130

American Missionary Association (AMA), 4

Architecture, 46

Arithmetic, 11, 35, 46, 51–52, 63, 65, 84

Arnett, Trevor, 124

Artifacts, 21–23, 74

Aspirations, 24, 139, 143, 152–153

Association of American Colleges, 124

Association of Negro Colleges and Secondary Schools, 100

Astin, 138, 152

Astronomy, 11, 35, 46, 49

Atlanta Baptist Female Seminary, 6–7, 11, 31, 63–66, 68

Atlanta Baptist Seminary, 32, 63, 65, 68, 73–75, 78

Atlanta riot, 76

Atlanta schools, 121

Atlanta University; Library 124; (System) Center, 125–125, 130–131, 137, 140, 146; Laboratory High School, 119, 122–123, 126, 129

B

Bachelor's Degree (Bachelor of Arts), 3, 49, 52, 127

Bacote, Clarence, 13, 35, 123, 130

Bands of Hope, 70

Baptist, 4–7, 11, 28, 32, 63–68, 73–79, 97, 118, 130, 155, 163

Beecher, Catherine, 72

Bennett College, 21, 24, 27, 29, 133

Bethune Cookman College, 29, 94

Bethune, Mary McLeod, 29, 94

Black colleges, 3, 13, 26, 29, 32, 34, 55, 77, 126, 130, 137, 143

The Blue Book: A Decorum Guide for Spelman Women, 149
Boarding, 49, 51, 66, 70, 75
Brill, 88, 89, 99
Bureau of Refugees, Freedmen and Abandoned Lands (Freedmen's Bureau), 3–4, 32
Buttrick, 80, 92, 97

C
Calculus, 51–52
Calisthenics, 46
Calling hours, 137
Carnegie Foundation for the Advancement of Teaching, 18, 34, 36, 42, 44, 45, 58, 59, 156
Ceremony, 23, 145
Chapel (*see* Sisters Chapel)
Character, 5, 6, 20, 27, 43, 67, 79, 81, 88, 128, 134, 137, 148
Chemistry, 49, 60, 93, 117, 120
Chisolm, Shirley, 139
Christian, 1, 6, 11, 27, 53, 56, 69–71
Christianity; education, 56, 69, 93
Christian Endeavor Societies, 70
Christian temperance workers, 70
Christianization (-ized), 64
Church workers, 9, 35, 58
Churches, 3, 32, 67, 118
Citizenship, 5, 19, 43, 47, 160, 161
Civic engagement, 167, 168, 170, 171
Civil rights movement, 160, 168
Civil War, xiv, 3, 49, 52, 65, 82
Clark, 122, 130, 131, 133, 151, 152
Clark Atlanta University, 146
Classical curriculum; education, 9, 58; languages, 35, 53, 63, 158
Clausen, 134, 151
Climate, 24, 31, 138
Clubs (organizations), 19, 42, 125, 159
Coeducational, 25–27, 54, 65, 122, 133
Cole, Johnetta, 27, 33, 37, 138, 142, 145, 147, 150–152

Collegiate status, 74, 75, 92, 94
Columbia University, 29, 33, 34, 59
Competition, 20, 44, 121, 144, 163
Commission on Interracial Cooperation, 122
Community, 4, 20, 21, 23, 24, 43, 44, 46, 48, 56, 88, 94, 121, 133, 134, 137, 138, 140, 141, 143–145, 148, 155, 165–167
Conduct, rules of, 84, 87
Congo Mission Circle, 67
Conversations, 27, 37, 137, 142, 150, 152, 167
Corley, Florence Fleming, 24, 28, 29, 32, 34, 35, 37, 51–53, 59–61, 80, 157–159, 161
Cornell University, 54
Cosby, Bill, 139, 140, 169
Cult of True Womanhood, 29, 76, 82
Cultural: events, 13, 18, 34, 42, 120, 125, 128, 132, 159, 169; religious, 148; resources, 121, 127, 158; values, 21, 23, 124, 134
Culture, 1, 7, 10, 17, 18, 125, 131, 133, 136, 146, 156, 160, 161, 164; organizational, 21, 134
Curriculum: academic, 7, 8, 10, 16, 19, 31, 40, 43, 45, 49, 77, 85, 94, 144, 159; breadth and depth of, 18; classical, 35, 53, 63, 158; content of, 7, 8, 36, 47, 57, 77, 89, 130; core, 127; domestic arts, 54, 66, 88, 120, 158; expansion of home economics, 46, 54, 55, 86, 88, 89, 92, 96, 117, 127, 149; liberal arts, 17, 20, 41, 44, 120; utilitarian, 9, 83, 94; vocational, xv, 10, 13, 38, 46, 47, 53, 54, 67, 69, 83, 85, 87, 88, 91, 94, 95, 156, 158

D
Department of Education, 89, 93, 96, 97, 99, 122, 123
Discipline, 137, 141, 143, 147
Diversification: faculty, 132; students, 138, 139, 166

Division of Labor, 121
Domestic: arts and sciences, 88; hygiene, 65; science, 53, 54, 158; skills, 9, 21, 66; studies, 158
Dormitories, 137
Dorm mothers, 145
Dress code, *see* Policy
DuBois, William Edward Burghardt (W. E. B.), 9, 10, 35, 81, 95

E

Ebenezer Missionary Baptist Church, 147
Economic depression, 117, 118
Etiquette, 77, 157
Education: academic, 82, 125; comprehensive, 119, 133; elementary, 3, 92; higher, 6, 10, 13, 15–17, 20, 21, 27–29, 32, 37, 39–41, 43–45, 47, 48, 50, 52, 54, 56–61, 74, 80, 81, 92, 96, 152, 153, 160, 161, 166; industrial (practical), 10, 35, 36, 84, 85, 87, 95; intellectual, 13, 84; liberal arts, 83, 121, 127, 171; society, 12, 17, 19, 21, 27, 41, 43, 46, 53, 59, 67, 79, 85, 133
Electives: postsecondary, 45, 127; vocational, 158; elocution, 49, 53, 158
Emancipated, 2, 5
Empowerment, 21, 142, 168
Endowment, 52, 117, 118, 122, 164, 169
Engineering, 46, 149
English, 46, 49, 51, 55, 69, 72, 75, 84, 117, 120, 123, 127, 158
Enrollment, 45, 66, 78, 92
Entertainment figures (entertainers), 91
Equal opportunity, 91
Ethnocentrism, 11
Ethos, 58, 133
Everts Ward, 81
Evolution, 1, 7, 10, 21, 43, 46, 159, 160
Expectations, xiii, 12–14, 21, 24, 27, 75, 77, 85, 134, 147, 149, 156, 158, 160
Ex-slaves, 3
External funding, 118
Extra-curriculum, 18, 42, 77, 120,

F

Faculty, xiii, 9, 11–14, 18, 23, 25, 26, 33, 34, 42, 49, 84, 85, 90, 92–94, 96, 100, 119, 120, 123, 124, 127, 130, 132–134, 137–140, 144, 146, 150, 160, 165–168, 170
Family structure, 133
Federal funds, 89
Feigl, 139, 152
Fine arts, 13, 14, 119, 126
Finishing school, 52, 157, 161
Fisk University, 123
Foreman, Clark, 122
Forestry, 46
Formal academic curriculum, 8, 10, 159
Founders, xiv, xv, 1, 4, 6, 7, 9, 11–13, 23, 24, 35, 57, 58, 63, 66–71, 75, 77, 84, 85, 94, 128, 155
Fragmentation, 18, 42
Fraternal organizations, 3
Fraternities, 19, 42
Free(d) Blacks, 3, 4, 52
Freedmen's Bureau, 3, 32
French, 49, 52, 77, 117, 123, 127
Friendship Baptist Church, 6, 63, 65, 163
Funding, 3, 13, 33, 35, 84, 88, 95, 117, 118, 121

G

Gates, Frederick T., 73
Gender, 13, 17, 21, 26, 34, 41, 127, 144, 149, 150, 157
General Education Board, 34, 80, 88, 91, 95, 100, 118, 120, 124
Geography, 49, 67, 69, 87
Geometry, 11, 35, 46, 52
Georgia State Teachers and Educational Association, 93
Germany, 87
Giles, Principal (President) Harriet, xiv, xv, 1, 4, 5, 11, 31, 32, 77, 78, 81
Giovanni, Nikki, 140
Girls' school, 66

Giving back, 24, 141
Glenn, 151
God, 5, 71
Graduation, 25, 49, 52, 123, 149, 157
Grammar, 11, 35, 46, 51, 67, 69, 74
Granddaughters Club, 83
Greek, 49, 51, 53, 133
Grover, Caroline, 65, 135
Grover-Werden Memorial Foundation, 22
Guinn, Major Robert, 85, 86, 96–98, 100, 129
Guy-Sheftall, 28, 29, 31, 32, 35, 37, 60, 61, 78, 79, 95, 140, 152

H
Haley, Alex, 139
Harlem Renaissance, 125, 126, 131
Harris, Patricia, 28, 60, 139
Harvard College, 16, 40
Harvard University, 46, 59
Heathenism, 64
Hicks, 135
Hidden Curriculum, 8, 18, 28, 34, 42, 77, 159
Higher Education, purposes of, 6, 10, 45, 50, 54, 56, 57, 81, 160
High School, 20, 44, 67, 72, 86, 89, 92, 93, 100, 117, 119, 123, 129
Historically Black Colleges and Universities, 26, 27, 130, 133, 143
History, 1, 6, 7, 9, 10, 13, 16, 20, 23, 27–29, 32–36, 40, 43–45, 52, 53, 55, 57–59, 61, 75, 85, 87, 91, 93, 94, 117, 119, 120, 123, 126, 127, 129
Homemakers, 9, 58, 97
Home economics, 46, 54, 55, 86, 88, 89, 92, 96, 99, 117, 127, 132, 149
Home Mission Society (Publications), 28, 75
Hope, John, 94, 121, 122, 130
Household arts, 86, 88
Hughes, Langston, 139

I
Ideologies, 7, 21
Inaugural address, 140
Industrial: department, 66–68, 71, 85; education, 10,35, 36, 84, 85, 87, 95
Inferiority, 2, 49, 56, 157
Institutional values, 21, 134
Instruction: educational, 3; religious, 148
Instrumentalist, 19, 43, 161
Integration, 18, 42, 165
Intellectual education, 13, 84
Internal environment, 134
International Health Division of the Rockefeller Foundation, 94
International Sunday School Association, 87, 97, 98
Interviews, alumnae, 134
Involvement, 24, 122, 138
Iron Gates, 22

J
Jeanes Fund, Anna, 87, 95
Jesus, 5, 64, 65
Jewish students, 17, 41
Jim Crow, 15, 28, 60
Joint faculty appointments, 120
Jones, Dr. Sophia, 69

K
Kinfolk, 27, 151
King, Bernice, 140
King, Coretta Scott, 140
King, Jr., Martin Luther, 168
Kissinger, Henry, 139
Kruger, 135
Kuh and Hall, 22, 37, 133

L
Laboratory School, 122, 123, 129
Ladylike behaviors, 149
Lamson, Edna, 82, 90, 100, 101
Langdon, 139, 152
Latin, 51, 53, 75, 117, 120, 123, 157
Laundry work, 75, 120

Leadership, 1, 2, 4, 7, 9, 10, 12, 14, 22, 25, 26, 50, 64, 87, 124, 126–128, 134, 138–140, 142, 143, 149, 150, 158, 159, 163–171

Lectures, 14, 69, 95, 120, 126, 130, 135, 139, 147, 159

Liberal: curriculum, 17, 34, 41; education, 2, 15, 20, 34, 36, 39, 44, 46, 49, 50, 58

Liberal arts college, education, 13, 51, 54, 55, 117, 121, 126, 131, 144, 163, 165

Locke, Alain LeRoy, 125

Logic, 11, 35, 46, 56, 165

Lyon, Mary, 72

M

MacVicar: Hospital, 75, 76, 81, 88, 93, 96, 118; Malcolm, 72

Male professors, 25

Manley, Albert, xiv, 28, 33, 130, 135, 137, 139, 152, 163

Manners, 63, 76, 137, 148, 149

Manual labor, 46

Marian Wright Edelman Childcare Center, 139

Men's colleges, 48, 52

Mentorship, 134, 148

Merton, 21, 36, 133, 151

Metaphysics, 46

Ministers, 3, 6, 32, 45, 67

Mission Statement, 22, 164

Missionary: training course, 72, 74; women, 4; work, 6, 12, 53, 63, 69, 83

Model School, 65, 70, 72–74, 81

Moral: character, 6, 67; development, 148

Morehouse College, 26, 32, 63, 91, 92, 94, 119, 121–123, 128, 130

Morehouse, Dr. Henry L. (H. L.), 65, 73, 79

Morris Brown, 79, 130, 131, 146

Mott, Lucretia, 72

Motto, 6, 22, 77, 142, 159, 166

Mount Holyoke, 73

Music, 10, 11, 35, 46, 49, 53, 69, 83, 120, 125, 126, 128, 135, 141, 158

N

National Association of Collegiate Deans and Registrars in Negro Schools, 93

National Convention of Colored Baptists, 73

National Interracial Conference Normal School, 121

Natural science, 51, 53, 157

Neo-humanist, 19, 43

New England, 9, 16, 31, 40, 57, 64, 68, 73, 78, 97

New Negro Movement, 125

Newsome, Warren, 145

New York Normal School, 73

Nineteenth century, 3, 17, 29, 33, 40, 46, 47, 51, 53, 55, 56, 59, 69, 149, 166

Norms, 21, 23, 27, 50, 65, 77, 133, 134, 149

North Carolina State Department of Education, 93

Northeastern Seminaries, 1, 11, 57

Northern: Methodists, 4; missionary societies, 3, 4; philanthropies, 117

Nurse: medical technology, 118; registered, 89; training course, 33, 54, 69, 72, 73, 75, 76, 86, 89, 117, 118, 129

Nursery school, 126

O

Oberlin College, 9

Occupational, 1, 20, 44, 53, 139, 152

Opportunity, 140, 152

Oread Collegiate Institute, 9, 31

Ornamental Subjects, 53, 161

Organizational Saga, 133, 151

Outcomes, 24, 152

Overseas, 87

P

Packard, Principal (President) Sophia, xiv, xv, 1, 4–6, 11, 12, 31, 32, 63–69, 72, 77, 79, 80, 148, 156–159

Participatory Learning, 138

Pedagogy, 77, 123, 158, 171

Phelps-Stokes Fund, 122

Philanthropies, 85, 117

Philosophy, 9, 19, 35, 43, 46, 51, 53, 55, 56, 58, 60, 119, 127, 133–135, 137, 157, 158, 161, 165

Physical: activity, 88; cultural artifacts, 22, 23; plant, 63, 73, 76, 88, 91, 94, 127, 155; sciences, 46

Physiology, 55, 69, 135

Policy: dress code, 95

Political agenda, 140

Political figures, 91

Post-Emancipation, 3, 28

Predominately White Women's Colleges, 27

Presidential administration, 8, 14, 63, 77, 140, 156–158

Presidents, xiii, xiv, xv, 1, 7, 8, 10–12, 14, 21, 27, 28, 33, 35, 36, 73, 78, 80, 83, 90, 94, 134, 148, 151, 155, 157, 160, 163

Principals, 1, 11, 14, 65, 67, 69, 70, 77–80, 135

Private schools, 3

Psychological factors, 27

Public schools, 1, 53

Q

Quadrivium, 10, 11, 35, 46

R

Racial parity, 91

Racial uplift, 7, 9, 29, 63, 85, 148

Racism, 27, 125, 150, 151

Rationalist, 19, 43

Read, Florence M.: administration, 12–14, 33, 117, 126, 127, 158, 159; President, 13, 28, 72, 93, 117, 120, 126, 129, 140, 141, 150

Reconstruction, 49, 52, 56

Red Cross, 81

Reed College, 94

Refinement, cultural, 79, 148, 158

Religion, 6, 14, 55, 56, 64, 67, 70, 75, 147, 161

Responsibility, 3, 14, 54, 120, 125, 137, 138, 141–143, 148, 164, 165, 167

Reynold's Cottage, 22

Rhetoric, 11, 35, 46

Rites of passage, 23

Rituals, 23

Rockefeller: Abby Aldrich, 137; David, 139; estate, 12,77, 79, 94; Foundation, International Health Division of the, 94; John D. III, 12, 67, 73, 75, 81, 93, 99, 139; Laura Spelman, 118, 129; Laurance, 139; Lucy Maria, 93; Memorial Fund, 118, 129; Nelson, 139; Winthrop, 139

Role model, 14, 24–26, 134, 139, 145, 148–150

Rosenwald, Julius, 118, 120, 129

Rules of conduct, 84, 87

S

Sabbath, 136

Sabbaticals, 93

Sage, Dean, 124

Sale, John, 74

Satisfaction, 138

Savage, 11

Save (as in souls), 64, 68, 77

Scholars, 79, 88, 138, 140, 169, 170

Scholarship, xv, 18, 19, 42, 43, 156, 164, 165

Schools: rural, 84, 86; women's, 53, 57

Science Building, 91

Sebrechts, 148, 149, 153

Segregated, 3, 14, 17, 41, 75, 76

Selassie, Haile (Emperor of Ethiopia), 139

Self-confidence, 138

Self-discipline, 141, 143

Seminaries, 1, 11, 26, 28, 35, 51, 57, 74, 77

Senior Bench, 22

Service, 7, 21, 35, 45, 50, 67, 83, 86, 89,

118, 122, 130, 134, 142, 143, 165–168, 170, 171

Sexism, 27, 151

Sisterhood, 21, 134, 141, 144, 145, 148

Sisters Chapel, 22, 93, 124, 147, 148

Slater Foundation, John T., 68, 73, 96

Slaves, 2, 3, 6, 15, 32, 52

Smith-Hughes Act, 89

Social: agency, 91; awareness, 138; condition, 5; consciousness, 147; uplift, xv, 9, 24, 86

Socialization, students, 8, 11, 13, 18, 21, 23, 24, 26, 27, 34, 37, 42, 69, 70, 76, 77, 83, 90, 91, 120, 125, 133–135, 137–139, 141–143, 145–149, 151, 153, 160

Social life, 16, 40, 64, 67, 88, 18

Social-psychological theory, 133

Societies, 3, 4, 19, 42, 70, 11, 130

Society of Social Purity, 69

Socioeconomic factors, 27, 170

Sociology, 32, 46, 55

Southern Association of Colleges and Schools, 101

Southern Methodists, 4

Spelman: Annual report, 31–33, 37, 66, 70, 78, 80–82, 94–101, 129, 132; Board of Trustees, 33, 83, 85, 92, 95–97, 100, 117, 128; College, xiii, xiv, xv, 1, 4, 7, 8, 10, 11, 13, 14, 18, 19, 21–23, 25–28, 31–33, 36, 37, 42, 43, 45, 53, 57, 59, 61, 63, 71, 75, 77–82, 85, 90, 92, 94–101, 118–125, 127–137, 141–145, 147, 150–152, 155–157, 159, 160, 163–167, 169–171; college hymn, 22; elementary school, 86, 117, 118; faculty, 13, 14, 84, 85, 90, 92, 120, 145, 150; high school, 93, 119, 123; junior high school, 117; legacy, xiii, 155, 163, 171; *Messenger,* 22, 32, 69, 71, 78, 80, 94, 95, 97–101, 135, 136, 151, 152; presidents, xiv, 90, 151; seminary, xiv, 11, 12, 31, 33, 37, 68–70, 72, 75, 78–82, 91, 92, 94–101,

152; senior high school, 86; woman, 23, 27, 141, 142, 148

Spelman, Mr. & Mrs. Harvey Buel, 68

Spheres, 2, 6, 13, 29, 32, 47, 57, 59, 61, 121

Sports, 19, 42, 88, 141

Standardized Tests, 90, 93; *see also* Thorndike McCall Reading Scale, 90; Otis Group Intelligence Scale, 90; Ayers Spelling Scale, 90; Binet–Simon Tests, 90

Stewart, Donald, 33, 140, 142

State Department of Education, Georgia 89, 93, 99

Student government, 143

Student Interracial Study Group, 93

Subjugation, 50

Suffield Academy, 31, 67

Summer school, 93, 98, 120, 130

Sunday school teacher, 87

T

Talented tenth, 9, 10, 75, 181

Tapley Hall, 93

Tapley, President Lucy Hale, 98

Teacher certification, 93

Teaching, cooperative 120

Teacher's: Professional course, 74, 76, 88, 89; Professional department, 33, 83

Temperance, 70

Traditions, 13, 18, 19, 23, 34, 42, 49

Training: hand, 67, 134, 151, 155, 159, 171; head, 84, 132, 134, 144, 151, 155, 159, 117; heart, 134, 144, 151, 155, 159, 117; industrial, 29, 66, 84, 89, 96; moral, 14, 32, 56, 57, 66, 84; religious, 84; spiritual, 21

Trivium, 10, 11, 35, 36

Trow, 152

Troy Seminary, 52

Twentieth century, 23, 53, 149, 156, 163, 164, 166, 169

U

Undergraduate curriculum, 20, 27, 44, 46

United States Secretary of Health, Education and Welfare, 139

United States Secretary of State, 139
University and Colleges Committee of the National War Savings Committee, 86, 97, 98
University of Illinois, 54
University of Michigan Medical College, 69
University Players, 126
Upton, Acting President Lucy Houghton, 78, 81–83, 94
Upward mobility, 6, 91

V

Values: faculty, 24, 34, 160; institutional, 21, 134; student, 23
Vassar College, 9
Verbal cultural artifacts, 22
Vocational education, 10, 46

W

War effort, 87
Washington, Booker T., 9, 10, 35, 83, 84, 95
Wellesley College, 9
Western civilization, 49
Wheatless and heatless days, 87

White flight, 17, 41
White Shield Societies, 69
Whiting, Albert, xiv, 6, 28, 33, 130, 135, 137, 139, 152, 163
Willard, Emma, 52, 72
Women: Black, xiii, xiv, xv, 1, 2, 4, 7, 12, 21, 24, 26–29, 34, 37, 48, 49, 51–57, 59, 60, 72, 133, 138–140, 148, 150, 153, 156, 157; professors, 25; students, 1, 21, 24, 25, 37, 54, 138
Women's American Baptist Home Mission Society, 118
Women's: colleges, 2, 21, 24–27, 29, 34, 37, 48, 49, 51–57, 59, 60, 72, 132, 138–140, 148, 150, 153, 156, 157; studies, 34, 60, 151, 167
Worldcentric, 138
World War II, 127

Y

Young, Elizabeth Barber, 29, 34, 47, 48, 55, 59
Young Women's Christian Association (YWCA), 69
YWCA, *see* Young Women's Christian Association